The Origin
of Culture and Civilization

The Cosmological Philosophy
of
The Ancient World View
Regarding Myth, Astrology, Science,
and Religion

By

Thomas Dietrich
aus Fritzlar

THE ORIGIN OF CULTURE AND CIVILIZATION
PUBLISHED BY TURNKEY PRESS
2100 Kramer Lane, Suite 300
Austin, Texas 78758

For more information about our books, please write to us, call 512.478.2028, or visit our website as www.bookpros.com.

Library of Congress Control Number: 2005929009

ISBN-13: 978-0-9764981-6-2
ISBN-10: 0-9764981-6-2

10 9 8 7 6 5 4 3 2 1

Zeno consulted the oracle to know what he
should do to attain the best life, and that the
god's response was that he should take on the
complexion of the dead. Whereupon, perceiving
what this meant, he studied ancient authors.
Diogenes Laertius

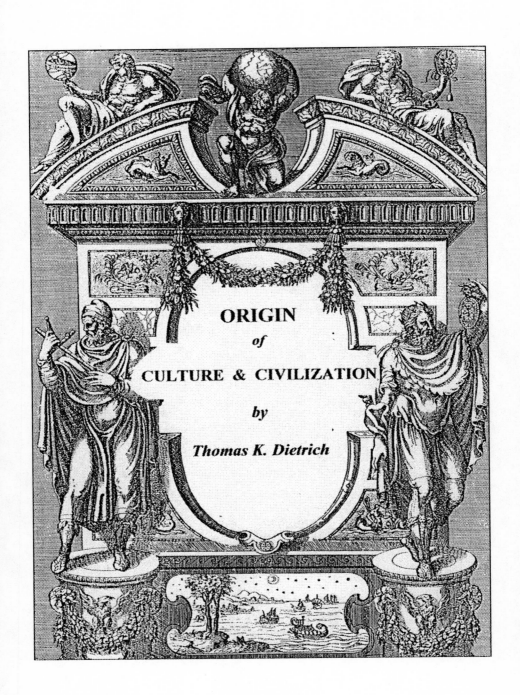

ORIGIN

of

CULTURE & CIVILIZATION

by

Thomas K. Dietrich

THE ORIGIN *of* CULTURE *and* CIVILIZATION
Ancient Ideas about Myth, Astrology, Science, and Religion.
by Thomas Dietrich

TABLE OF CONTENTS

Introduction to Cosmological Philosophy

We are going to introduce a new way of looking at ancient history and philosophy. To begin, we are going to consider that some of the ancients held sophisticated scientific knowledge which they transmitted to posterity in the guise of astrology and mythology. This book is a philosophical exposition of these two subjects which will help us to understand many aspects of the ancient world, our perception of mankind, and our relationship to God.

The Beginning

Ireland is one of the oldest countries on earth that may have experienced a continuity of culture and science stemming from the ancient heritage of the Atlantic, and therefore possibly Atlantis. There is good reason to call this island *Ogygia*, "the most ancient place."

One of the foremost of all the Irish crosses stands within a neglected graveyard nearby the Kilkenny Road. Its iconography is almost shatteringly different from anything we have ever seen. Its arms are decorated with intertwined serpents proceeding from a mystic spiral knot. At the top of the cross and above this unusual knot are the gaping jaws of a creature, whose mouth looks like that of an alligator's. All this is depicted above three very simple and natural looking four-leaved flowers. On the opposite and western side of this cross there appears a solar symbol at the center of the stone circle. We will learn as we proceed that the so-called sun pictograph may actually also allude to the solar system's cycle around the center of our galaxy.

Our cross exhibits some very complicated and advanced mathematical and geometric principles which one would not normally associate with any stone creations in this backwater of the island. Indeed that which is represented is so very sophisticated that it will force us to alter our perception of the history of science.

The Geometry and Math Shown on the Stone Cross

The diameter of this stone circle, taken from within its rope molding, times 3.14, or *Pi*, produces the height of the cross.

The cross is based upon a 2 x 1 rectangle made up of two adjoining squares. The cross arm is placed at 0.618, or *Phi*, of the uppermost square.

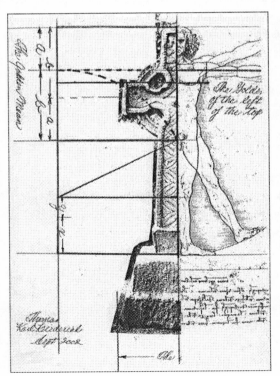

Every line of the ornamental iconography of this cross is based upon sacred geometry, Fibonacci numbers, and simple divisions of the two fundamental squares.

Pi and *Phi* are associated with the geometry that Pythagoras brought out of Egypt. One can only ask, "What are these factors doing in Ireland, associated with a pre-Christian cross which is decorated with mysterious cosmological icons?"

Furthermore and most remarkable of all is that if we take the Vitruvian Man drawn by Leonardo da Vinci, and superimpose him upon the true height of the cross, we find a perfect correspondence of the exact construction lines of the man and of the cross.

When we see the two joined together, the interlaced rope-work of the cross corresponds to the man's intestines. The twists and windings of the large intestine are symbolized in the ancient practice of creating mazes. It is well-known that mazes are an integral part of many of the mysterious initiations of the ancient mystery schools and occult societies.

In astrology, the bowls are related to Virgo, the exaltation of Hermes/ Mercury, god of science and knowledge. Astoundingly, the mysterious knot from which two of the serpents evolve is in the position of the man's esophagus and the vocal cords, which are the instrument of the voice, speech and *logos*. The central boss of the cross is over the man's stomach, below which is his navel, the center of man's spiritual circle. The center of the square around the man represents man's material nature which is marked by his genitals. The cross's stone circle is tangent to this center of the square. This stone circle seems to embody man's embryonic seed cell, from which the extremities of his arms, legs, generative organs, and head will develop and extend.

The major question to be asked is, "What are Egyptian, Greek, Roman, and Renaissance geometric principles doing here regulating the design of an ancient Irish cross, whose iconography has nothing to do with Christianity and therefore allows us to assume that its origin is prior to the time of Christ?"

Our first response was, "Not so fast, *da Vinci!*" The answer is that we need to look at a larger historical picture of science and culture before we can ascribe the credit of origination to anyone, or any nation. But, what an utterly fascinating puzzle, when one considers that Leonardo's construction lines absolutely cut the identical lines that construct this primeval Irish cross.

We will talk more about this cross in a later segment. If a detective were to investigate this case they might discover that history mentions that the nearby locality was notorious for its deep-rooted druidic traditions. It has even been shamefully admitted that a gospel of Saint Patrick's time was drowned in the nearby River Suir, pronounced like the English word "sure."

No native snakes are said to live in either Sardinia or in Ireland. But the symbolic stone serpents upon the Killamery Cross represent the very snakes that St. Patrick had been sent to cast out of Ireland forever. St. Patrick's battle is with the Serpent Knowledge of the Druids. Patrick needs to tell the Druids about his God, who was born on the special extra days at the end of the year like so many of the primeval gods of antiquity. The extra days between the fulfillment of the old cycle and the beginning of the new cosmic cycles were regarded as sacred windows of time. Within the space of this brief period of Holy Time, the worn-out beliefs and idols must be tossed down from their exalted pedestals and abandoned. New beliefs and ceremonies must be instituted.

The underlying drama of the history called *The Contention of Patrick and the Druids* is that the Druidic Crosses have already predicted the advent of the Universal Messiah, and therefore have preceded Patrick's evangelical mission. In fact, almost each and every one of the Druids of Ireland converted to Christianity, not just as proselytes or new believers, but as the very knowledgeable priests of the new religion. Patrick could not, and would not allow Christianity to become a continuation of the Serpent Knowledge; yet upon reviewing Irish law, he pronounced it to be acceptable and in accord with the natural law. It is because of this mandate that Roman law was never introduced into our island. Because of this very special history, Irish Catholicism became a chimera-like creature reflecting a union of extremely ancient as well as modern traditions.

The Killamery Cross is one of a group of seven extraordinary and prototypical crosses called the Ossory Group. In the hills above these crosses is an astronomical observatory called Knockroe. This observatory is like a miniature Newgrange. Its directional sights perfectly mark the position of the winter solstice. One very remarkable feature about Knockroe is its extreme antiquity. This may be deduced from the fact that Knockroe had fallen into decay in very olden times, because an ancient road was discovered to have been built right over the middle of this very special site. Knockroe was therefore old and forgotten even in ancient times.

But sadly, far below at the foot of the mountain, in the misty and disheveled churchyard, stands our cross, silent and aloof, with an important message to tell. But, there is no one there to hear it!

Why have we been deaf to its message for so long? The reason is the simple fact of Ireland's forced isolation from the world stage because of its tumultuous history, to which it is still emotionally subservient. If this stone cross were discovered in some sealed underground chamber in Egypt or Greece, then half the world would come to attempt to decipher its meaning and revealing iconography.

We realize the importance of its message, and we will examine neglected and rejected pathways of inquiry. These will serve as the mystical keys that open the doors to the past. We will learn that astrology and mythology both can be used to confirm the antiquity of the Atlantic regions. Ultimately we may even challenge the absolute priority of Egypt.

We will introduce ideas based upon pure physics and astronomical cycles. These were the foundation stones of ancient thinking and philosophy. Indeed their philosophy was a mixture of history, religion, and astronomy which they unified under the term cosmology.

The reader will see that there is a Cycle of World Culture which is moving *very gradually* from the West toward the East, from the Atlantic to the Mediterranean. But, there is also a lesser and more rapid cycle, the Cycle of Civilization, which moves in the opposite direction from the Middle East to the Atlantic. Therefore, Civilization and Culture are opposed elements. These opposing cycles represent the clockwise and counterclockwise, the positive pole and the negative; they are night and day, and good and evil. Yet without the contention of these cycles, life would be without meaning and without history. Culture by itself is too stagnant and conservative. Civilization by itself is too adamant and war-like. Together and through their confrontation they produce the magic of the drama of life.

Classical mythology presents us with a sequence of the generations of the gods. This sequence is a scientific account of the history of Culture, and the progress of the astronomical Cycle of Culture. This cosmic cycle will also tell us where on the earth these separate generations of the gods lived and acted out the history of their unique age.

This progression of Culture has nothing whatsoever to do with the advance of Civilization. The advance of civilization—which means cities, nations, and empires—proceeds from the East and moves westward. Civilization follows the physics of the astronomical cycle called the Precession of the Vernal Equinoxes.

Why have we not been instructed about the great astronomical cycles which seem to direct Culture and Civilization? Why have these matters been such an illusive mystery for so long? First of all, the content of astrology and myth has never been seriously considered to present valid scientific information. Yet both these subjects form a considerable portion of the entire opus of classical literature. I have always wondered, "Why has so little been made of so much information?" We will learn how to use astrology and myth to discover the cosmological philosophy and thinking of the ancient people.

Second, we are in the infancy of discovering that the ancients had an incredibly expanded knowledge of the universe. Most of the illuminating research stems only from 1915, the 1960s, 1970s, and 1990s. It is only most recently that we have learned that the ancient people aligned their megalithic structures in accord with the celestial bodies and in relation to the astronomical cycles. The ancients adored the heavens as a means of communication with the divine. Because of the extremely long history of their observations, they discovered cycles that we are only now beginning to become familiar with again. We modern people have just begun to recognize and tentatively explore the movement of our solar system's circuit around the center of our own Milky Way Galaxy.

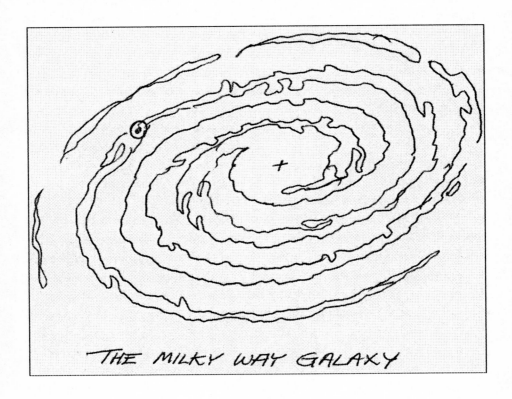

THE MILKY WAY GALAXY

Modern people have surmised that the center of our galaxy is in the neighborhood of the direction of Sagittarius. But, the ancient cosmologers had long ago marked this direction, and had given special recognition and a unique form to the picture of the zodiac constellation of Sagittarius.

As yet, Modern science does not predicate any special meaning, effect, or influence to the fact that our solar system circles the galaxy. The ancient people, up to the last great astronomers of the Mayan, actually based their history and cosmology upon the workings of the galaxy. I do not feel that the ancient scientists kept their cosmic knowledge a secret, but rather, they regarded it as appropriate to the higher levels of human study. Therefore, the knowledge of this greater cycle was mostly transmitted to the select few of their chief scientists and priests.

Let us spend some time with these ancients. We will attempt to see the world and the cosmos with their ancient eyes. But we must first be open-minded in order to investigate the germs of true science which they often wrapped within a popular, or *demotic*, cocoon of poetry, myth, and astrology.

We cannot advance scientifically, nor can we form a philosophically correct image of this world without the information that the ancient people have so patiently collected for us, and have transmitted over such immeasurable periods of time.

Like the Cross of Killamery which we discussed above, there is an important message to be told, and to be heard. This message has been carefully preserved for us, if we will but take the time to learn how to read its meaning.

The Antiquity Puzzle
and the Mythology Code

The appearance of early man upon the globe shows us a broad range of examples of rude development to almost inexplicable examples of high technology. Modern theory is that humans have evolved from natural roots. This has served us as a very good working thesis which is eminently teachable, and upon which we can hang much of our research and conclusions.

We are not going to question whether this theory is true or not, because it has been such a practical and useful tool of science. We are, however, going to challenge its time frame which is unquestionably too conservative and has led many investigators to form sophomoric and illegitimate conclusions.

We will review a great part of our cultural tradition which will guide us to discover a true and corrected viewpoint of the history of this planet. We are going to try to rediscover what the ancients thought about this world, and we will try to learn from them in order to form a more correct philosophical and scientific standard that may be used for all future research.

I believe that the ancients will have many interesting things to show us because they had discovered the ultimate concordat of history, science, and religion. Their research had discovered what amounts to the Unified Field Theory. Their philosophy produced the final cosmology in which nature, physics, God, and man all fitted together into one complimentary and congruent system.

Their cosmology presents us with a world under the auspices of many balancing and reoccurring astronomical cycles, which in their regular courses cover every portion of the globe in a very democratic fashion. This cosmic system assures us of the constant communication between God and humanity, a communion whose history is not in terms of thousands of years, but rather, in terms of millions of years. We will read about all those things which will give credence to this view. Unfortunately we will also discover that every place upon the surface of the globe is subject to periodic and increasingly forceful natural change. The great variety of natural disasters perpetually interferes with what we call human progress. This is probably a very good thing because some of the things that we do are not socially, environmentally, or philosophically beneficial. It is for this reason that we should be amazed at the quality of scientific and cultural heritage that has been transmitted down to us over these incomprehensible time periods.

In order to make our discoveries we will need to try to enter the minds of the ancient people and learn to deal comfortably and freely with the subjects and terms that they used. We will therefore consult several misinterpreted and discredited disciplines such as myth and astrology. Granted, at first this sounds a bit voyeuristic and alarming. But really, you will have to have patience as we demonstrate their scientific underpinnings which will serve as the very foundation stones of a new theory about the cosmology of ancient people.

My one great pride has been the absolute dedication to the actual material of the ancient writings and reports. These are not hidden in the Vatican or in the clandestine libraries of secret societies, but all the works cited in this book are commonly available. Neither have I used the crutch of extraterrestrials in order to rescue our conclusions. Extraterrestrials are basic astronomical phenomena covering a wide range of meteorological and divine aspects.

Beginning our Investigation

Unfortunately, the name *Atlantis* has become synonymous with antiquity. I personally dislike the fact that this name has been so overused and prostituted. Even as a young man, I resolved to discover the root of this story, that it might for once be investigated upon its merits, and not be ill used as a convenient catch all for things which we cannot otherwise conveniently explain.

What follows, therefore, is a detective story of sorts. While archaeologists sift through tedious layers of soils and civilizations, I have spent my life leafing through ancient books; looking for facts and clues to the *Puzzle of Antiquity*. However, there will be no hair-raising adventures. Our satisfaction will be a deeper intellectual satisfaction of true discovery which gives us a philosophy which will be a foundation to our thoughts for the rest of our lives.

I am among those who thought that the novel, *The Da Vinci Code* was extremely gripping and well-written. But, our work is not this type of mystery of deception and intrigue, spun and woven about an artificial plot. Our plot is humanity itself, a subject of which no one should tire. We are going to look into human cultural and civic origins from an antiquity, context, and age that will be marvelous to contemplate. In fact the more we get used to great periods of time, the more we will become assured of a reality that so carefully comprehends all things and finds even our limited existence an important part of the fabric of life.

First of all, let us get a taste of the special cosmological thinking of the ancient people. There is a very ancient story told by the Roman writer, Plutarch, in his work concerning *Isis and Osiris*. It begins thus:

It is told that Rhea secretly co-joined herself with Cronus. Helios saw what had transpired, and he proclaimed that Rhea should not be permitted to give birth in any month, or any year. Hermes lived with the goddess, and he, too, loved her. He resolved to help her, and therefore challenged the moon goddess, Selene, to a board game. Hermes proceeded to win $1/70^{th}$ part of each day of the year from Selene. These portions he put together; and they made up five days, which he placed behind the 360 days of the year. These days are still called the added on days; and it was during these extra five days, that Rhea gave birth to the gods.

To Helios she bare Osiris and Harueris. By Hermes, the goddess brought forth Isis. And, to Cronus; the goddess, Rhea begat Typhon, who tore out of her womb; and Nephthys, whom some relate to Aphrodite, Teleute, or Nike.

You would really have *had* to *have* read an extraordinary amount of classical literature to become excited by this story. But, at the moment, we are just learning. Please believe me, this story is very intriguing. The story tells about how ancient people thought about gods, science, and history. This story is about science . . . It is about astronomy . . . It is about calendar reform. This same story is also about religion, namely, their greatest gods. This story is about history, . . . and it is about myth, . . . and different generations of the gods overlapping the time periods and cycles of chronology. THIS STORY IS ABOUT CULTURE and it is told after the innocent fashion of children who speak quietly about the most awesome and grave matters. It resembles children teaching sages the correct words to speak to us. I become emotional each time I hear this tale because I realize how very old and sacred this elegant story is.

This is what makes cosmological thinking so unique. For in the mind of the ancient people there is no science without religion, or religion without science. There is no history without myth, and no myth without history. And, there is no astrology without astronomy, and visa versa.

Everything that the ancients talk about is a giant woven tapestry of all the conditions of life. Every detail is considered on a multiplicity of levels: myth, astrology, science, and religion. Nothing really has intrinsic meaning, that is, nothing has meaning of itself. Everything only has *contextual* meaning, that is, it has to fit in with everything else. Its definition of itself *has to fit in with all the other things that surround it* and serve to define those other things; and thereby illuminate the greater context. Such thinking breeds an infinite respect for the order of all things in nature and the divine.

How did I get started in the pursuit of this particular thesis? I was at my first philosophy class at the University of San Francisco. The professor began by saying that we would study Hans Vyinger's philosophy called "As if." His idea is *that whether we believe in God or not,* we should act as if we do believe, because it makes our life so much easier. I interrupted the professor by saying that while I did not fully know how much my education was costing my father—I would now retire to the University Library to try to justify his expenditure. I did go to the library, and spent my two years there reading every classical work, as well as the great scholarly German, French, and European researchers and commentators.

I was very happy to be out of that classroom, because, even as a child; I have always been intimidated by ignorance, instinctively fearing the danger and unpredictability of this sad deficiency of mind and spirit. What I discovered in the library was a new world of poets, historians, and philosophers who had a very different way of looking at the world—*different* to the staid academic or the presumptuous political propaganda concerning a very narrow and regulated view of the origins of Western Civilization.

First of all, it became quite apparent that there was some kind of general truth to the stories of Atlantis and a technologically advanced people residing on the shores of the Atlantic Ocean. Diverse poets and historians all had their little bit to add. Most importantly, the Greeks and the Egyptians fully admit that their ancestors and their gods came from the land to the west of them: the Land of Night, *first of the ancient goddesses,* and her companions, the goddesses Sleep and Dreams. A place where the sun sets and the moon rises, a land of past generations and the fountainhead of culture and science.

Some of the writers, citing sources more ancient than themselves, hinted that some of the episodes of the voyages of Odysseus, and *even,* Jason and the Argonauts actually took place outside the Pillars of the Mediterranean Sea, out upon the broad Atlantic Ocean. Well, why not, they had already admitted that the Gardens of the Golden Apples of the Hesperides *(the Westerners)* were in Morocco, and that the Isles of the Blest were the Canary Islands just off of that shore.

I have found that even those whom we call the ancients had difficulty dealing with the antiquity that appeared before them. It is a part of human nature to forget the past. We build our palaces upon the promontories of a haunting and jagged coastland, only to be surprised to see them fall into the ocean at the next earthquake. The very shop fronts of Pompeii were built of the very tufa stone of the previous lava flow.

What really confirms this Western Theme (west of Egypt & Greece) is the detailed record of the god Atlas, who discovered the great cycles of the cosmos and named the majority of the stars. Atlas's contribution to the science of astronomy is unparalleled and unquestioned. Atlas's discoveries are documented by all the ancient sources, and reconfirmed again by even modern researchers. Because of his achievements he is depicted holding *the orb of the heavens* upon his shoulders. In the story of the Labors of Hercules, this hero relieves Atlas of his burden, thereby suggesting that the Libyans and the Egyptians copied their sciences from this *Western God,* Atlas. The renown of Atlas was so great that they named the ocean after him and also the mountain range where he conducted his observations. The very Pillars of Hercules were more anciently called the Pillars of Atlas. Also, most of the Greek tribes trace their origin from the famous seven daughters of Atlas.

The cultural connection of Greece, Asia Minor, and the eastern Mediterranean with Morocco is indisputable. But, with the additional formidable tradition of the sciences coming from Morocco, I think that we can feel confident in our assumptions of an Atlantic origin of Culture and Science.

My story continues as I lived with my retired father in Ireland for some 13 years. There I became a stone carver and sculptor, and studied under the eminent Seamus Murphy who carved the busts of the Republican Heroes of Ireland who were involved in the first foundation of the state. My interest in antiquity was not diminished, but rather accelerated when I discovered how far reaching the Irish had documented the past history of their island.

This locale where we lived was called the Romantic Slievenamon, a place of fairy tales and heroic sagas of Finn Mac Cool and his son Oisin. Nearby was the scene of the last witch-burning in Europe, as late as 1894. My wife's grandfather was on the jury deciding the fate of those who were involved in the burning. No more than a few miles away, stand the imposing Ossory Group of the oldest know Irish Crosses, most of them designed and sculpted from pagan roots. Upon the mountain are many stone places and underground forts, and the Rock of the Spinning Wheel of the Fairy Women. The Irish Tourist Board used to say that every Irish resident could have one ancient Irish monument for themselves, and there would still be a very sufficient number left over for others.

What I am getting at is that there was really a lot to do and see there. But what totally shattered my wildest expectations was the depth of the histories regarding the many invasions of Ireland, the many names that the island had held, and the many people that it had hosted over its incredibly long existence.

The most important overview and compendium of Irish history was composed by the Reverend Jeoffry Keating in 1625 AD. He studied in the College of Salamanca for 23 years, and upon returning home traveled the country to locate and consult all the ancient documents of his homeland. Some of the histories that he saw were destroyed by savages in the course of the years. It is not generally known that the true Irish were compelled to study abroad because their own educational institutions were in the control of a foreign power, who naturally promoted their own agenda. Keating as a dedicated antiquarian was not critical of his sources. He faithfully presented what others had accounted worthy of recollection. It is unique to Ireland that the national and regional histories, and pedigrees of the rulers, were orally reviewed on a regular basis, as well as at the assemblages at Tara. Modern scholars and critics like to disparage and poke some fun at the 17th century Reverend Keating. Yet, his work remains the most consulted of the ancient historical manuals. This disparagement of a dedicated Irish scholar again is an unfortunate aspect of the willful control by a certain other nation of Ireland's own pristine traditions.

Concerning our thesis of the Western and Atlantic origin of science and culture; the Reverend Keating informs us that the most ancient conquerors and inhabitants of Ireland were Sea Kings from Morocco. In Irish they were called the Fir Moricchi, *the men from Morocco*. Sometimes, they were just called the Fir Mor, or *the men from the sea*, but, always of African origin. These Sea Kings were skilled navigators, administrators, astronomers, and builders of the great forts and castles upon the island. They may possibly be the earliest recorded "tax-collectors" in all of history.

You may imagine my surprise and delight that Irish history confirms the accounts of the Greeks and the Egyptians. Irish history substantiates and lends vibrant color to the picture of a heroic, scientifically advanced, and cultured seafaring people upon the Atlantic. We must not neglect to mention the Morini and the Aquitaine mariners, as well as the deep-sea voyaging Veneti of Carnac in Brittany. But, the Fir Mor of Ireland are an especially interesting genealogical study. This is because the Fir Mor do not disappear into the mists of time, even after many future invasions of Ireland by different people. The Fir Moricchi legends, their names, and their pedigrees are adopted through intermarriage to form a dominant cultural foundation of what we call Irish. It is not until the popular rebellion of the artisans and mechanics of 54 AD; that Firmorian pedigrees were legislated to be, *henceforth*, illegal by the decree of 79 AD.

Many of the Fomorians (this has become the popular form of Fir Morian and Firmoricchi) who remained in Ireland embraced the island as their new beloved homeland. The story of their adoption of new settlers, or their own assimilation into the hosts of the conquering invaders is a model and classic study of a society absorbing new immigrants. Their neighbors in Brittany were not so fortunate. On a very ill-starred day, when their normally swollen and protective seas disastrously turned into a deadly glassy calm,

Julius Caesar easily annihilated the superior fleet of the Veneti. In typical Roman triumphal fashion, Caesar ordered every man of their nation to be killed, and their histories and documents burned.

Unfortunate for us and our research; the Veneti just happened to be the designers, builders, and guardians of Carnac, the world's largest megalithic astronomical observatory! The area is rich in tombs and everything megalithic. We have visited Carnac and nearby Gavrinis, where the carved spirals upon the huge boulders cry out their identity to those of Newgrange in Ireland. At this moment in time, Newgrange is regarded to be older than the pyramids. We will also relate the foremost tradition in this region of Brittany, that of the *Seven Holy Bishops*. Likewise, this legend of the Seven Holy One's is intimately connected to many regions of Ireland.

At this stage I became quite engrossed with the unfolding picture of the great range and antiquity of Atlantic coastal history. It was no wonder, then, that the Greeks and Egyptians should give testimony to these talented navigators and astronomers of the Atlantic. Because of the astronomer Atlas, and many other references; it seems that Morocco was truly a focal point in very olden times. There is no doubt that Morocco was a colony of the real Atlantis. Morocco was a place which survived and retained many of the traditions of the former legendary island stronghold. In its own special history Morocco became the homeland of what we may call the proto-Phoenicians, who later settled Libya and Syria. Much later again, their descendents revisited all these places of their origin, as was the case of the mythological Cadmus, who founded 100 great trading cities on the coastlands of Morocco.

No one can doubt that Morocco was a focal place of Origin. It was a region that we could genuinely study as a real geographical place and not just an idea or a legend. It further struck me that Morocco was a springboard to the development of the Mediterranean. It was the honored homeland of prodigious colonies which settled far into this Middle Sea, even to places above the Black Sea and beyond the Red Sea.

As I read on I noticed that Homer and the other poets ascribed great prominence at a later time period to Libya as a place of culture and of the gods. As Morocco was *step one* in the transmission of culture and science from Atlantis; now, Libya became *step two*. As we read about the history and legends of Libya, we notice that they had adopted most of the traditions and the place names of Morocco. We will see, regarding the name Triton, that this name was brought from Atlantis to Morocco, to Libya, and finally to several cities in Greece. This is not unusual when we see that colonists in our modern era transported many European names, such as New York, New South Wales, New Amsterdam, throughout the globe.

Just as Atlantis and ancient Morocco were devastated by earthquakes, Libya was also visited by natural disasters which destroyed and obliterated its former glory. Libya suddenly became a semi-desert, and over long periods of time, it became a true desert. We know this because of the ancient reports that there had been a land of paradise and plenty in Libya. Apparently, at an early stage the desert was actually a prosperous ocean-lake swamp with innumerable islands. Today there are still the remains of thousands of miles of underground aqueducts which the people used, for long periods of time, to stave off the onslaught of the impending drying-out of the land.

My wife and I had the opportunity to visit northern Sardinia and Corsica which have an ancient connection with Libya. The Greek historians and olden traditions of Sardinia report that the first conquerors of their island were seafarers from Libya. This is extremely important because, just like the Fir Moricchi of Ireland, these Libyan seafarers are the scientists, astronomers, and builders of Sardinia.

Not too many people are aware of the thousands of impressive megalithic astronomical observatories that cover the island of Sardinia. In fact, it was only in 1980, during our visit there, that Professor Massimo Pittau published his *La Sardegna Nuragica*. His work, written in Italian, was quite daring in suggesting that these beautiful stone fortresses might have implications to science as astronomical observatories. Professor Pittau was the first to demonstrate the connection of these structures with underground water spirals, as is the case with the subterranean water courses over which Carnac in Brittany is founded in the land of the sea faring Veneti. Professor Pittau also showed that these massive castles were regarded as sacred structures, and that many of them were taken over by the Catholic Church and given the appropriate names of Saints, which typified the special characteristic of the site.

The usages and traditions of these islands remind one clearly of a connection with the many traditions of Ireland. The mountains of Corsica are surmounted by impressive Cyclopean stone forts built around gigantic natural rock formations. Filotosa is Corsica's most renowned astronomical observatory. This site seems to contain a seat for a resident prophetess in the midst of a natural stone cavity. Most unusual, however, are the stone pillar figurers portraying the planets. These were aligned along sight lines of the usual rising places of these wandering heavenly bodies. Unfortunately, in the *excitement* of the discovery of these stone planetary figures, they were dislodged from their original positions and assembled in a circle near the center of the site. However lovely this arrangement may have appeared; this imprudent relocation totally obliterated any possibility of the scientific investigation of ancient planetary cycles. Incidents of this type remind us to call for a better understanding of the cosmological philosophy of the ancients.

All of the above information presented a mighty fortress of evidence for the Origin of Culture and Science in the West. The final proof came from the Divine Ptolemy himself in his geographical works. Most probably, as a resident of Alexandria; one would imagine that he would assign the priority of The Prime Geographic Meridian to his adopted city, which was the capital of the sciences of the world at that day. The nearby Pyramids have been called the greatest geodetic markers of all time. Yet, Ptolemy respected and retained the more ancient Prime Meridian founded upon the Canary Islands in the Atlantic Ocean. Even long before Marinus of Tyre, these islands were the place which the ancient cartographers had held in high and sacred esteem. For sheer honesty and intellectual integrity, our studies must admire Ptolemy. If his inspection of maps showed that a refined tradition of map-making placed the main meridian in the Atlantic, he would not alter that position unless he had a scientific reason to approve such a change. For me, Ptolemy's positioning of the Prime Meridian is one of the paramount proofs of Western Origin upon the Atlantic coastlands. Ptolemy had all of the scientific evidence of the world at his disposal in Alexandria. I feel that it would be wise to respect his conclusions.

I think that anyone may be able to see that my investigations naturally grew and matured out of themselves. That is, as the truth of Atlantic priority of culture and science became unquestionable, other things naturally fell into place. Namely, if the original Atlantis was out there somewhere; and the next step was Morocco; after which, the next step was Libya; and the following step was Egypt—*then*, it must be presumed that the directional trend of Culture and Science flows from the West toward the East.

The predominant interest of all of the ancient people, that we studied, centered on *astronomy*. All of these ancient people were obsessed with this science; whether they were: Atlas, or the Libyan builders of the Nuragica of Sardinia, the Fir Moricchi of Ireland, or the Veneti of Brittany. Were they all obsessed because they had discovered something? When we look at the astronomical complex at Chaco Canyon in New Mexico, we must be amazed at the extraordinary *precision* with which their studies of the cycles of the moon and sun were calculated and expressed by means of interrelated structures which were a few miles to over 400 miles apart! Anna Sofaer, the discoverer and interpreter of Chaco Canyon, also relates the mystery that this religious site was ceremonially closed with great effort and time. Our conclusions must be that the obsession with astronomy also includes an obsession with religion. This obsession extended to the belief in astronomical cycles of history and myth.

As our investigations continued we came to the realization that the ancients thought cosmologically. That is, their *worldview* was that science, religion, and history are woven together into one fabric of life. These separate disciplines are different expressions of one unity of God, nature, and man.

Many researchers into astronomy and mythology have tried to relate the different generations and successions of the gods to the astronomical cycle of the Precession of the Vernal Equinoxes. This is a stunning idea because it follows the consequent development of the cosmological reasoning which the ancients used. The only problem with this exciting idea is that the succession of the gods does *not* follow the Precession of the Vernal Equinoxes!

Precession does however mark the progress of another important aspect of history, namely that of cities and the political reality of this world. This cycle marks *Civilization* and the development of city states and empires. Astronomically, Precession is quite rapid as it takes only 2,160 years to move through one sign of the zodiac and onto the next. We have all been taught that civilization came from India and the Far East, from Ur, Chaldea, and Babylon; and onto Palestine, Egypt, Greece, Rome, and Europe. Precession actually marks this historical sequence of events and determines the flow of Civilization from the East to the West. But, its course is much too rapid to deal with such august and important matters as religion, gods, science, and culture.

Gods and Culture come from the West, gradually and slowly. This astronomical cycle of Culture seems to accord with the ancient record of myth, the sequence of the gods, and all the amazing discoveries that we have found in the regions of the Atlantic seaboard.

Everything that we have spoken of seems to jive, fit, and meld together into a grand scheme explaining Culture and Civilization. Before we are swept away with our own self-congratulation we must pass the ultimate test. This test will see if the succession of the gods is mirrored by the astronomical cycle of Culture?

The generations of the gods, from the most recent times toward the most ancient of times, starts with Zeus/Jupiter. Before him came Cronus. And before Cronus there came other gods; which were preceded by Uranus.

During the time of Christ until 2,160 years before Christ—Precession was in the region of Aries. From 2160 BC to 4320 BC—Precession was in Taurus. Aries and Taurus have nothing to do with Jupiter and Cronus. And therefore, the cycle of Precession did not describe the succession of the gods. But the Cultural Cycle revolves contrary and opposed to Precession. Following this cycle we see that Jupiter fits into Pisces, which the astrologers call the lunar house of Jupiter. We also see that Cronus fits into the sign of Aquarius, which precedes Pisces, and which the astrologers call the lunar house of Cronus. Myth elegantly synchronizes with the Cycle of Culture!

All these facts are all *too much* of a coincidence to be a lucky chance of historical coordination with an astronomical cycle! We will carefully investigate the details and nuances of these theories as we proceed.

To conclude, we would like to say that many of our investigations throughout this book illuminate the cosmological thinking of the ancients. This, in itself, is a worthy study. We began this lecture with the cosmological tale of Hermes, friend of the goddess Hera, winning parts of days from the moon goddess. We also noticed the utter simplicity of the tale. You will remember the story of *The Purloined Letter* by Edgar Allen Poe? The *secret* was that if you wish to hide something successfully, you would attach it to a ribbon and hang it in plain sight on the front of the mantelpiece of your fireplace. This is exactly what the ancients were doing. They were encoding their deepest mysteries in the transparent simplicity of a child. Their religion and science were wrapped in a cocoon of myth and astrology.

This is part of the explanation of why this cosmological philosophy was never before brought to light. The basics of this worldview were hidden under a mantle of disregarded myth and discredited astrology. Secondly, the reader will soon notice that many of the writers upon which we have drawn as prime sources are not the names that we have become familiar with at our schools. They are rather names which have been denied the prominence that they deserved, such as: Nonnos, Sicilus, Skytobrachion, the Reverend Keating, F. Boll, Mr. and Mrs. Schwaller de Lubizc, Underwood, Hapgood, Schliemann, and many others. Most of these great investigators fall into the category of the underappreciated, the occasionally ridiculed and despised, and in some instances the actively disenfranchised. But once again, the heart and determination of the soul will win the day, and the mystery of antiquity will be solved when the stone that the builder rejected has become the corner stone!

The Chronology of the Cosmic Kingship

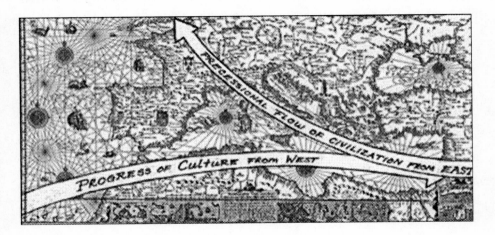

Every student of history has heard of The Rise and Fall of the Roman Empire. In retrospect, it is difficult for us to imagine that this forceful and advanced civilization controlled a great portion of the Western World, but it is now no longer in existence, except in the storybooks of history. It really is something to reflect upon, how quickly things change in the world!

It seems that over the past 6,000 years that civilization has come from the East and traveled *westward.* This development featured the political power of Babylon, Assyria, and Persia. Following the triumphs of these nations came the rise of the Greek city-states, culminating in the Macedonian Empire of Alexander. Then came the rise of Rome to world dominion. But when the Roman Empire was in the last phase of its demise, the power and leadership in this part of the world reverted backward to Constantinople. After the Dark Ages the Renaissance brought light and power to Italy and Europe. The Age of Discovery enabled Europeans to dominate and influence the entire planet. After many wars, the political power now seems to reside in Great Britain supported by its allies such as the United States of America as well as England's former colonies within its worldwide sphere of influence.

On a very simplistic level, there seems to be an observable and remarkable trend of world power evolving from the East. There are, of course, many variations and flashbacks. But again, we are not discussing culture or science, but only sheer political and imperial domination and influence. Therefore, I do not think that anyone could deny the direction of this movement of world power from East to West.

This trend is a natural astronomical phenomenon which is contingent upon the Cycle of the Precession of the Vernal Equinoxes. The location of world power and civilization flows westward upon the face of the globe in accord with Precession moving through the heavens.

Political power in the world is exactly what the root of the Greek word means: *polis*, a city (political). Or in Latin: *civis*, a city (civilization). It is the natural consequence of this cycle, to illuminate and exalt the power of the cities in its path. This directly causes what we will call the Cycle of Civilization. As stated earlier, the Precessional Cycle takes about 2,160 years to move 30 degrees, or one full house of the zodiac. We will therefore notice that the reign of these empires of the city-states is brief. It is never longer than a 2,160 year period. And more often than not, the period of great worldly power is usually less than a millennium of a thousand years.

We know that astronomical phenomenon promotes life here on earth. We acknowledge the sun and the moon's gravitational pull on the tides and upon the blood and water content of human and animal bodies. These same forces likewise determine the generative life cycles of the vegetative kingdom. Because astronomical cycles exert an influence upon humans and nature, they therefore also influence cities and nations. This is because the cycles mark a specific geography over an extended period of time. It is as if the astronomy of the heavens proclaims, "This is where time is now; and this is where things will happen." Because these cities are the earthly focus of this cycle they seem to foster more creativity within their own population as well as drawing talented individuals from other cities. The very minute preponderance of the physics of a repetitive astronomical cycle serves to create a noticeable advantage of one city over another over the course of many years.

I have omitted the mention of Mesoamerica, China, Japan, and especially Egypt in the historical course of civilization. In favor of the appropriate simplicity of our demonstration, we will only focus upon Egypt which has of course played a major role in the progress of civilization. Yet, Egypt's colonial and imperial aspirations were very modest in respect to the technology that this federation of cities possessed. Egypt's achievements in art, science, architecture, social organization, and religion are unparalleled in world history, and are the envy of all nations. The very chronicle of their rulers and history surpasses the 2,160 year maximum that other nations were not able to achieve. I believe that Egypt is *not* an example of civilization; but rather, Egypt was an example of Culture. That is, Egypt was the homeland of Culture prior to the advent of the new cosmic age during which the greater cosmic cycle has moved to demarcate Jerusalem as the new cultural locality and the new Heavenly City here upon earth.

If a slow moving astronomical cycle designates a cultural holy place, and during the course of great periods of time moves onward to find a new place of inspiration; then we must consider that there have been favored cultural places in the far distant past prior to Egypt. We will also consider that these former cultural places were located to the west of Egypt and Greece. And we will further notice that the traditions of Egypt and Greece confirm that their gods and their science came from the regions to the west of them, thereby attesting to the influence of the astronomical Cycle of Culture. Moving backward in time, these divine cultural places were Libya before Egypt, and Morocco prior to Libya. Therefore, we also believe that the legend of Atlantis is not a fable or a philosophical paradigm, but, that it was indeed a genuine locality upon the face of the globe prior to the cultural dominance of Morocco. Briefly the point we are trying to introduce is that civilization is a rapidly developing process highlighted by a rapidly moving astronomical cycle. But when we mention Atlantis, Morocco, Libya, Egypt, and Jerusalem we are speaking about Culture, an extremely ponderous astronomical cycle moving eastward in a contrary direction to Civilization.

Without a doubt, the primeval Atlantis had many colonies upon the entire Atlantic seaboard. Apparently one of the major colonies was also destroyed by the ravages of earthquakes about 9,000 years before Solon visited Egypt. The destruction of this colony occurred much closer to our own time than that far distant era when the original Atlantis was overwhelmed. This similar event rekindled the memory of the older Atlantis mythology. Therefore, the sum total of all Atlantis tradition was applied to this similar earthquake which destroyed a colony of Atlantis located upon the seaboard of Morocco.

This evolution of history into myth is part of the fundamental nature of all stories. The world-engulfing flood of Noah did not occur some few thousand years ago. But rather, as Albiruni tells us in his *Chronology of Nations*, there have been many cycles of regional floods and natural devastations. Every time one of these minor cataclysms occurs, its regional history is joined together with the story of the universal event, in this case that of the world-engulfing flood.

All cultures and civilizations steal, borrow, and appropriate the very best and most important information from their predecessors. Every nation appends ancient histories onto their own identity and experience of their own regional disasters. Nations tend to absorb scientific ideas until they actually believe that they have become the true and original discoverers of those very ideas that their ancestors had stolen. For in the course of time, as nations and cities rise and fall, the survivors easily appropriate the glory when there is no one left to challenge their claims. All this is very natural and it is exactly how civilization and culture interact. It is for these very reasons that it is possible that ancient information is preserved over millions of years.

As far reaching as these assertions may seem, there is very dramatic proof in the record of human recollection which will attest to these matters. The mythology of the Greeks is a compendium of their very own ancient traditions, and those that they have learned about from the Egyptians. And again, the Egyptians had borrowed these vital traditions from people who had come before them, namely the Libyans, the Moroccans, and the Atlantians.

There is a simple reason why mythology has never been regarded as a font of scientific information. First of all, many people just do not have a taste for this type of bewildering prose, recounting episodes of gods behaving badly. We have difficulties seeing the reason or meaning behind these bizarre interactions of supposed immortals whose conduct is sometimes ludicrous, immoral, and all too animalistic. However, this absurdity is a protective guise over some of the most important information in the universe.

Examination will show that mythology accurately describes the west to east directional flow of the Cycle of Culture here on earth which mimics the Cycle of Galactic Progression in the heavens.

Below, the classical sequence of the gods is listed, according to Greek and Egyptian tradition, in relation to the cosmic periods of time in which they appeared and dominated. Again the reader should notice that the sequence is not in relation to the Precession of the Vernal Equinoxes and Civilization, but counterclockwise and in relation to the Cycle of Culture.

Greek	*Egyptian*	*Cosmic Period*
Uranus	(Hephaestus)	Scorpio
The Great Titans	(Helios)	Sagittarius
Hyperion	(Agathodaemon)	Capricorn
Atlas & Cronus	(Cronus)	Aquarius
Olympian Zeus & Hera	(Isis & Osiris)	Pisces

This human recollection of the Generations of the Gods is a cultural recollection. It seems incredible that human memory can encompass such vast realms of time. But as we said above, smaller but similar events, occurring on regional stages, continually serve to reanimate the true history of cultural events.

Numerous other researchers have toyed with the idea of relating the mythological gods to the signs of the zodiac. Many of these ideas remained in their notebooks and were not published at large. Below is one such attempt from Franz Boll in his *Sphaera*.

		I	II	III	IV	V
1	♈	[Athena]	?	?	?	⚹—
2	♉	Aphrodite	Selene	Demeter	Ares	Hermes
3	♊	Apollon	Herakles	Hephaistos	Hera	Kronos
4	♋	Hermes	Ares[1]	Zeus	Pan (?)	Aphrodite
5	♌	[Zeus]	?	?	?	?
6	♍	[Demeter]	[Selene]	[Demeter]	?	[Hermes]
7	♎	[Hephaistos]	[Herakles]	[Hephaistos]	?	[Kronos]
8	♏	[Ares]	[Ares]	[Zeus]	?	[Aphrodite]
9	♐	[Artemis]	?	?	?	?
10	♑	[Hestia]	Selene	Demeter	Aphrodite[2]	Hermes
11	♒	Hera	Herakles	Hephaistos	?[3]	Kronos
12	♓	Poseidon	Ares	Zeus	Hermes	Aphrodite[4]

Hopefully we have begun to establish the idea that the ancients thought cosmologically. They distrusted the accuracy of yearly measurement over greater periods of time as well as the variability of cycles and the changes in the rotational and orbital speeds of heavenly bodies. The advance of the Precessional Cycle would also cause feast days to fall behind in the calendar. Therefore they established a scientific cosmology where *time* only meant a heavenly position. As an example, the feast of Osiris will be held when the sun enters the sign of Pisces. The ancients remembered that the god Osiris first made his appearance to mankind during the cultural age of Pisces. In this way, history, astronomy, and religious celebration are scientifically and accurately unified in the one medium of cosmology.

We also noticed that the ancients were extremely religious. The final expression of every form of their technology was a temple to their gods. This may not have been totally to gratify their devotion, but rather, God was the final frontier of all their sciences. As well, their pragmatic scientists used Revelation to coordinate points of geography with regions of the heavens in order to develop and synchronize their science of cosmology. For example, the god Cronus was born in Morocco during the Cultural Age of Aquarius. Therefore the global region around Morocco corresponds to the heavenly region of Aquarius.

The ancient priest/scientists established a direct congruency between earthly geography and celestial position which in turn opened the door to all the other sciences. In our further chapters we will report on the New Madrid Earthquake in America which closely approximates the congruency which the ancients achieved.

Most of the following articles are intended to demonstrate the Atlantic Origin of Greek, Egyptian, Mesopotamian, Mediterranean, European, and Irish culture. Of course, each country and nation brings its own particular flavor of civilization to these traditions. But, history will show that science and religion feed upon the past, and that more things have been borrowed, stolen, and copied from antiquity, than have ever been originated in newer times.

We will now begin by establishing a context in African Morocco, the colony of Atlantis, and our best example of the seat of ancient culture. After setting this firm foundation we will follow the progress of culture to Libya, then on to Egypt, and finally on to the Holy Land.

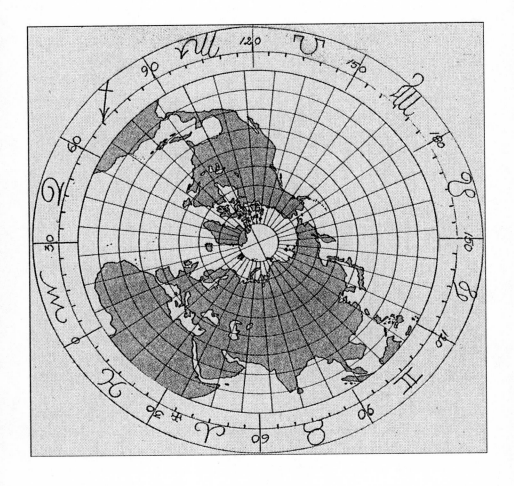

PART I:

WESTERN GENESIS

Introduction

The idea of a Western Genesis first came from the Egyptians themselves. They related a strange story of an advanced people who lived to the *west*, on the bounds of the ocean. But, their unique, ringed, capital city of Atlantis was destroyed by monstrous earthquakes long ago.

Plato, the celebrated Greek philosopher, told this story in his *Timaeus*. Because of his excellent reputation, Plato assured that the tale of Atlantis would enjoy a permanent vogue in Classical, Renaissance, Medieval, and modern times.

As a student of classical philosophy and Greek literature, I became aware of the vast quantity of references to a Western origin in Greek history, mythology, astronomy, science, geography, and poetry. This was a strange confirmation of the tale told by Plato. As well, there seemed to be a peculiar and mysterious undercurrent of tradition, that is, the Greeks also had memories of a more ancient homeland.

Chapter 1

Plato and Solon

Plato was an eclectic endowed with considerable good taste and a love of the ancient. Diogenes Laertius in his *Lives of the Eminent Philosophers* declares that Plato mixed together doctrines of Heraclitus, the Pythagoreans, and Socrates. Early in life, he lost the love of his own original compositions. For when he was about to compete for a prize with a tragedy he had composed, he listened to Socrates in front of the theater of Dionysus. Apparently, Plato was so impressed by what he heard that he consigned his own poems to the flames and attached himself to the great man.

The story of Atlantis appears in Plato's *Timeaus,* in which he explains that the story was brought by Solon from Egypt (from the city of Sais, which had a strong connection with Athens). In the *Critias,* he says that the Egyptians translated the Atlantic names into their own tongue, from which Solon was able to render them into Greek. Solon transmitted the story to his brother, Dropides, who is the great-grandfather of Critias, who is an uncle of Plato's mother, Perictone. The motivation for the transmission of this curious tale may have been that Solon traced his descent, through great antiquity, to Neleus and Poseidon. And, of course, Poseidon was said to have been the first ruler of Atlantis. Plato's father also traced his descent to Poseidon.

One matter that has always concerned scholars is, "Why does the Atlantis story appear in the *Timeaus,* which is mainly a cosmological account of the formation of the world?" Diogenes Laertius reports that Plato traveled to Sicily where he purchased a book from the relatives of Philolaus, a noted pupil of Pythagoras. It was from this book that the *Timeaus* was transcribed. Aulus Gellius also confirms this borrowing of Pythagorean philosophy as the source of the cosmological part of the *Timeaus.* Pythagoras himself was a Tyrrhenian, a very ancient and notable seafaring people, who share many similarities with the Atlantic navigators.

It is difficult to reach any definite conclusions from this background material, and impossible to explain the thousands of books written about Atlantis. Berger (*Pauly-Wissowa Encyclopedia*) says that the myth was thought to be true at the time of Columbus. Spanish and German writers referred to America by the name of *Atlantis.* Theories of an advanced, ancient people of high culture, who settled the world, were put forward by Olaf Rudbeck in 1682, Bailly in 1779, and Muller in 1844. In 1777 Baer attempted to trace the biblical origins of Genesis to Atlantis.

I cannot think that it would be profitable to regurgitate the wealth of modern thinking concerning Atlantis when we have already traced the very simple and plausible source back to Egypt by way of Solon. It is our intention to remain close to the original sources throughout this work. These sources already present enough food for thought to occupy our attention concerning the origin and transmission of history over long periods of time.

At this stage, the best question to ask would be, "Are there any other ancient writers that speak about Atlantis?" There is one, indeed, named Dionysius Skytobrachion, who lived in Alexandria in the middle of the 2nd century BC. Diodorus Sicilus uses this writer extensively as an authority for his own work, saying, "This writer has composed an account of Dionysus and the Amazons . . . and many other matters in which he cites the versions of the ancient writers."

Let us, then, have a look at this other story of the Atlantic regions, to see how it compares to the one that came to us by way of Egypt through Solon and Plato.

Chapter 2

Skytobrachion and the Other Atlantis

Let us now follow another account of the Atlantic people who lived in the regions of the West, in what is now Morocco and Algeria.

Diodorus Sicilus (iii.53–55) gives us an account which he has preserved from the writings of the earlier historian, Skytobrachion. It is he who reports,

> We are told, namely, that there was once in the western parts of Libya, on the bounds of the inhabited world, a race that was ruled by women . . . As mythology relates their home was on an island which, because it was in the west, was called Hespera, and it lay in the marsh Tritonis. The marsh was near the ocean which surrounds the earth and received its name from a certain river Triton which emptied into it; and this marsh was also near Ethiopia and that mountain by the shore of the ocean which is the highest of those in the vicinity and infringes upon the ocean and is called by the Greeks Atlas . . . They subdued many of the neighboring Libyans and nomad tribes, and founded within the marsh Tritonis, a great city which they named Cherronessus after its shape . . . The first people against whom they advanced, according to the tale, were the Atlantians, the most civilized men among the inhabitants of those

regions, who dwelt in a prosperous country and possessed great cities; it was among them, we are told that mythology placed the birth of the gods, in the regions which lie along the shore of the ocean . . . The story is also told that the marsh Tritonis disappeared from sight in the course of an earthquake, when those parts of it which lay towards the ocean were torn asunder.

If Skytobrachion's account is correct, and I see no reason to dispute the direct simplicity of what is reported; we should use this as the foundation of our inquiry. That is to say, that an Atlantis colony existed in Morocco, near Mt. Atlas, and that Greek and Egyptian culture identified this region with the birthplace of their gods. *The birthplace of the gods,* is, I believe, also a way of saying *the birthplace of culture.*

The *Timeaus,* Plato's account of Atlantis, came by way of Solon, who quotes the Egyptian priest as saying,

> It is related in our records how once upon a time your state stayed the course of a mighty host, which, starting from a distant point in the Atlantic Ocean, was insolently advancing to attack the whole of Europe and Asia to boot . . . for in front of the mouth . . . of the Pillars of Hercules: there lay an island which was larger than Libya and Asia together, and it was possible for the travelers of that time to cross from it to the other islands, and from the islands to the whole of the continent over against them . . . but that yonder is a real ocean, and the land surrounding it may most rightly be called . . . a continent. Now in this island of Atlantis there existed a confederation of Kings of great and marvelous power, which held sway over all the island and over many other islands also, and parts of the continent; and moreover, of the lands here within the Straits they ruled over Libya as far as Egypt, and over Europe as far as Tuscany . . . But, at a later time, there occurred portentous earthquakes and floods . . . and the island of Atlantis in like manner was swallowed up by the sea and vanished.

Skytobrachion's account of the island of Hespera, in the Tritonian marsh near the ocean by Mt. Atlas, is very helpful in illuminating Plato's account of Atlantis. As we will see, Greek tradition assigns great importance to this Tritonian Marsh and river Triton, by the mountain of Atlas. For the Greeks,

Morocco was the cultural birthplace of their gods and their traditions. We may assume this because the Greeks say that their gods came from Morocco. And, also, the Greeks applied the name Triton to the rivers upon which they sited their first settlements in Greece. This is exactly what colonists have always done, practiced the perpetuation of names from their former homeland. As well, among many of the Greeks, there has always been a special reverence for the tradition of Atlas. And this is because most of the Greek tribes trace their ancestry directly back to the daughters of Atlas.

The Egyptian priest's account in Plato is definitely of much greater antiquity than these events in Morocco. It stems from a more ancient time when America was Atlantis. This was a time of a worldwide empire, controlling parts of the North and South American continents, the islands of the Atlantic Ocean, Europe as far as Tuscany, and Africa as far as Egypt.

Upon rereading and comparing Plato to Skytobrachion one conclusion seems evident. Skytobrachion's Island of Hespera in Morocco appears to have been the important centerpiece of the many colonies upon the Atlantic. Hespera was overwhelmed by earthquakes and disappeared 9,000 years before Solon went to Egypt. The disappearance of Hespera on Triton in Morocco brought to mind and reanimated the recollection of the fabulous myths of the much older original Atlantis of the Americas. Hespera now became the carrier of all Atlantis Mythology.

In respect to the above conclusions; we will faithfully use Skytobrachion's account of Hespera on Triton, and distinguish it as the leader and foremost of the Atlantic colonies. For, it is here in Morocco that the traditions of the very ancient gods, the astronomical and cosmological sciences, and architectural technologies were preserved and communicated to people around the world. We ourselves are the heirs to these traditions.

Some Noteworthy Intricacies within Mythological History

Prior to the disappearance of Hespera beneath the waves, this colony had a long, rich, and brilliant history as a leader of many other colonies along the coastlands of Europe and Africa. We will investigate some of the regional histories that still point back to the cultural primacy of Morocco. We will also consult myth in order to give us a sequence of rulers in those far distant times. Namely that the Heaven-Holder, Atlas of Morocco, was honored by having the nearby mountain and ocean named after him. But, we should also realize that before Atlas, this ocean held the title of the *Cronian Sea,* after the god Cronus. And before that, it was called *Ocean,* after the god Ocean. One might therefore be led to the conclusion that since the Egyptians and Solon call it *Atlantis*—that this must refer to Morocco at the time when the name of Atlas distinguished these regions. This is not necessarily true.

Often though, the locations and names in a story are adjusted to make sense to the present auditors of the myth. That is why the Egyptians, or Solon and Plato, translated the name of the ruler of Atlantis as Poseidon. This was because Poseidon of Libya was a more contemporary Earth-Holder who was closer to the time of the Greeks and the Egyptians. The astronomical and scientific traditions of Atlas were handed down to posterity by Poseidon. But truthfully the name of Poseidon is only associated with Libya, and it is therefore much younger than the era of Hespera on Triton in Morocco.

We may, therefore, imagine that the *real* ruler of the first Atlantis in the Americas was the god, Ocean. He who is the oldest of all the maritime gods!

There are definite images of a marsh along the Moroccan coastline near the supposed Garden of the Hesperides.

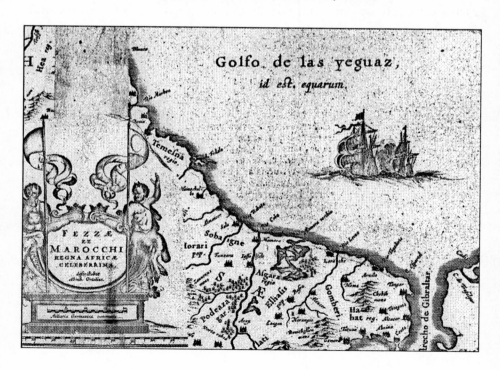

Our best hypothesis is the notion of a 9000 BC Atlantis colony, located in a swamp in Morocco. A very interesting map by Abraham Ortelius shows a swamp with five large islands at a place called *Mamora Vecchia*, or Old Mamora. The old forest of Mamora supplied the magnificent timber for the vessels of the Corsairs of the Barbary Coast. The map of Ortelius shows islands in a swamp located between Larache and Marmora. Note the spelling of Morocco which is like the Fir Morocchi of Irish history.

With the eradication of the Old Wood; the water table would naturally have sunk, and all traces of the swamp would have disappeared as well. This wood and swamp was south of Larache, on the River Lecuz, known in antiquity as Lixus; the home of Anteaus, the giant who fought with Hercules. Ancient Lixus is also considered to be the legendary site of the Gardens of the Hesperides. It is an extremely ancient area which saw the occupations of Atlantic Phoenicians, Carthaginians, and Romans. Larache, itself, might have rivaled modern Tangier as a major trading port were it not for the dangerous offshore sand bars which restricted the access of modern vessels.

Abraham Ortelius (1527–1598) was called the father of modern cartography. He was directed into his career by none other than the great Gerardus Mercator, with whom he traveled throughout Europe collecting maps and information. Abraham was a member of the influential Ortelius family of Augsburg, Germany. He was a student of Classical History and a collector of books and coins. He was assisted in his research and map gathering by his wealthy patron and friend, Gilles Hooftman, lord of Cleydael and Aertselaer. Ortelius's good scholarship prompted him to credit 87 persons as the authors of maps which he produced in his own work called, *Theatrum Orbis Terrarum*. In 1575 he became geographer to Phillip II of Spain.

Ortelius's depiction of the Marsh of Mamora appears on his own 1595 map of Fessae and Marocchi. The above swamp also appears in the most complete detail in a map dated 1656 by Nicholas Sanson (1600–1667), the father of French cartography. Sanson's map is dated 1656 and he gives full credit to Ortelius. Yet, Sanson's coastline is extremely detailed and articulated. His rendition of the swamp, while in the same location below Larache, is quite different with only two islands shown.

Nicholas Sanson is credited with adopting the new scientific methods of mapmaking. He was the founder of the firm of Sanson who supplied Atlas's of general charts of all parts of the world. He also produced groups of maps showing places of the ancient world.

Sanson also produced a map showing a swamp with several islands in the region of Marmora. Perhaps this map and that of Ortelius were copied from a very ancient map showing the Tritonian Marsh and the Island of Hespera? Sanson is also notorious for his map of California as a complete island! Yet, on the same map he shows Hudson Bay in accurate detail.

We can only conclude that Sanson, the pioneer cartographer, through his business and interest, was a great collector of olden maps of all parts of the world. Could it be that Sanson and Ortelius had included the Island of Hespera in the Tritonian Marsh on their maps of Morrocco?

The answer is—possibly or maybe not. It does, however, show that such an island swamp could have and did exist at Old Mamora, nearby most ancient Lixus and Larache.

The 1565 Venice map from Ptolemy shows no details of any swamp in these regions called Fez and its Seven Provinces by later geographers. Ortelius seems to be the first to show the swamp in 1595. Among those who depict the Marsh of Mamora are: Purchas and Hondius in London 1625, W. J. Blaeu of Amsterdam in 1636 (Ortelius credited), M. Merian of Amsterdam in 1640 (credits Blaeu and Ortelius), then comes the Sanson map of 1656 (who also credits Ortelius).

I think that it is permissible to say that because of Columbus and the other voyages of discovery at that epoch—that many of the formerly prized and secret maps of the past were seen to be out-of-date and out-moded. And furthermore, that these old fashioned maps were taken out of the safe repositories of the kings and the great merchant city leagues. Therefore, these once prized and secret maps entered into circulation once again, and became accessible to the agents of the cartographers, who were giving good money for any antique maps full of supposedly out-dated information. I believe that it was in the context of these yard sales of old maps that some very interesting and perhaps accurate pieces of ancient cartography, once again, saw the light of day.

Chapter 3

Confirmation on the Atlantic Island of Ireland

Ireland is of such great age that its antiquity was recognized in classical Greek literature. The historical annals of the kingdom of Ireland admit that the island was conquered at various times by Giants and pirates from Africa. These facts lend confirmation to the Greek and Sardinian reports that their ancient heritage had its origins on the Atlantic and Mediterranean coasts of North Africa.

From the beginning, Ireland has always been associated by the Greeks and Romans with the name Ogygia. The Reverend Jeoffry Keating in his *General History of Ireland* (first published in 1625) relates that Plutarch calls it Ogygia, which in Latin signifies, *Insula perantiqua,* that is, the most ancient isle.

The most illustrious Greek poet Homer in his *Odyssey* (vii.244) sings, "There is an isle Ogygia, which lies far-off in the sea. Therein dwells the fair-tressed daughter of Atlas, guileful Calypso, a dread goddess." The goddess Calypso clothed Odysseus in immortal raiment, and detained him there for a period of seven years. They are said to have produced Latinus, the ancestor of the Italians.

Hesiod (*Theogony*, 359) makes Calypso of a much older generation, saying that she was sprung from Ocean and Tethys. In accordance with our thesis, this would suggest that Ireland may have been a part of the empire of the primeval god, Ocean. If this were the case, then Ireland would truly be one of *the* most ancient of all bastions of culture and tradition. But Ireland has been conquered so very many times that one of their historical documents is simply called *The Book of Invasions*. If America is the modern melting pot of immigrants from around the world then Ireland was that same melting pot for the ancient world.

Keating says that the first historical name of Ireland was *Inis na bhfiodhbhuidhe*, which signifies "the Wooded Isle." Homer (*Odyssey*, i.50, vii.245) records, "Tis a wooded isle, and therein dwells a goddess, daughter of Atlas of baneful mind, who knows the depth of every sea." Atlas knows the depth of every sea because he was among the greatest of all the mapmakers.

Plutarch, in *Concerning the Face Which Appears in the Orb of the Moon* (pp. 941–945) tells us that westward of Britain lies Ogygia and other islands, in one of which Cronus is confined. The sea is called the *Cronian Main*, and is watched over by the giant Ogygius or Briareus,

> Later in time Heracles came there to rekindle Greek culture, and he and Cronus receive the highest honors there. Every thirty years when the planet of Cronus, that is Saturn, enters the constellation of Taurus, some of the people of these islands go on a seafaring pilgrimage to the far West. They visit a people who are holy and prophetic, and spend their time among them in sacrifices and celebrations, and in discourses of philosophy and astronomy.

Greek traditions also tell of Apollo coming down from the North, from the Hyperborean Island. It is also said that there are similarities in Ireland to the sacrifices in honor of Demeter and Core which are celebrated in Samothrace. These facts are reported in Strabo (4.4.6) and Plutarch. But, we do not wish to be distracted from our point with the wealth of Greek tradition about Ireland and the mysterious islands of the North Atlantic. It is enough to say that the Greeks connect Ireland with Atlas and Cronus.

The Invasions of Ireland

The ancient annals, the historians, and the folklore of Ireland tell us that their island was inhabited by the *Fomorians,* a race of Atlantic sea-kings who descended from the Giants of Africa. In Sardinia, Spain, France, and England we also meet with a wealth of legends concerning Giants. Quite simply, I believe that this is a reference to the descendants of Ge and Uranus. The *Ge-gantes* are a people born of Ge. For, it says in the Irish *Stair Ercuil* (p. 123) that Antaeus was the governor of Morocco, and he was called a Fomorian. This Antaeus is also called Mac Terra, a son of Ge, the Earth.

There are many variations of the name Fomorian: *Fomor, Fomra, Foghmoir, Fir-mor,* and *Fomhoraicc.* I favor the last example: Fir = man and Morocchi = Morocco. All of the above forms mean the same thing—"men from the sea." The prefix "fo" comes from "fir" when it is followed by an "m." It is still common in Irish speech to refer to a person as a German-man. Irish history confirms this practice by calling one of their great tribes the *Fir-Bolg,* or, the men from Belgium.

As is common in the histories of every nation on earth, the conquerors appropriate by adoption the illustrious genealogies of the more ancient inhabitants whom they have defeated. In great part this is achieved through intermarriage with the ancient stock. All conquerors feel fully justified in practicing this most universal custom.

Ireland is no exception to this rule. Keating (p. 74) complains of the confusion of adopting former names, "The four sons of Partholanus were Er, Orbha, Fearon and Feargna. We should observe that Milesius [a much later conqueror] had four grandsons of the same name."

We do not wish to get into a long dissertation about Irish genealogy. Suffice it to say that there is evidence that the Fir-Morocchi occupied Ireland before the first invasion by Partholanus. These Fir-Morocchi, or Fomorians (as most people speak about them in modern usage), are mentioned in the battles of every subsequent invasion of Ireland. O'Flaherty in his *Ogygia* (p. 11) finally suggests that the Fomorians may most probably have been the aboriginal inhabitants of Ireland.

O'Donovan (p. 101) writes that traditions of Partholanus are still remembered in Co. Leitrim and Ballyshannon, and that, according to Mac Firbis, this Partholanus was compelled to give battle to the Fomorian, Ciogal Griccenn-cosach, near Lough Swilly by Magh Itha.

The historians say that Ireland was depopulated by a serpent or plague, until the coming of Nemedius. Curiously, it is the Fomorians who are commissioned to build two royal palaces for Nemedius, the new conqueror of Ireland. O'Donovan (p. 101) quotes Mac Firbis who says, "The Fomorians were they who first waged war with the country in the time of Nemhidh and his children . . . Gann and Seangann two kings of the Fomorians; Conang son of Feabhar, and Morc son of Deala were the most illustrious persons of the Fomorians." Their main fortress was called the Tower of Conaing, and also the Tower of Glass, on the island of Tory off the coast of Donegal. The Nemedians succeeded in taking this castle of glass where Conuing was slain. Nevertheless, according to Keating (p. 79) Morc returned with a fleet from Africa and took possession of the whole island.

The Nemedians fled the island. But several hundred years later, they returned under the name of the Fir-Bolg. Again, their main commanders, curiously, had the identical names of the Fomorian kings, Gann and Seangann.

The next invasion of Ireland was by the famous Tuatha de Danaan. They were renowned for their great love of music, celebrations, fables, poetry, and dancing. Charles O'Connor (*Dissertations.1753*) says that the Fomorians reinvited the Belgians, the Fir-Bolg; and in conjunction with them fought against the Tuatha de Danaan, in the battle of Moy-Turey, near Lake Arrow.

The second king of the Tuatha de Danaan was Bres, son of Elathan Mac Dalbaech, a king of the Fomorians. This Bres was later discredited in a satire by one of the poets, and Nuada of the silver hand, the first king, reascended the throne. Bres then enlisted the aid of the Fomorian, Balor, of the reinhabited Tory Island. Balor's daughter, Ethlinn, became the mother of the third king of the Tuatha de Danaan, the renowned Lug Lamfada, the longhanded, also called the master of all arts.

Lastly, there came an invasion of the Gadelians, under the command of Miles, the King of Spain. The second great battle of the Gadelians was fought at Teanhuighe against the Fomhoraicc pirates. Later, the fourth Gadelian king fought against Stirne, son of Duibh, son of Fomhoir.

In more modern times, in 54 AD, there occurred a great uprising of the rent-payers, artisans, masons, and builders who were the remnants of the Fomorians and the former conquered races of Ireland. These rebels elected Cairbre Cat's Ears to the throne. This Cairbre was no less than a descendant of Labhra Liongseach (whose ancestry and myth are steeped in the traditional style so particular to the Fomorians). The next rebel leader was Elim, a descendent of Fomhoir. Keating, in his book on *Genealogies,* tells us that after this revolutionary monarchy was put down in 79 AD, "That the national assembly decreed that all non-Milesian or non-Gadelian pedigrees became illegal in the future records of the Kingdom of Ireland." Thereby, every association with the heritage and traditions of the Fomorians was forever cast aside, and illegitimized. The once proud and noble Fomorians were now relegated to the oblivion of a children's story or a local fable.

The Fomorians

The Reverand Keating (p. 124) writes,

> We meet frequently, in the Irish histories, with many voyages made by a sort of Africans, who often landed upon this island; and there we have an account of certain stars, and the names of them, that were worshipped by the mariners, and were supposed to derive a power from the god of the sea, either to misguide the ship, or to conduct her safe into the port.

Keating (p. 78) continues by saying that the Fomorians,

> Fitted out a fleet, and strengthened themselves with a standing army, and by these military methods harassed the unfortunate Nemedians, and obliged them to bring the tax and contributions laid upon them . . . for they demanded two parts of their children, of their cattle, of their milk, butter and wheat . . . The Africans employed a woman to be the general receiver of their tribute.

Some earlier Irish historians tried to assign a Hamitic or Semitic origin to the Fomorians. But, O'Flaherty in his *Ogygia* writes, "Fomhoraigh . . . over-sea people who infested Ireland during the time of the first colonies; of Hamitic origin, and from Africa they assert them all to be; except only for those first Fomorians to whom they assign no home place or origin."

O'Flaherty also comments, "But they say that some Fomorians which are called ours, have come from the land of the Danes, the Swedes and Norwegians." And he cites Socer, the Fomorian King of Finland.

In conclusion, it would seem most probable that the most ancient Fomorians were from Morocco in Africa, and that they stemmed from ancient Atlantic peoples. Furthermore, that these Moroccans came to Brittany and Ireland, and also colonized much of the North Atlantic including the Scandinavian coastlands. It would seem that later in history the name Fomorian came to be applied to all pirates or raiders from the lands of the Northmen. The name may also have been applied equally to the Carthaginian and Moroccan Phoenicians who ventured into the North Seas. Again, I think that these later episodes of raids and piracy would have rekindled memories of the legends of the original and most ancient Fomorians.

In ancient times, Ireland could only be reached by sea. Any invasion would require an organized flotilla and an armed force. The African Fomorians were acclaimed as deep-sea mariners who traveled by the stars. They were the acknowledged architects and great builders of mighty fortresses, castles, and sacred sites. Monmouth, the medieval British historian, even attributes Stonehenge to the African Giants. He further asserts that Stonehenge was first erected in Ireland, from where it was magically transported to England by Merlin. In addition to astronomy, seafaring, and building, the Fomorians were successful in establishing lasting government and social institutions. They are the first tax-collectors of recorded history. Until their name and glory was eradicated and legally expunged from Irish history, the Fomorians were the most powerful, influential, and enduring families and tribes of Ireland. They had survived almost every invasion and incursion of new people to their holy and sacred island.

Chapter 4

Confirmation on Cadiz, the Balearic, and Sardinian Islands

The histories of some of the Mediterranean islands and Cadiz compare to many of the events of Irish history. This correspondence will help us to illuminate one well-defined picture and a real historical context in the western Mediterranean and the North Atlantic regions down to Morocco. This image will focus upon Morocco as the birthplace for the origin of culture, science, and religion.

Armstrong, in his *History of Minorca*, writes that the Balearic Islands were first ruled by a race of Giants. After them came Geryon, the monarch of Spain, who annexed these islands to his kingdom. Much later, in 452 BC, the Carthaginians overcame the islands and built great cities there.

Concerning the history of Sardinia, Pausanius relates (*Phocis.17*) that the first settlers were Libyans under the command of Sardus. He was a son of Hercules, and it was after him that the island was named. Later, Artisaeus, the son of Apollo, came from Boeotia to settle in Sardinia. He was married to a daughter of Cadmus, who was a descendant of Libya, and of Egyptian-Phoenician stock who had settled in Boeotia. The next conqueror of Sardinia was Norax from Spain, a son of Hermes and Erythia (Cadiz), who was a daughter of Geryon, the monarch of Spain.

Let us digress for a moment in order to capture the background of that most famous trading emporium, Cadiz, also called Erythia, Gadira, and Gades. Cadiz is among the most famous of the Phoenician strongholds on the Atlantic. Yet, in the reports of genealogy and mythology this island-peninsula must be listed among the very ancient places of all antiquity. Apollodorus in *The Library* (II.v.10) tells us that Erythia was an island near the ocean, which was later called Gadira (Cadiz). The sacred cows of the Sun were kept at Erythia, which was named after one of the Hesperides. This island was inhabited by Geryon, son of Chrysaor by Callirrhoe, a daughter of Ocean. The reference to the god, Ocean, places it in the deepest antiquity, long before the advent of the Phoenicians.

Geryon is said to have had the body of three men who were grown together and joined into one at the waist, but then, parted again into three from the flanks and thighs. The tri-formed Chimera of the Tyrrhenian also follows this threefold combination. This kind of metamorphic symbolism may belong particularly to the Atlantic regions.

Hercules was to steal the cattle of Geryon who also possessed the two-headed watchdog, Orthus. This hound was begotten by Typhon and Echidna, who also sired the Chimera. Since, the Chimera was the mascot of the mysterious seafaring Tyrrhenian; we may allege that these navigators also came from these Atlantic regions.

Echidna is one of the earliest genetrix of Atlantic culture. She is the daughter of Tartarus and Ge. She is actually called the mother of the dragon, who spoke with many and divers sorts of voices, and who guards the apples of the Hesperides. As well, Echidna is the mother of the mysterious Sphinx that appeared in Greece.

Returning again to events in Sardinia, it is reported that after Norax, grandson of Geryon, there came Iolaus, with Thespians and men from Attica. Then Athenians arrived under Ogrylus. After the Trojan War some of the followers of Aeneas settled in Sardinia. But all of these Greek colonists were utterly eradicated by Libyans who reconquered the island. Pausanius concludes by saying that in figure, fashion, and mode, the Sardinians are most like the Libyans.

These accounts from the Mediterranean islands present a historical context very similar to the records of the Irish in their *Book of the Invasions*. Namely we have: African Giants, African Libyans, Spanish Monarchs of

Atlantic origin, Greek settlers with Atlantic and Libyan roots, and finally, a recapture of the islands by Libyan Africans.

Corsica and Sardinia contain a wealth of megalithic structures similar to those found in Ireland and Brittany. The mountaintop precincts and fortresses of Cucuruzzu and Capula have only been recently rediscovered. The astonishing planetary and astronomical observatory at Filitosa, though mentioned in 1810 by Merimee, has only come under some superficial critical inspection since 1954. At this site, the stones depicting the specific risings of the planets were actually removed from their special locations before their scientific function could be surveyed, analyzed, and appreciated.

On Sardinia there are thousands of astronomical observatories and round towers which inclued some rare instances of Ogam writing. About one hundred of these exceptional towers are huge fortress-like structures built of massive Cyclopean stone work. But, it was only in 1980 that these wonderful structures came to be appreciated through the enlightened publication of *La Sardegna Nuragica* by Massimo Pittau.

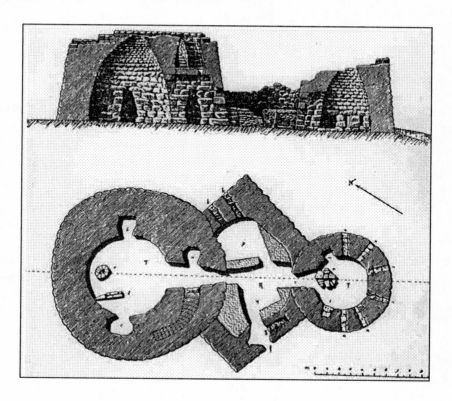

Mythological Review

The genealogies of the Greek and Egyptian traditions may be taken as the most certain guide to checking and reviewing the sequence of universal history. These genealogies present a logical and consistent system which exhibits a science of pedigree, which we can use as a guideline to confirm our historical picture.

The histories report that Geryon, Phoenicians, Libyans, and Carthaginians are connected with the events of these islands. Let us review what genealogical sciences have to say about these people:

LIBYA was descended from Io of the family of Inachus. Inachus was the son of Ocean and Tethys.

POSEIDON and Libya had two sons, Belus and Agenor. Belus became the ruler of Egypt. Agenor went to Phoenicia and had the following children: Europa, Cadmus, Phoenix, and Cilix.

GERYON, the son of Chrysaor, was descended from Poseidon. It was he who severed the head of the Gorgon. An alternate and earlier form makes Geryon, *not* of the generation of Poseidon, but from the generation of Ocean. In this case, Chrysaor is identified with Callirrhoe, who was a daughter of Ocean. This Geryon of Gades in Spain, was called a triple-bodied giant, whose cattle were stolen as one of the labors of Hercules. Before this adventure, Hercules sets up his famous Pillars at the entrance of the Mediterranean, though some say these already existed and belonged to Atlas.

In our review of Ireland we saw that some of the ancient Fomorian names were reused and taken up by subsequent invaders and conquerors of the island. This is such a natural consequence of the intermarriage of peoples that it hardly merits our comments. Other than that; we should notice that when names are reused, they obviously belong to different generations in time. Therefore, in the above case, it is highly likely that there was a Geryon from the generation of Ocean, and that there was *probably* a later Geryon from the generation from Poseidon.

One other matter that spawns confusion is the use of the terms, Ancient Sea Kings and Ancient Sea Peoples. We have already discussed the etymology of Fir-Mor, as being, Men from the Sea. The Fomorians and the Morini of Atlantic France, and the citizens of Aquatania already qualify in their names as ancient sea people. We do not need another generic term to hide the identity of people that we already know existed. Within this group of Mysterious Sea People comes the enigmatic seafaring Shardanes depicted on the temple walls of the tomb at Medinet-Habu. We have just been told by the leading Greek historians that the Libyan Admiral Sardus, had conquered Sardinia. It goes without saying that at this period of time, the Libyans dominated the seas. There is really no mystery here at all.

Chapter 5

Atlantis in Andalusia, Spain

In 1928, Elena Maria Windsor-Whishaw wrote her *Atlantis in Andalucia*. This work is a classic study of the ancient history of Spain including megaliths, cyclopean structures, the Atlantean city of Niebla, ancient minning, and the Sun Temple at Seville. Her work underscores many of the viewpoints that we are trying to advance.

Dona Elena, as she was affectionately called by the natives, advanced the theory that the Tartessus region of Spain had been colonized by Atlanteans during the period from 40,000–12,000 BC. She cites mythology in which Gadir inherited Poseidon's kingdom outside the Pillars of Hercules. This name is naturally related to the famous Cadiz or *Gades*, but also to Gadea on the Rio Tinto nearby Niebla, the site of an ancient mill and a stone-age fortress. Later on this region was conquered by the Libyan Empire. Again, this is the same sequence of history that we encountered in Ireland, Sardinia, and the Balearic Islands. Actually, this Niebla is of such antiquity that the citizens entertain legends of a great world drought and flood, which their city survived. They also recall voyages to far distant islands across the Atlantic.

The reason for the probability of such olden legends and architecture, which even includes samples of the rare stone-age cement, is that the Rio Tinto region was forever noted for its mining of gold, silver, and copper. This activity is of such great age that anyone can see evidence in the mines of silver extracted next to untouched gold, where in other places the gold or copper have been mined right next to where silver veins lay untouched. This reflects the supply and demand market conditions over substantial periods of time. This antiquity is confirmed by the prehistoric fields of slag which have accumulated on a gigantic scale.

Furthermore, Dona Elena (p. 145) writes,

> It has been pointed out again and again that there is a striking similarity in the bronze arms and implements of countries so widely separated as Switzerland, Denmark, Ireland and Africa . . . 400 bronze arms, ornaments, etc., dredged up in 1923 . . . at the port of Huelva, show such a likeness to bronze arms . . . found in the other countries named, as to leave no doubt of a common origin.

Throughout history, Niebla (Iberian: *Ilipla*) was the greatest fortress in the whole region extending from the river Guadiana to the Guadalquivir. Its walls, with no less than forty watch-towers, still stand practically complete on a plateau 100 feet above the bank of the Rio Tinto (known as the Iber in ancient times). On the east side of the ancient city is the man-made harbor, the *Desembarcadero*, 1,000 feet long by 100 feet wide to 15 feet deep. Numerous wells of 24-inch diameter have been dug in ancient times through 100 feet of limestone in order to reach the water table beneath the fortress. Only slaves would be used to dig in such confined space and to such a depth. And only a fortress of great age and many assaults would need internal wells. Yet, the Rio Tinto was often polluted from the mining, and hence its colorful name.

There is an unusual abundance of prehistoric mills on the Rio Tinto, especially at Gadea. Some of these resemble the beehive shape of the Tomb of Atreus, and also employ building methods identical to the gallery at Tiryns, thereby giving the appearance of ancient Minoan civilization in Greece.

Furthermore, Dona Elena reports (p. 91) on the folk memory of the people of Palos who recall visits to the Antilles. Because of these traditions many of them eagerly joined the expedition of Columbus, along with Irish sailor, William Ayres of Galway whose native city also entertained similar, old stories of far-off Atlantic islands.

In chapter XI, Dona Elena writes that the rulers of ancient Tartessus had been harassed for many ages by the Phoenician traders who established Gades as their base. The final fall of the Phoenician city of Tyre to Nebuchonodosor in 574 BC lead to the expulsion of the Phoenicians of Gades, and initiated the new era of trade with the Greeks. Very soon, however, the two- century-old Carthage in North Africa stepped in to offer a new mother country to all dispossessed Phoenicians upon the Atlantic and Mediterranean. Thereafter, Gades became a refuge of very mixed populations solely interested in trade and manufacture, "and having little or no racial or national instincts to bind them to the soil." Briefly, King Theron, of the Balearic Isles, tried to help the native Tartessians; but finally, the Carthaginian Phoenicians overran all of Tartessus—"and they were implacable in their triumph."

Until 1145 AD, a majestic, bronze statue stood at the entrance of the Bay of Cadiz. This statue was 9 feet tall and rested upon a foundation of 44 square feet. Strabo calls it the statue of Chronos, who is the African variant of the Iberian god Gargoris. The statue represented an old man with a long beard; one of his hands stretched toward the south, toward Africa, holding a large key, the symbol of his dominion over time.

Dona Elena also comments (p. 168) upon the amazing structures of ancient Iberia from the time of the Tartessus culture. Even in the period as late as 1248 AD, the original ancient city walls of Seville were "six miles in circumference with 176 towers at equal distance one from another."

Dona Elena's final conclusions may be summarized as follows: The first conquerors of Spain were colonists from Atlantis interested in the gold, silver, and copper mines along the Rio Tinto.

After long periods of time, invaders came from northwestern Africa, including people from Libya. This mixture of Atlantean, African, and Europeans produced the ancient race of the Liby-Tartessian (p. 173).

Her conclusions echo the identical histories that we have discovered to exist among the Irish, to the North; unto the Sardinians in the Mediterranean. There really can be no further doubt of the truth of the mythological history of the ancient Atlantic regions. There is such an abundance of local traditions and national histories that all confirm in unison a brilliant sequence of culture and science, beginning upon the Atlantic seaboard.

Of great interest are the examples of megalithic culture still preserved in these regions. Dona Elena, in Chapter XIV, describes the most perfectly preserved sun temple in all of Europe. In ancient times, Seville was the capital of the Tartessian culture. It was called Tharsis. At 6.5 meters below the present level of Seville is a building called *El Laberinto*, the Labyrinth, which includes remains of the ancient Temple of Hercules. Columns from this temple were 40 feet in height. The Temple was rediscovered in the 16th century by workmen cleaning out a well. The domed roofs are of stone-age cement called *hormazo*. The Chapel of the Sun Temple is constructed by brick vaulting, niches, and ribs of exquisite workmanship, but stemming from an ancient megalithic period. Seven square channels slope upward, perhaps to follow or mark some astronomical phenomena.

Dona Elena also reported (p. 226) that Gargoris of the Iberians is the Cronus of the Greeks, whom the ancient Libyans had called Saturnus. These three names were then later worshiped under the one name of Hercules within this temple of Seville.

We have already spoken of Hercules's journey to the island of Erythia (Cadiz) to capture the cattle of Geryon. Zuniga quotes an olden local tradition that says that Hercules learned mathematics and astronomy from his relative Atlas of Libya, who accompanied him to Seville to help build the great temple there. There are numerous prehistoric constructions in the area. Dona Elena's conclusions (p. 234), based upon traditions and archaeology, are that Seville is "the City of the Libyan Athena, the Tartessian *Dea Genetrix*, the Christian *Ops Regina*, and to-day this region is called the 'Land of the Blessed Virgin.'"

PART II:

MAPS OF THE ANCIENT SEA KINGS

Introduction

E ver since the publication of *Maps of the Ancient Sea Kings* by Professor Charles Hapgood in 1966, the world has taken a renewed interest in the achievements of ancient science and cartography. Hapgood's book was based upon the research and the collections of ancient maps put together by the Swedish scholar, A. E. Nordenskiold. Hapgood showed that there were accurate representations of the American coastlands that predated Columbus. More extraordinary, he brought forth precise maps of the coast and interior of Antarctica that could only have been charted prior to the last Ice Age! That is, the detail of streams, mountains, and coastlands, with rivers running into the sea, could only have been charted when Antarctica was not covered by ice.

As a reward for his heroic insight and pioneering efforts, Hapgood was shunned by his peers, close associates, and fellow academics during his lifetime. Nevertheless, his achievement is continually quoted and recognized by every major new work about ancient science and technology.

Some of these antique maps employed extremely complicated projection techniques which were unrivaled until the late Renaissance. A few of the maps have not been equaled until our own modern era. These extraordinary maps were said to be the work of the Agathodaemon, Third God of the First

Dynasty of Egypt, which Manetho dates at about 36,525 years ago. There was also another person of this same name who copied the maps of Ptolemy.

It should be obvious that there have been as many schools of cartography and map research as there have been city-states and nations engaged in naval trade and empire: Phoenician, Tyrrhenian, North African, Crete, Rhodes, Veneti, Venetians, Genoa, Constantinople, Lisbon, The Hansa League of Northern Europe, The Dutch East Indies Company, and so on. It is well-known that Christopher Columbus traveled as far as Galway in Ireland looking for maps and knowledge of western trade routes, and northwestern passages to the Orient. Columbus did this because nearly every olden city along the Atlantic seaboard had traditions of their sailors visiting far-off places and islands across the Atlantic.

There is also a wealth of spuriously documented or preliminary research and hearsay concerning feats of navigation which need to be investigated further. I personally met a diver, employed by a very prestigious institute, who said he had discovered numerous Chinese junk-type vessels under the surface of the San Francisco Bay. In 1973, the Geology Service of the U.S. Navy discovered a multitude of donut-shaped stone anchors off the coast of Palos Verdes near Los Angeles. They were made of a cristobalite rock found in Southern China—though some have seen a resemblance to a stone type found near Monterrey. Further anchors were found off the Mendocino Coast of Northern California. These were dated at 2,000 to 3,000 years old using the deposits of manganese that had formed layers upon these artifacts. In 1984 more Palos Verdes anchors were brought to the surface, and these were definitely dated at 3,000 years old. "Even old Spanish documents describe oriental ships off the Mexican coast in 1576" (*Corliss*, p. 21). In the ancient shipbuilding yards of Canton, China, which date from 221 BC, the dry dock pits show that vessels of 60 ton displacement and 30 meters in length were being built (*South America on Ancient Maps* by Nito Verdera). In *Ancient Seafarers* (1991), Heinke Sudhoff shows photographs of Libyan stone slabs discovered in Ecuador. These portray elephants and Libyan script. One of these slabs is now in the museum at Carthage in Libya.

Later on, we will speak about the professor at the University of California at Santa Barbara who discovered an ancient ship building site on the Catalina Islands in an uplifted strata of considerable geological antiquity. He demonstrated that these ships were caulked with tar from the La Brea pits of Los Angeles. His artifacts, research papers, and small museum unfortunately burned down some years ago.

There is also the curious research produced by Ivar Zapp and George Erikson in *Atlantis in America* (1998). Their study uncovered the gigantic, granite stone orbs of the Diquis Delta of southwest Costa Rica. Some of these balls measure over 9 feet in diameter and weigh as much as 20 to 50 tons. These stone spheres were milled to within 2 millimeters of perfection, a feat which seems incomprehensible in respect to their antiquity. The authors claim that these spheres were arranged in groups forming sight lines pointing directly toward Easter Island, Stonehenge, and the Pyramids of Giza.

There is also the unbelievable 120-million-year-old stone fragment with a relief map of the Ural Region of Russia. So far neither the technology behind its creation, nor the hieroglyphic-syllabic language has been understood. This is the so-called *Map of the Creator,* which depicts gigantic civil engineering works, canals, weirs, and dams of a tremendous scale which could only have been built in order to service immense populations. The map appears to be but a tiny segment of an entire world map broken up over time by natural geologic forces in this region. The Center of Historical Cartography in Wisconsin, USA, is among those studying the map at this time (*Farshores Ancient Mysteries News.com*).

The Ancient Worldview

Our intention is to rediscover the underlying philosophy of ancient thought. Their ideas were that nature proceeds in many cycles within cycles. As minor cycles keep turning and reoccurring they are modified by the slight advance of the higher cycles. This creates a theater for nature in which many things seem almost to stay the same—while many other things seem to change ever so slightly.

Within this system, the cycles present natural and divine themes during the daily, monthly, annual, precessional, and galactic cycles. Therefore, according to the ancients, it is possible for things to come into being, to change, to be destroyed, and then to reappear in a slightly different form.

Consequently, it is very possible that scientifically advanced civilizations have existed before us, and have suffered destruction. Though sometimes some of their wisdom endures, and has been carefully preserved as unique cultural and scientific treasures.

This assertion is all too painfully apparent when we place the maps of Ptolemy side by side with the mysterious Master Portolano of the

Mediterranean (1300 AD). The same may be said when we compare early European maps alongside the exquisite Phoenician geography of Marinus.

Finally, there are many instances of so-called mistakes copied from older maps to the latest current versions. The examples are: the western bulge on the sub-continent of South America, the representation of California as an island, the Northwest Passage above Canada, and the appearance of the Swamps of Old Mamora in Morocco. Perhaps, we should be cautious before we dismiss these revealing glitches in geographic representations. They may be true maps of how the earth looked in the past.

Some Background History

L. A. Brown in his *Story of Maps*, acquaints us with the amazing quality of the Babylonian star data which describes the "Saros" cycle of 18 years and 11 days, or 223 lunations. At the end of this Saros Period, the moon very nearly returns to her original position in the sky with respect to the sun, her nodes, and perigee. Also, Venus returns in almost 8 years to a given point in the sky, and Mercury does the same, but only once in 46 years; Saturn takes 59 years, Mars 79 years, and Jupiter 83 years. Brown claims that this proves that accurate and uninterrupted observations had been made over long periods of time, especially the ability to predict lunar eclipses with great accuracy. Before we conclude too much of the Babylonians, it should be noted that the return of the lunar cycle was known throughout the entire globe.

Around 640 BC, Berossus of Babylon is credited with bringing together Chaldean, Egyptian, and Greek astronomy in his school on the island of Cos, at the mouth of the Gulf of Halicarnassus.

Eratosthenes of Cyrene, born in 276 BC, became head of the Library of Alexandria. He calculated the circumference of the earth to be between 25,000 and 25,200 miles which is close to Herschel's measurement of 24,899 miles. He also introduced a Prime Meridian, running north to south, through the city of Alexandria. His other nine meridians were based upon well-known positions of cities and places, and therefore not at regular distances from each other. Eratosthenes's calibration of global circumference is based upon a deep well at a substantial, but known, distance from an obelisk casting a shadow at the specific date when the sun is directly overhead and seen at the bottom of the deep well. The setup for this calculation has always struck me as being too text book and scientifically convenient.

Though, the actual geometry and math could be done by a child. Something is just not right with this story. I would wager that this calibration apparatus had been constructed for that purpose long before the time of Eratosthenes, who claimed the credit.

Poseidonius (130–151 BC) of Rhodes made an excellent calculation of the distance of the sun from the earth. According to Cleomedes, he also calculated the circumference of the earth to be about 24,000 miles. This distance is misquoted by Strabo who instead recorded a sum of 18,000 miles, a figure which led to the confusion of Columbus.

Marinus of Tyre (c.120 AD) made his observations in that oldest and largest city of Phoenicia. His works are lost, and we know of him only through the commentaries of Ptolemy, who accepted many of his calculations. Unfortunately, it seems that he accepted the misquoted figure by Strabo of 18,000 miles for the circumference of the earth. Marinus also seems to have accepted an important meridian going through the Fortunate Islands, which Ptolemy later adopted. Nordenskiold reports that the geographer Masudi (955 AD) declared that he had seen maps drawn by Marinus of Tyre, and that they were better than the maps of Ptolemy.

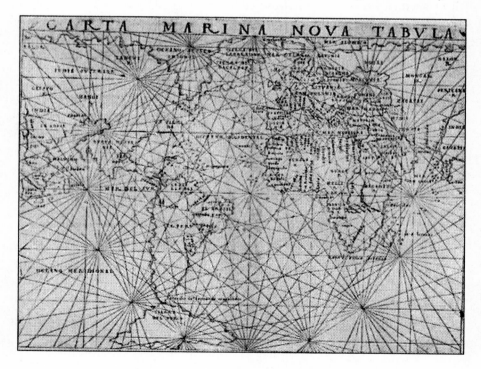

Ptolemy (c.100–178 AD) said that there were two ways of making a portrait of the world. One is to reproduce it on a sphere, and the other is to draw it on a plane surface. The globe is the most accurate but it needs to be extraordinarily large to present local detail. In order to preserve accuracy, projection of spherical geography upon a plane surface requires special conical and modified, spherical-geometric projections involving the trigonometry invented by Hipparchus.

Ptolemy (following Marinus) decided to locate his Prime Meridian not at Alexandria, but passing through the Fortunate Islands. From this most important position it was only a matter of spotting each place according to its latitude and longitude. He devised a compromise projection methodology whereby the meridians would be drawn as straight lines equidistant at the equator and converging at the North Pole. The parallels of latitude would be laid down as arcs of circles having a common center at the North Pole. Ptolemy also insisted on inserting the parallel through the Island of Rhodes, because so many distances had been determined in relation to it that the island had become a standard line of departure in map drawing and the calculation of distances. Even the later Mediterranean Portolanos demarked Rhodes with a white cross surrounded by red color. Rhodes has some special, significant connections in myth. Triton and Rhode were the issue of Poseidon and Amphitrite, daughter of Ocean. As well, the descendants of the Phoenician Cadmus held the hereditary priesthood of Poseidon on the Island of Rhodes.

We will see later, in our discussion of astrology, that Ptolemy was an excellent compiler of ancient information. But, he was ever a reluctant philosopher and proponent of his own conclusions. It is for these reasons of fidelity to his sources that he is so well regarded down to the present day. If we try to follow Ptolemy's thoughts, and try to get into his head for a moment, we may be able to better understand the origin of some of the mysteriously accurate ancient sea charts.

1. Ptolemy, though an Alexandrian, did not adopt the Prime Meridian of Alexandria, selected by his famous predecessor, Eratosthenes, who had already correctly estimated the size of the earth. The only reason that I can see for this extraordinary slight of Eratosthenes is that the Library of Alexandria did not

contain any ancient maps that employed a Prime Meridian located in Egypt.

2. Ptolemy, for no immediately apparent reason, adopts the usage of the Phoenician, Marinus of Tyre, in establishing his Prime Meridian in the Atlantic by the Isles of the Blessed, the so-called, Fortunate Islands. Why would he do this? Why would he abandon his adopted country of Egypt in favor of the Phoenician interpretation? The only reason that I can give is that he discovered very ancient charts in the archives of the Library of Alexandria that also demarcated the Fortunate Islands as the Prime Meridian. Above everything, Ptolemy was the epitome of a very faithful researcher. He only followed the information that was overwhelmingly presented to him.

3. It would be difficult to recreate what kind of science flourished in Tyre at the time of Marinus. We are acquainted with the fact that the Phoenicians were the eminent merchants and well-traveled seafarers of antiquity. If there were any people on the planet that might have had access to sophisticated maps gathered from more ancient geographers, one would think that the Phoenicians would be the best candidates as collectors of information that would advance their mercantile interests.

4. If these astoundingly accurate maps were of Phoenician origin, why is their Prime Meridian not located in their own city of Tyre?

The Mystery of the Prime Meridian as a Sacred Marker

The reader will already have guessed that the Prime Meridian is one of the important keys to the solution of the mystery of the ancient sciences. It rather confuses the issue that the English astronomer Flamstead had the audacity to presumptuously place the ultimate scientific marker through his island!

In antiquity, Prime Meridians are founded only upon holy places of divine revelation. Because the geographical place of revelation is the ultimate astronomical calculation of the correspondence with heavenly time here upon the earth. Neither instruments nor human intellect can determine this place which is manifest through one of the highest and majestic of cosmic cycles; that cycle which is the revolution of our solar system around our Milky Way Galaxy. The location and the time of birth of a great revelation enabled the priest/scientist to formulate this *coincidence* between a geographic place and the start of a new universal cycle of cosmic time.

First, we must be acquainted with the fact that, even in antiquity, there was some confusion as to whether the Prime Meridian was in the Canaries (Fortunate Isles) or the Cape Verde Islands.

The true Prime Meridian of the ancient people is most probably the Cape Verde Islands because it pinpoints the line dividing the cosmic time periods of Capricorn and Aquarius. That dividing line between Capricorn and Aquarius was a very important revelation of ancient times. Today we are fortunate to live very close to the time of one of the greatest of all revelations. Jerusalem is the seat of the new revelation of the Messiah. Jerusalem becomes the Heavenly City descended from on High, and it geographically pinpoints the astronomical line dividing Pisces and Aries, on earth and in heaven.

Cape Verde Islands	16 North, 24 West
Jerusalem	31 North, 36 East

If we add 24°W plus 36°E, their sum equals 60 degrees, or two zodiac signs. The distance between Jerusalem and the Cape Verde Prime Meridian is 60 degrees. These places are also located on the Ring of Fire, a natural phenomenon which attends significant places on the globe.

What is truly amazing about all this is that it explains another ancient mystery, namely, the phenomenal mapping and astronomical center located in the Diquis Delta in Costa Rica. Ivar Zapp, in his *Atlantis in America*, describes these perfectly spherical monolithic sighting stones arranged in patterns showing the directions to such places as Easter Island, Stonehenge, Malta, the Great Pyramid, the Cocos Islands, and the Galapagos. Could it be that these scientific shining, polished orbs were the original spheres or Apples of the Hesperides?

It is no coincidence that the capital of Costa Rica, San Jose, is located at 9 North, 84 West, which is 60 degrees west of the Cape Verde Islands, and 120 degrees west of Jerusalem. Each of these places is, astonishingly, 60 degrees removed from each other! How could the ancient people have ever penetrated such a system? Was religion the final step to the resolution of the sciences? Was this the reason that Ptolemy adhered so determinedly to the Atlantic Prime Meridian?

The resolution of the controversy between the Canaries and the Cape Verde Islands is easily demonstrated. That the Cape Verde Islands were an original Prime Meridian is proved by the fact that Pope Alexander VI and his advisors used them to determine The Papal Line of Demarcation concerning the explorations and rights of Portugal and Spain. Territories on either side of a boundary line 100 leagues west, later adjusted to 370 leagues west, of the Cape Verde Islands were granted as personal property to their Royal Majesties. One must be assured that maps in possession of the Papal Library were carefully consulted in marking this important Line of Demarcation.

It is apparent that Costa Rica and the Cape Verde Islands were important guidelines for marking the ancient globe. Once the grids were established; it could be easily inferred that the next great revelation would take place in the longitudinal area of Jerusalem.

Chapter 1

On the Nature of the Prime Meridian and Greenwich Mean Time

As we have already remarked, one of the most influential books of our century is *Maps of the Ancient Sea Kings* by Charles Hapgood. One of the awkward questions he poses concerns the national origin of these charts. These exceptionally accurate maps appeared to have been copied and transmitted by mapmakers without any reference as to where they came from.

One fact always presents itself. Most of the maps were drawn in reference to the Canary or the Cape Verde Islands in the Atlantic off the coast of Morocco.

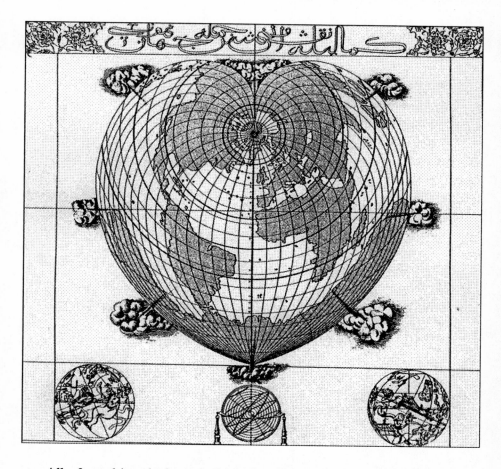

All of our historical, mythological, and genealogical research points to Morocco as the birthplace of Western and Middle-Eastern culture. All the facts seem to suggest that the ancient cities of Morocco were colonies of a great Atlantic Culture. These colonies copied, fabricated, and preserved these maps which have been handed down to our culture.

Most of the oldest source maps are longitudinally graduated around the equator from 0 to 360 degrees. On some rare occasions, the graduation is in terms of hours and minutes from west to east. The Prime Meridian where this graduation begins and ends is either directly upon the Canary Islands or the Cape Verde Islands. Sometimes even the Azores are used as the Prime Meridian. The graduation from the West toward the East is significant because it defines the West as the starting place. This is also in accord with our thesis that Culture begins in the West.

Hapgood made his scintillating discoveries simply by reading the *Facsimile Atlas to the Early History of Cartography with Reproductions of the Most Important Maps Printed in the XV and XVI Centuries*, first published in Stockholm in 1889 by the famous explorer and scholar, A. E. Nordenskiold. This knowledgeable researcher informs us that the excellent, original maps or *portolanos* were used by merchants and seafarers of the Mediterranean and Atlantic seaboard for traveling from port to port. These portolano maps contained no graduation degrees from west to east. They were *loxodromic* charts based upon a central compass point describing a large circle, upon which symmetrical points were arranged to become a particular compass rose, or point, through which straight lines were drawn toward coasts. The sole purpose of this layout was to establish points for compass readings.

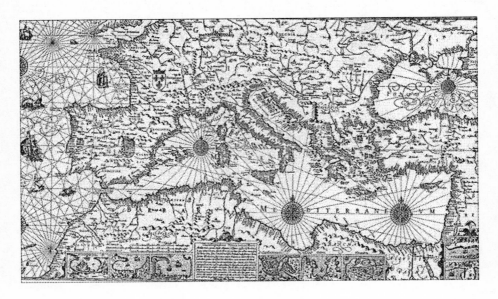

These portolanos have been attributed to the Byzantine Empire. Nordenskiold tells us that later copies and renderings of these maps were provided with, "meridians and parallels on a projection of equidistant parallelograms." This type of projection is identical to the methodology used by the Phoenician, Marinus of Tyre. And Ptolemy concurs saying that Marinus constructed his maps after this fashion.

Based upon the study by N. H. Brehmer, and in his own mind, Nordenskiold concludes that the prototype of all modern atlases is most likely of Tyrian, or in other words, Phoenician origin. These conclusions seem to stand to reason, seeing that the Phoenicians were the greatest traders and merchants of the ancient world. In regard to our particular thesis of Western origin, it is reported by Nonnos that Cadmus, the Phoenician, established over 100 cities upon the Atlantic shore of Morocco. This Phoenician presence on the Atlantic is irrefutable and beyond controversy.

But, even though the Phoenicians are credited with the introduction of weights and measures, coined money, and the alphabet, I firmly believe that the later or recent historical Phoenicians were more *carriers* of science and invention, rather than the genuine originators. These later Phoenicians really succeeded in putting everyone else out of the trading game. Through their monopoly they controlled the highly valuable information of the day. And, once they had succeeded in monopolizing the information, they also succeeded in taking credit for the origination of its science.

As far as we know, the Romans invented propaganda. And they certainly did not spare their hatred and vindictiveness for their chief rivals, the Phoenicians of Carthage. The Romans condemned them as utter pragmatists, who adopted cities only if they suited their trading purposes. We must try to separate this propaganda from fact. The earliest, ancient, and mythical, Phoenicians were indeed transmitters of culture and science. I think that we, or the Romans, would not have so very much to say about the Phoenicians if they were not a very important people who figured in much of the history of this planet!

L. A. Brown (p. 139) in his *Story of Maps* also discusses the *Mysterious Portolano of 1300 AD* which Nordenskiold attributed to the Phoenicians. Brown says that several copies of these exceptional charts of the Mediterranean and the Black Sea had just appeared at this time. These charts lacked parallels and meridians, yet they fully compared to a modern chart of the same area drawn on a Mercator projection. "How could this be the case, hundreds of years before Mercator?" Brown questions, "Could it be that some ancient chart maker solved the riddle of the *conformal projection*, and either purposely covered up his tracks, or lost its coordinates because of a copyist who felt that they only cluttered the picture? It is highly probable." The early portolanos of Genoa do not contain wind roses, though a single one appears on a Catalan example in 1375. The later Pinelli charts were laid down against a background of wind roses connected by intersecting rhumb lines, or loxodromes.

To me, it seems that ancient maps portray the known world as the Trading Empire of the Phoenicians. Ptolemy had also followed the lead of the Phoenician, Marinus of Tyre, in establishing the inhabited world to extend 15 hours, or 225 degrees, from the Euphrates to the Canary Islands. I am fully convinced that this particular portolano map has forever influenced our picture of history, civilization, and culture as pertaining to this particular area of the globe.

Other complications arise in our quest for the origin of these early scientific maps. During the Age of Discovery, one of the most prominent and prestigious schools of cartography was founded in the Canary Islands. This fact must confuse our search in establishing an Atlantic source for these ancient sea maps. For, it will be nearly impossible to differentiate the real ancient source from the newly developed product of this revitalization of the Canary Islands' school of cartography. This circumstance definitely complicates our search for the genuine origin.

G. R. Crone, in his *Maps and their Makers,* tells us that in 1381 the envoy of the French king asked King Peter of Aragon for a copy of the latest world map. He was presented with a work by Abraham Cresques, a Jew of Palma on the island of Majorca, who was cartographer and instrument maker to the King of Aragon, from whom he received special privileges and protection. His work was carried on by his son Jafuda, who because of the wave of persecution, converted to Christianity in 1391, receiving the name of Jaime Ribes. He accepted the invitation of Prince Henry of Portugal, where he instructed the Portuguese in cosmography and the making of charts. Crone says, "This link between the Majorcan school and the beginning of Portuguese overseas expansion is of obvious significance."

Prior to Cresques, Angelino Dulcert of Majorca had produced a world map dated 1339 AD. Nordenskiold relates that the oldest surviving world globe was produced by Martin Behaim, originally of Bohemia, who married the daughter of the governor of the Azores, where he served as astronomer and cosmographer. It seems remarkable that there is always some connection to the Atlantic islands!

The *Super Portolano* could have been made by the ancient Atlantic Phoenicians, or by the mythical Agathodaemon, or by Atlas of Morocco, himself. Obviously, there were talented navigators of Genoa and Venice, who might have discovered this special accurate map of the Mediterranean. But the most promising candidates, who may have discovered the true ancient source maps, would have been the Jewish refugees from the Almohed persecutions, who settled in Morocco, the Canaries, and the Cape Verdes. Crone says that these refugees included scholars who could interpret the works of Arab scientists. And this contact between practical and skilled seamen, and those versed in cosmology and astronomy, must have unquestionably led to the Age of Discovery. For, when men have the command of several languages and can read documents from several cultures, then indeed, science will flourish.

Schwaller de Lubicz in his *Sacred Science* (p. 46) completely supports this theme, saying that Islam was enriched by the works of the Library of Alexandria (which influenced such Persian converts as Avicenna, Musa al-Khwarazmi, and Ibn Jabir). Islam had installed itself in Spain with the last of the Umayyads, and instructed many great men of the Middle Ages at the University of Cordoba. It was the scholars of Islam who translated and commented upon the Greek writers whose doctrines were retransmitted to the Christians by Jews coming from Spain (e.g., Maimonides). With the conversion of the Persians to Islam, knowledge originating in India, China, and Babylon was joined with the science drawn from Alexandria. Unfortunately, the Christian conquest of Islam in Spain led to the looting and destruction of the library at the University of Cordoba. The destruction of this important library once again demonstrates the danger of attempting to centralize information; instead of having many independent repositories.

Next, we should address the difference between the Cape Verde Islands and the Canary Islands. Those islands which the ancients called the Isla Fortuna, or the Isles of the Blest, are the Canary Islands. The Cape Verde Islands were notorious as the major outpost of the African slave trade. Both island groups were used by the mapmakers as the place of the Prime Meridian. Both groups were natural starting ports for trans-Atlantic voyages because the natural ocean currents guide ships directly to the Caribbean. The return trip is just as easy by following the currents of the Gulf Stream to Ireland and Britain. From there one could follow the natural currents down to Morocco. The natural currents of the Atlantic form this triangle of easy trade and communication, which was used long before the time of Columbus.

Crone informs us that Mercator was also interested in the problem of terrestrial magnetism, and accepted the general observation of navigators that the line of no magnetic variation passed through the Cape Verde Islands.

Accordingly, Mercator wrote, "Since it is necessary that longitudes of places, should for good reasons, have as origin the meridian which is common to the magnet and the world . . . I have drawn the prime meridian through the said islands." At Mercator's time this may have been a correct fact, however we know that the Magnetic North Pole is subject to changes in position over time. Magnetism is not the answer. The location of the Cape Verde Islands reflects an important cosmic relation to our globe. At this point, it may be revealing to trace how our modern day Prime Meridian was established.

Greenwich Mean Time

Even those of limited education are aware that our present day calendar originated in Egypt, and that the Romans and the Pope reformed the calendar to the present standard which is accepted worldwide.

In this same way, we have come to accept, and take for granted, the demarcation of Greenwich Mean Time. This is based upon a small observatory, some little distance out of London. Here at this seemingly insignificant place, a longitudinal parallel has been *arbitrarily* run from the North Pole to the South Pole, where the hours of the official earth's day begin. Here also, at this place, longitude is reckoned as zero degrees, and the rest of the globe is divided into 180 degrees west and 180 degrees east.

Dicearchus and Hipparchus had already used the distinctions of longitude and latitude. The modern organization of these divisions was a consequence of the necessity of finding longitude at sea for the great fleet of Charles II of England. The Royal Astronomer, Flamsteed (1646) prepared star maps at the National Observatory at Greenwich, and arbitrarily called his position zero degrees longitude.

Even as a child, this fact intrigued me. I knew that Great Britain had been the predominant world power since the sinking of the Spanish Armada, and that the sun never set upon its Empire. But I wondered if this gave them the right to control time and geography as well.

The English established a Prime Meridian because they actually had a world empire. Therefore, one of our conclusions might be that the Canary/ Cape Verde Prime Meridian had been established by the last great world empire. But, was the ancient Prime Meridian the product of an ancient political empire, or an ancient cultural and scientific dominion that had at one time enlightened the entire world?

We have called this book, *The Origin of Culture and Civilization,* because we are continually alerted to the amazing interplay of these two very opposed forces. Civilization deals with the enticements of this world, such as power and empire. Culture deals with the spiritual reality which transcends this world. Yet, often these two forces work to assist each other.

If we look at the direction of the compass roses shown on the van Keulen map below, we can no longer be blind to the ancients' achievement of a significant scientific and cartographic system. This map represents a copy of the Master Map of the Atlantic Sea Kings.

Not only does it use the Canaries as its Prime Meridian of 0 to 360 degrees, it also uses the Canaries as the focus of its *Eight Wind System of Compass Roses.* On this map the roses are further divided into 32 segments of the pie around the Canary Islands. We may notice that these 32 rays transect numerous places of historical and cultural significance. Another master map is a Venetian interpretation of the *Carta Marina Nova Tabulas* of 1548; which comes from Marinus of Tyre. He, however, uses the equator below the Canary Islands as the prime focus and the center of his system of wind roses.

Spherical, astronomical computation and reference is easiest under the system where a circle comprises 360 degrees. Reference and measurement upon a plane surface is simplest based upon a right-angle cross. Each 90 degree right-angle is easily bisected to form two 45 degree angles. This is the basis of the Eight Wind System of Compass Roses, because 360 degrees divided by 8 equals 45 degrees.

The world map (c.1714–1720) below was created by Gerard van Keulen. One will easily ask—"What does this van Keulen know about ancient map-making?" Here we find another example of the political and pragmatic world assisting and preserving scientific material for the benefit of culture.

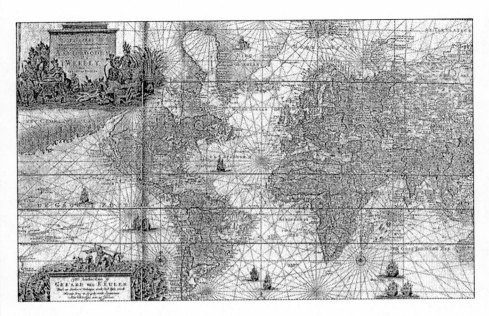

Johannes van Keulen of Amsterdam was born 1654. His father was a stockholder of interest in both the Dutch East and West Indies Companies. Being involved in such worldwide ventures, he interested himself in maps; and, furthermore, established a business in 1677, under the name of *The Crowned Pilot*, making and selling nautical maps and charts. In 1743, he was distinguished as the "Offical Chartmaker of the Dutch East Indies Company." This distinction allowed him a more familiar access to the Examiner of the Amsterdam Chamber, and the maps and secrets of the East Indies Company. By outrageous good fortune, five of the most notable chart-makers closed-up, wherefore, Johannes simply obtained their entire collection of copperplates. Even more importantly, he took possession of their manuals and source maps.

His son, Gerard van Keulen, took over and greatly expanded the flourishing firm. He also aggressively hunted down and collected important pieces of cartographic art and science. His great collections are now in the private hands of numerous private European libraries and archives, purchased at auction in 1885, when after 200 years, the firm closed it doors forever

So, that is the background as to how some very secret and sensitive information of antiquity got placed upon Gerard van Keulen's world map. Namely, that the Canary Islands were the Prime Meridian was no great secret. But that they were the Prime Focus of world geography—that was a great secret! And just as the Marsh of Old Marmora mysteriously appears on the maps of two of the great early cartographers—it just as quickly disappears forever as an absurd curiosity of early modern science.

The Madeira Solution

The true cosmic Prime Meridian is located at the Cape Verde Islands, while the geographic Prime Meridian for making world maps was shifted to the Canary Islands. This was most probably because the Canaries are nearest in latitude to the center of the most temperate zone of human habitation and activity. Curiously, a cord connecting the astronomical globes of Puerto Rico and Jerusalem more closely passes between the Madeira and the Azores Island groups.

In conclusion, we must say that truly sophisticated and highly scientific maps can only be the product of a culture that has achieved the pinnacle of long-term astronomical observation. L. A. Brown relates that Strabo realized that there was a special union between terrestrial and celestial phenomena.

Brown's own comment is, "Progress in the science of cartography has never moved ahead of developments in astronomy, and our world map of today has been made possible largely because of the high degree of accuracy achieved by astronomical observers."

If Brown knew the real truth—he would be compelled to say that our incredible progress is the fruit of some very excellent examples of ancient cartography; based upon millenniums of their long-term astronomical observations and theories.

Chapter 2

The Trade Secrets of the Phoenicians

The Phoenician sea merchants were the vehicle of the enlightenment of the ancient world. In their wide travels they discovered and retained the traditions and inventions of mankind, and distributed them throughout the globe from India to America.

In the late classical era these people became so cosmopolitan that their personal national heritage became an obscure and decadent mixture of the many Mediterranean and Mid-Eastern nations with whom they came into contact. This was especially the case with the Phoenician Punic colonies in North Africa and Spain. In general they tended to ally themselves intimately and culturally with the natives of those nations among whom they settled. At the time of Alexander the Great they possessed no unified national history, but only the traditions preserved in their various cities which were largely disrupted by the Syrian-Palestinian wars.

In accordance with their maritime activities, the Phoenicians adopted a policy of destroying any information relating to themselves or their trade rather than allowing it to pass into the hands of their competitors or enemies. In the modern sense, they instituted the practice of safeguarding their mercantile routes and trade secrets. We might well believe that it was the

Phoenicians who circulated reports of outrageous sea monsters, and theories of a flat earth where vessels fell over the edge of the ocean should they travel out too far. They were indeed the forefathers of misinformation and information control.

Strabo (3.5.11) says that in former times the Phoenicians of Gades (Cadiz in Spain) carried out all the trade in the Atlantic Ocean,

> And when once the Romans were closely following a certain Phoenician ship captain in order that they too might learn the markets in question. Out of jealousy the ship-captain purposely drove his ship out of its course into shoal water. And after he had lured the followers into the same ruin, he himself escaped by a piece of wreckage, and received from the state the value of the cargo that he had lost.

L. A. Brown in his *Story of Maps* (p. 8) relates that all nations had their maps and related logs locked up in the innermost vaults of their palaces. They only allowed partial copies to be distributed to their captains. Divulging such secrets was a treasonable offense. The Englishman Robert Thorne was one of the very few ever to successfully steal information, in this case a map and a report on the West Indies out of the archives of Seville. It was an old Spanish custom of weighing charts, not to mention log and code books, *with lead*, so that they could be quickly jettisoned should an enemy try to board their vessel. All maps and charts of the New World were deposited for safekeeping in the archives of Seville, and only a limited number of copies were made for the use of the most trustworthy Spanish sea captains. None of the original maps of the great explorers were allowed to be engraved or printed, so that the primary documents relating to Columbus, Cortez, and Magellan are lost forever. Entire editions of ancient books and maps were purposely destroyed by the Spanish authorities to safeguard their monopoly.

Another factor which has contributed to the loss of ancient cartography in the Near East was the burning of the Library of Alexandria. Ptolemy Soter and his successors had avidly embarked upon a program of collecting maps all over Greece and Asia. Their scouts had instructions to spare no costs acquiring material for their magnificent Museum Library which by their extraordinary efforts was to become one of the most legendary library collections of all time.

The Phoenicians apparently tried to frighten navigators from exploring outside the gates of the Mediterranean, for the Irish *Stair Ercuil* (p. 73) records that Hercules (whom the Phoenicians especially honor) planted four columns, and an image of himself, at the entrance to the Atlantic Ocean with the inscription, *"Let no one of Adam's race go to seek land or country on the other side of these, for there is no land there."* It could be inferred that the Phoenicians propagated a deliberate policy of misrepresenting the facts to protect their commercial interests.

Many prized documents and records of the past were lost in the burning of Carthage and its famous library. A very interesting example of a work which survived is given in Plutarch's essay, *Concerning the Face that appears in the Orb of the Moon.* His article seems to recount a very special form of Atlantic religious philosophy; which is well worth reading and studying. Their enemies brutally destroyed the Phoenician cities, and in some instances they even salted the ground upon which they were built. It seems that the Phoenicians usually initiated the destruction themselves once they determined that their cities were close to being taken. It is reported that during the siege of Carthage, the wife of Hasdrubal burnt the holy temple of Asclepius on the citadel, and herself along with it. Also, Caesar tells in his *African War* that it was Juba's design to collect all his treasure, children, wives, and citizens in one place, and to consign everything to flames.

Josephus (*Apion*, i.6) mentions the Phoenicians, alongside the Egyptians and Chaldeans, as possessing a very ancient and permanent record of the past. In their mythological accounts, the Phoenicians claim to have invented all the arts and sciences. The coast of Syria, where one element of the Phoenicians lived, became a meeting place of the East and the West. It is therefore difficult to segregate that which is truly original to the Phoenicians.

Eisfeldt (*Pauly-Wissowa*) says that while the classical authors agree that the Phoenicians introduced the alphabet to the Mediterranean, the oldest example (c.1500 BC) found in Byblos, is a pseudo-hieroglyphic script composed of syllables, seemingly, a combination of Egyptian and Babylonian styles. Nevertheless, it was the Phoenicians who perfected the convenient systems of records by numbers, weights, and scriptures. These became the models for modern business procedures.

Strabo (16.2.22) writes,

After Sidon one comes to Tyre, the largest and oldest city of the Phoenicians, which rivals Sidon, not only in size, but also in its fame and antiquity, as handed down in numerous myths. Now although the poets have referred more repeatedly to Sidon than to Tyre (Homer does not even mention Tyre), yet the colonies sent into Libya and Iberia, as far even as outside the Pillars, hymn rather the praises of Tyre.

Strabo continues that although this city was taken by siege by Alexander, the Tyrians managed to restore their fortunes through their excellent seamanship and trade, and the superior nature of their dye, the Tyrian purple, extracted from the shellfish near their coasts. The height and stories of their houses were even greater than those of Rome. They paid a great amount of money to be adjudged autonomous by the Kings and by the Romans. The citizens of Tyre pay extravagant honors to Hercules. The number and the size of their colonial cities is evidence of their power in maritime affairs. This, too, was the city of the famous cartographer, Marinus, upon whose authority Ptolemy relied in his mapmaking.

Strabo (16.2.24) writes that the Sidonians are skilled in many beautiful arts, as the poet Homer points out. They are philosophers in the sciences of astronomy and arithmetic, having begun their studies with practical calculations and with night-sailings; for each of these branches concerns the merchant and the ship owner. Geometry was invented from the measurement of lands when the Nile overflowed its banks, changing the former boundaries. This science is believed to have come to the Greeks from the Egyptians, *while astronomy and arithmetic came from the Phoenicians*. At present by far the greatest store of knowledge in every other branch of philosophy is said to have come from these Phoenician cities. Posidonius says that the ancient dogma concerning Atoms originated with Mochus, a Sidonian, who was born before Trojan times.

The Phoenicians sent out colonies to Thrace, Thebes, Athens, the Greek islands, Rhodes, Crete, and Cyprus; and also as far afield as India, Spain, North Africa, and Morocco. The Punic Phoenicians of North Africa adopted much of the culture and religion of Libya, and became part of a distinct historical context separate from the Syrian Phoenicians. Some commentators actually assert that these North Africans were the original ancestors of all

Phoenicians. There are great differences of opinion regarding the racial origin of these people.

There can be no doubt that the Phoenicians were a very ancient and original people who invented and transmitted science and culture. In Greek mythology they are said to have sprung from the most ancient Atlantic roots, and later became related to Egyptian and Greek families. One of their great demi-heroes, Cadmus, is said to have established 100 cities in Morocco on the Atlantic. Since Cadmus is said to have followed a cow to the foundation place of his city of Thebes in Greece, it may be assumed that these events took place during the Precessional Age of Taurus. Otherwise this quaint anecdote would not have been attached to his mythology. Cadmus is most noteworthy; because he and his myth are the most Hellenized versions of true Phoenician stories and culture. Cadmus allows us to approach the distant and removed character of this race, and view them on a Greek level.

It appears from the stories about Hannibal that the Phoenicians were the only people who had ever successfully trained the African elephant. They, too, are said to have invented glass manufactured for their trade around the world.

The Phoenicians received a most horrible reputation from the Romans, with whom they were in constant rivalry in trade and naval competition. In Western tradition we have become heir to the propaganda disseminated by the Romans regarding the untrustworthiness of these people. Again, my view is that they were a most ancient people; but, historically, we meet them in their most decadent form. The Romans portrayed them as selfish connivers, utterly pragmatic merchants and businessmen, who adopted strategic cities only for the purposes of trade, without any feelings of patriotism or allegiance to their adopted nations. In a word, these most ancient peoples had become parasites of those countries which they shamelessly adopted for their own purposes.

Most importantly, the Phoenician maps, especially those of Marinus of Tyre, not only became the maps of all future Mediterranean traders but helped to determine our modern concept of the place of origin of Western civilization, culture, and history. These Mediterranean maps became the ideal picture of the geography for the home of Western Culture in the mind's eye of all future academic professors.

The Phoenicians created the paradigm of self-sufficient river and coastal fortress strongholds. These could grow and supply their own food, produce their own industries, and fortify their domains against the attacks of others. These Phoenicians were not only fiercely independent of other nations and people, but, I would imagine that they were quite independent within their own society. This was because their society required such a wealth of talented navigators, merchants, astronomers, fabricators, carpenters, mechanics, builders, masons, and naval architects. Such a society would of necessity be very democratic, ruled by the leading tribes (*demos*) who would have elected a king as its head.

The Phoenicians' exquisite, self-sufficient, coast-side and island fortresses served as a model to all later mercantile city-states, such as Venice, and all cities engaged in piracy and trade. Olden maps of Libya show the famous city of Carthage occupying its own island, and snuggly tucked into the corner of a great bay. These Phoenician fortresses had to be impregnable because of the great wealth that their merchants generated.

In conclusion we should recognize several important matters regarding the Phoenicians. First of all, we do not really know very much about them, because of their policy of self-destruction of their own history. Yet, the classical historians assign them the preeminence in, or credit them with the transmission of, written language, philosophy, mathematics, mapmaking, and astronomy.

The Phoenicians' were in Libya, Morocco, and Spain, and clearly appear to have monopolized all Atlantic travel and trade. They were not above falsifications and misinformation, which unfortunately confused and discredited the history of communication with the Americas. In fact, we must directly accuse the Phoenicians of perpetrating false reports and misinformation, which has directly influenced the very limited view of ancient history that is prevalent in our modern worldview.

Chapter 3

The Deep-Oceangoing Ships of the Veneti of Brittany

It has been our theme to develop the idea of an ancient culture thriving upon the eastern seaboard of the Atlantic Ocean. The superlative scientific and technological achievements of this culture were original to the Atlantic, and served to inspire the entire Mediterranean world. Fortunately, there are three examples of great seafarers whose homeland is the Atlantic Ocean. These are the Tartessians of Gadiera (Cadiz) in Spain, the Fomorians of Lixus in Morocco, and the Veneti of Carnac in Brittany.

Naturally, it is common to all seafaring merchants or pirates to have strong and inaccessible fortresses built upon islands, in marshes, or upon coastal crags. And this is for the obvious reason that their families might have protection while the sailors are at sea; plundering or trading. This type of mercantilism also generates great wealth and treasure, which necessitates strongholds to defend their acquisitions. The hazards of seafaring and journeys to foreign lands provide the material for sagas and stories of adventure. The long and boring times on board promote the love of song, dancing, and musical instruments. Long voyages also cultivate time for thinking, invention, star-gazing, card-playing, and board games. If we combine all these elements of the life of people who make a living from the sea: the adventure, the castles, the music, we can only conclude that here we have all the elements of romantic novels and stories such as *Amadis de Gaula* and the Arthurian legends of *the Knights of the Round Table*. These stories are without a doubt, of Atlantic origin. And interestingly, *Amadis de Gaula* was the backpocket romance of every Conquistador that traveled to New World.

The Veneti

One of the best documented group of ancient seafarers was the Veneti of Brittany in France. Julius Caesar gives us a splendid account of them in *The Gallic War* (iii.7–18):

> These Veneti exercise by far the most extensive authority over all the sea-coast in those districts, for they have numerous ships, in which it is their custom to sail to Britain, and they excel the rest in the theory and practice of navigation. As the sea is very boisterous, and open, with but few harbors here . . . The positions of the strongholds were generally of one kind. They were set at the end of tongues and promontories, so as to allow no approach on foot, when the tide had rushed in from the sea, which regularly happens every twelve hours; nor in ships, because when the tide ebbed again the ships would be damaged in shoal water . . . whenever the natives were in fact overcome by huge siege-works . . . they would bring close inshore a large number of ships, of which they possessed an unlimited supply, and take off all their stuff and retire to the nearest strongholds, there to defend themselves again...our own ships were detained by foul weather, and because the difficulty of navigation on a vast and open sea, with strong tides and few . . . harbors . . . Not so the ships of the Gauls, for they were built and equipped in the following fashion. Their keels were considerably more flat than those of our own ships, that they might more easily weather shoals and ebb-tide. Their prows were very lofty, and their sterns were similarly adapted to meet the force of waves and storms.
>
> The ships were made entirely of oak, to endure any violence and buffeting. The cross-pieces were beams a foot thick, fastened

with iron nails as thick as a thumb. The anchors were attached by iron chains instead of cables. Skins and pieces of leather finely finished were used instead of sails . . . because they thought that the mighty ocean-storms and hurricanes could not be ridden out, nor the mighty burden of their ships conveniently controlled, by means of sails. When our fleet encountered these ships it proved its superiority only in speed and oarsmanship; in all other respects, having regard to the locality and the force of the tempests, the others were more suitable and adaptable. For our ships could not damage them with the ram (they were so stoutly built), nor, by reason of their height, was it easy to hurl a pike, and for the same reason they were less readily gripped by grapnels. Moreover, when the wind began to rage and they ran before it, they endured the storm more easily, and rested in shoals more safely, with no fear of rocks or crags if left by the tide; whereas our own vessels could not but dread the possibility of all these chances.

Caesar goes on to describe the battle with the Veneti (56 BC) who arrived with 220 ships. The Roman fleet succeeded in disabling several of the halyards and sail rigging of the Veneti vessels, but he himself admits that on the day of the battle the ocean was unusually and exceptionally tranquil, which naturally favored his Mediterranean-type ships. He writes,

> When suddenly a calm so complete and absolute came on that they could not stir from the spot. This circumstance was in the highest degree fortunate . . . for our troops pursued and boarded the vessels one by one, with the result that of all the number very few, when night came on, reached the land. The battle, indeed, lasted from about the fourth hour to sunset.

It is incredible to think that the Romans, who controlled the greater part of the world and were heir to the engineering and sciences of the Greeks and Egyptians, by dint of a most fortunate happenstance of weather, were able to master one of the last great remnants of Oceanic people. This was a nation that was clearly equipped with superior oceangoing vessels.

We are thankful to Caesar for recording so much information about the Veneti, but he is also guilty of annihilating one of the last traces of this sea culture, "He therefore put the whole of their senate [of the Veneti] to the sword, and sold the rest of the men as slaves."

Strabo (iv.4.1) says that the Veneti are a tribe of the Belgae (Belgium) and further supposes that they established Venice on the Adriatic. However, while the Venetians fall into the pattern of ancient sea kings with their island state and maritime trade, Strabo also adds that some think that they came from the Heneti of Paphlagonia, who according to Homer in the *Iliad* fought on the side of the Trojans, and accompanied Antenor to his new settlement on the river Po. Strabo (i.3.2.) equates these Heneti or Eneti in skill of navigation with the Phoenicians who made longer voyages by sea than the men of later times. The similarity in the name of the Veneti and the Venetians is intriguing, especially considering their maritime culture, but it is better not to force a connection at this time.

Patrick Andre, *La Cite Gallo-Romaine Des Venetes,* reports that based on evidence found in their ruined temples, the Veneti imported items from far afield, such as white marble tinted with red veins like that found in the quarries of Italy. The Veneti inhabited such important centers as Vannes, their capital, Rieux, Castennec, Locmariaquer, Carnac, La Croisic, and the entire south coast of Brittany up to the Loire River. Pliny mentions a number of islands of the Veneti in the Gulf of Aquatania, Belle Isle is among them.

The area that the Veneti inhabited is renowned for several ancient sites, preeminent among them is Carnac. Colin Wilson, *Atlas of Holy Places,* writes,

> The greatest concentration of upright stones [menhirs] in Europe, 3,000 of them in all, stands just to the north of Carnac . . . all but 70 of the stones at Carnac are arranged in parallel rows . . . The only Carnac mound to be dated so far is St. Michel, and the tests there placed its origin at about 5000 BC. The Count de Caylus speculated that, "Carnac was the monument of an unknown race of seafarers . . . [who] later went to Britain where they built Stonehenge." In 1970, the scientific methods of Alexander Thom . . . revealed that Carnac had been set up by ancient *astronomer-priests* to observe the cycles of the sun and moon.

For the little that we know about the Veneti, they are indeed a treasure. They firmly establish a tradition of Atlantic navigators who also were builders and scientists who created vast stone astronomical monuments. The Veneti are also on record as the inventors of novel "Kog" oceangoing vessels, of a type which was unheard of in the Mediterranean. Jarno's research indicated that the Kog-type ship of the Hanse fleet, and those of Dantzig, stem directly from the model of the merchant ships of the Veneti in size, displacement, and equipage. An ancient ship discovered at Giens measured an incredible 37 meters long. This vessel was ironclad and of a naval architecture resembling the ships of trans-Atlantic exploration of the 16th century.

The Veneti also give substance to the Irish reports of the Fomorians, who were credited with building most of the ancient monolithic monuments of Ireland, Britain, and Scandinavia. It should be noticed that the megalithic architecture and spiral carvings at Gavrinis in the land of the Veneti are identical to those at the renouned Newgrange observatory in Ireland. As was reported, the Fomorians were well versed in the astronomical sciences and the nature of long, deep-ocean voyages.

PART III:

WEST OF EGYPT
IN THE LAND OF NIGHT, SLEEP,
AND DREAMS

Introduction

Our general goal is to establish a cultural context of religion, history, and science that existed prior to Mediterranean culture. We would now like to continue establishing this picture of an original culture that existed out upon the Atlantic shoreline long before the rise of Egypt, the Middle East, and Greece. We will paint this picture with the actual words of the Greeks and Egyptians themselves.

The Egyptians themselves admit that the story of Atlantis comes from very ancient times. But rather than relying totally upon the Egyptian account that was transmitted by Solon to Plato, we have chosen to focus on Skytobrachion's account which tells of a blossoming culture upon the coast of Morocco, a real place that still exists in our own time.

Up to this time, we have been told that the home of our Western tradition lies in the Near Orient where the latest great traces of empire are to be found among the ruins of architecture and in the philosophies, sciences, and religions which came from this region. It cannot be denied that the Middle East is a very special place upon the face of the globe.

Yet, in the far distant past, the Atlantic coastlands of Europe, North Africa, and Western Libya were the focal points of revelation, culture, and invention. Through the course of time and great upheavals of nature and human depredation, there remains little trace of this former endowment of heaven, nor of the skill of man.

Only the memories and records of the very olden poets, historians, and genealogists remain to testify to a land whose ancient glory is obscured by the shadow of *Night and Sleep and Dreams.* The West, where the sun sets and the moon rises, was the fascination of the Mediterranean world. To them it was the locality of heaven and the Isles of the Blest; the place of Paradise, and the Garden of the Hesperides and the Golden Apples; the birthplace of the gods and the doorway to the Underworld and Hades.

Here in these chapters, these ancient remembrances are assembled to recreate a picture of one of the earliest contexts that we can ever know of in all human history.

Chapter 1

Degradation of the Historical Fact and Nonnos of Panopolis

In the folktale, *The Pied Piper*, the setting is in Hamlin, on the banks of the River Wesser, many long years ago. This has always disturbed me. Because if the storyteller knew the locale, why didn't he know the time these events took place? This is exactly what makes this story fit into the category of a folktale—the want of a chronology. The names of the people in the village are not recorded, and The Piper's true name is never mentioned.

Yet it is quite obvious that the Piper is Harlequin, with his bold-checkered, or pied costume of contrasting black and white, or variegated colors. He is also Mannan Mac Lir, the Irish god of the sea, who delights in appearing in jester's garb or the tattered disarray of a beggar, trying to tempt us mortals before revealing his divine nature.

Fairy and folktales are for children and their grandparents because their meaning is deep, hidden, and imaginative. This is why most adults prefer history where, in the fashion of Shakespeare's plays, the persons, the place, and the time are clearly established in the introduction to the story. History, too, has its grievous defects in that it is composed and promoted by people in power to vindicate their views and actions. History is always written by the victors. Josephus tells us that the Hebrew scribes were afraid that

Alexander would level Jerusalem. So to propitiate him in his wish to be regarded as the much awaited Messiah, they altered the time frame of their own sacred chronologies.

Indeed, the Egyptians must be admired and regarded as those people who kept the best and most ancient records of their gods, demi-gods, the spirits of the dead, and their mortal kings. *The Egyptian History* of Manetho actually shows how dry and lifeless history becomes after the great passage of time. The resumés of the countless kings and dynasties are empty. Only occasionally does Manetho append a significant remark such as, "In his reign a lamb spoke." The moral of Egyptian history appears to be that events which we believe to be quite momentous at the time of their occurrence, frequently prove to be inconsequential in the perspective of universal history.

For this reason, the study of mythology is most revealing. Mythology actually records events which have real consequences in the progression of culture and civilization. In myth the names of persons and the places of the events are most often recorded. However, the time-frame is often occluded and hidden to the average reader. Yet, there is a definite sequence from the reign of one high god to the next. The stories of heroes are always confined to the reign of a particular main god, who characterizes his cosmic epoch, and thereby pinpoints time with astronomical certainty.

Mythology deals with events that are so far distant in the past that the tally of solar years would be confusing and beyond our concept. Therefore, the mythographers used the cycles of the heavens as their zodiac calendar and scientific timepiece. When mythographers say that Zeus assumed the form of a bull to have converse with a maiden, we know that the cosmologists are referring to the epoch of Taurus. And when Athena is born of the head of Zeus, we realize that events are taking place during the time of Aries, which is called the head of the zodiac.

All the stories about Olympian Zeus refer exclusively to the Cultural Age during the Galactic Cycle of Pisces. During this long, galactic time period of Pisces, the more rapid Precessional Cycle is completing many revolutions of its own. These Precessional revolutions serve to weave the many reoccurring universal themes, like a tapestry, in and out, over and under the main fabric of the dominant theme of the Cultural Age of the galactic region of Pisces. Therefore, the long and dominant theme is never overwhelming, but mixed and diluted by the many themes of the universe that the Precessional revolutions interject.

All the stories of Cronus/Saturn refer to the Galactic Age and Cycle of Aquarius which preceded Zeus by several million years. We will touch upon the workings and influences of these cosmic cycles in much greater detail as we continue on.

Heinrich Schliemann represents one of the truly great milestones in decoding mythology and the thoughts of the ancients. His archaeological methods were said to have been a bit over enthusiastic. Yet, his childlike faith in the reports of the ancients allowed him to become one of the most successful of the discoverers of antiquity. This man so believed in the works of Homer, that he kept a copy of his works in his back pocket, and used them as his road map to the discovery of Troy. Schliemann, would also have discovered the Minoan Civilization had not Crete remained in the hands of Turkish rule until 1898. In the meantime, trusting the writings of antiquity, he discovered the palace of Nestor at Pylos, as well as the noted pre-Hellenic ruins of Tiryns and Mycenae. Before the advent of Schliemann, Homer was speaking mythologically. After Schliemann, Homer was speaking about history. Schliemann's total acceptance of Homer opens the gates to our appreciation of the underlying reality of mythology.

As a general rule, all history and stories go through a simple regressional sequence. We will call this sequence the degradation of the historical fact:

> **History** is such that the persons, places, and the exact number of solar years that have elapsed, before the present time, are faithfully recorded.

> **Mythology** relates the names of persons and the names of places, but the time element is couched in terms of astronomical and astrological reference.

> **Folklore** concerns a certain locality, but often the time and the true names have been forgotten.

> **Fairy Tales** are stories wherein the time, the place, and even the names have become obscured and lost. They have become a part of the general human experience.

People have always appreciated the genuine reality of Folklore. This is because it is told over and over again in a local community which serves to correct any inaccuracies during the many instances of retelling the story. Usually, this folklore is even in song and poetic meter which serves to guide and direct the accurate telling, like the strings of a *quipu*. Dona Elena, the author of *Atlantis in Spain*, tells of a revealing incident where an old woman told her that her native city of Niebla had been conquered by, "Romans, *Moros*, and Carthaginians." The author asked her if her father read much history? "No, senora, no one in my family has ever had the pleasure of being able to read, nor has a book ever been seen in our house. His father told him, and *he* heard it from his grandfather."

Life on this planet is not just about the rise and fall of civilizations. It is about the appearance of prophets, men of God, inventors, geniuses, heroes, and persons of inspired intellect. These are the personages who are chosen to transmit culture and science which comes of inspiration from the divine source. Life is also about great floods, catastrophes, and meteors crashing through our atmosphere. The ancients recognized that there were higher celestial cycles. And they remembered the significant revelations of genius, and the momentous cataclysmic events. All these things they remembered through the agency of myth.

The absolute best clocks and calendars for historical and scientific purposes are the very heavens that surround our planet. This celestial timepiece is not subject to theory or interpretation. It is observable and final. But, it also requires a disciplined, formal religious-scientific community to insure that accurate traditions are passed on to the future.

Cosmology is based upon a principle that unites nature, humans, and God. On many occasions, God reveals His Spirit in human form. Of course there are many levels of revelation. We have recently witnessed the ultimate Revelation wherein God sent His Only Son into the world. This Revelation only takes place at the beginning of a certain Galactic Cycle. This Revelation also serves to define a specific holy geographical place on our globe, which the ancients referred to as the Heavenly City or the City of God. The place and time of this Highest Revelation are the most important of all scientific facts.

In this fashion, the birth of a person inspired by God (a god) or a hero defines exactly what time it is, and where that time points to on the surface of the world. Nonnos in his *Dionysica*, tells us about several revelations of the god Dionysius at different periods of time and at different places on the globe. He likewise informs us of the outrageous changes in the star pictures, and the movements of the constellations and the heavens. In the *Dionysica*, he describes the change in our perspective, here on earth, as our solar system is revolving around the galaxy. The Babylonian Star Catalogues of ancient and no longer to be seen constellations, confirms the reports of Nonnos. These Star Catalogues and Nonnos both attest to the fact that the ancients kept track of the movement of our solar system around the center of our galaxy. The constellations do not change, only our movement changes our position which brings about a new relative perspective of the stars.

There is little doubt that the ancients were trying to communicate scientific information to us. They did so in many, many forms and guises. Naturally, they portrayed their science in their numerous stone alignments and massive stone structures. They also conveyed many of the details of their long-term observations clothed in genealogy, mythology, and astrology.

Therefore, let us define at least three levels to the perception of facts and symbols. The first level is the Hieroglyphic, which concerns the absolute sacred meaning of a thing. In this sense a thing is examined on the highest spiritual and cosmic level. In these terms, it is only discussed within the Inner Temple of the Holy of Holies.

The second level of perception is the Hieratic, which is the priestly, scientific, and philosophical meaning of a thing. This aspect is discussed on the porticos of the Outer Temple, much in the tradition of the Greek philosophical schools.

The third level of perception is the Demotic, which is local, folk, and tribal. On this level a thing is discussed as an immediate or pragmatic concern of everyday people. On this level, even holy matters are satirized and humorously spoken of in dramas and the theater.

Each of these levels is important to the complete understanding of an idea. And each level is vital to the continued transmission of the idea throughout time, social upheavals, and natural catastrophes. We may appreciate that the Demotic relates to our yearly experiences. We can also see that the Hieratic relates to the Precession of the Equinoxes. At this level our social and tribal consciousness tries to perceive things and consequences at a national and global level. Lastly, there is the Hieroglyphic level of absolute form and universal spiritual reality. Only here do we attempt to see everything through the childlike eyes of God.

As we grow to understand levels of understanding, we finally appreciate how historical fact is presented, preserved, and related to different cosmic cycles. We noticed how Geryon, the ancient king of Spain, was characterized as tri-formed, as was the Chimaera of the same generation. They were related to the snake who guards the Apples of the Hesperides. In Ireland, we also noticed how the Fomorians were disparaged as having horse's ears and other humorous deformities. We may now understand that mockery on the Demotic level assures that history is remembered by the ordinary people.

Nonnos of Panopolis

Students of antiquity must regard Nonnos with especial reverence because he has shed light upon so many matters. In the first place, he so beautifully bridges the awkward land masses of antiquity with the modern territories of the New Revelation.

Nonnos flatly ignores the problem of any break in tradition. He simply pretends that Christianity is a continuation of the mythological sequence of the gods of antiquity. His attitude is, "Why assume that there is a problem?" He does this because he is consistent. He believes that the mythological heroes are related to the cosmic cycles. The appearance of Christ is part of those cycles. Christ may be the Highest Revelation, but time and the natural cosmic cycles go on to Eternity. Some could regard Nonnos as a teacher and doctor of the Church. What really is the problem, and why cannot Christ be a continuation and fulfillment of the past?

There are not many facts known about Nonnos, other than that he was born in the most ancient City of Pan, Panopolis, in Upper Egypt about 450 AD. It has been surmised that he studied in Berytus in Lebanon, after which he settled in Alexandria, where he wrote the *Dionysica*. This epic poem is written in the most exquisite fashion. In includes most of the stories of Greek myth of some rare and very early collections. It therefore, includes many original, obscure, and local legends, and materials of the Alexandrian poets. Primarily, the *Dionysica* deals with the various incarnations and histories of the god Dionysus. It remains the longest story-poem in all of Greek literature, surpassing the combined works of Homer. Stylistically it is evident that he was a master and innovator of the poetic arts. He actually attained a small following in his antique revival movement. That he was an extremely intelligent and well-read man goes without saying. Tony Prost says that Nonnos revived the 1,000-year-old formal language of the Homeric Epic. He was able to construct hexameters correctly using the archaic quantities of Greek vowels. Nonnos later became a Christian and paraphrased the *Gospel of Saint John* in poetry. Adolf Lumpe remarks that Nonnos makes no distinction when he calls both the goddess Rhea and the Virgin Mary by the name of "god-bearers." Lumpe also remarks that Nonnos had the facile ability to create the impression of a universal god, whether of a mythological or Christian background.

The creation and assertion of the mythological continuum moving throughout Christianity, is of course Nonnos's greatest contribution. His second great accomplishment is relating astronomical cycles directly to the historical sequence of myth. Nonnos divides time into World Months, which constitute a World Year, during which the Great Fire and the Great Flood appear at the proper season. He hints at an astrological religion, whose genius is Astraios, the hoary chief cosmologer called *The Ancient of Days*, who keeps his astrolabe hidden in a special box. He consults this model of the heavens to make his mathematical calculations. Another cosmic character is Aion-Harmonia, Virgin of the Stars, whose robe is nothing less than the heavenly-embossed Star Mantel of blue with gold stars. Sometimes the Virgin Mary is represented in this fashion.

Nonnos resurrects all of the ancient star lore about changes in the heavens during the long World Year. He mentions how Leo and Virgo, and other constellations have moved from their places to other parts of the heavens. Long before Gallileo, Nonnos calls the sun the *mesomphalos*, "Helios, central navel of the seven traveling planets." Nonnos gives credence to the idea of a specially sanctified religious city here on earth, "Which of the cities has the organ of the sovereign voice?" Most importantly of all, Nonnos recognizes that time is told by the cosmic clock, "The Ram [Aries], the center of the universe, the navel star of Olympus."

Nonnos seems to have written his *Dionysica* in Alexandria around 450 AD. About 50 years earlier in 391 AD, Emperor Theodosius ordered the destruction of all pagan temples. Theophilus, the bishop of Alexandria, complied with these directions and the Museum and its famous Library were most likely destroyed at this time. However, what is technically called The Library of Alexandria were several decentralized libraries, such as the Serapeum Temple and its daughter library to the main Museum Library. Also, there were storehouses of manuscripts for foreign export such as the ones that Julius Caesar accidentally burnt when he set fire to the enemy fleet in the Alexandrian harbor. There was also the 200,000 volume Library of Pergamus that Anthony gave as a gift to Cleopatra. Further extensions to the libraries were made by Caesar Augustus in 12 AD and Cladius in 41–54 AD.

In 2004 AD, Polish and Egyptian archaeologists have discovered 13 identical lecture halls belonging to the 5th century University of Alexandria. These halls had a capacity of 5,000 students each. As well, Alexandria continued to be the leading intellectual center for Christianity during these times. It is not hard to imagine that Nonnos would have had abundant select material at his hand. Within this context, the once hidden sacred manuscripts and writings had become profane. At this special time in history, many ancient and sacred materials were publicly revealed and looked over before being disparaged and discarded.

Above, we discussed that the Age of Discovery brought many ancient maps out of hiding, because people now thought that they had better knowledge and that the old maps were obsolete. So too, the book-burnings and the new Christian religion brought forth many a secret and sacred document—now thought to be outmoded. At the end of certain time periods, secret and hidden material often comes to light. Apparently, Nonnos lived at such a special time and availed of what was revealed. I freely admit that the cosmological background to my research into classical readings would never have been conceived without the insights and information from Nonnos of Panopolis. I, therefore, thank him profusely!

Chapter 2

Cultural Ages and their Cultural Gods

Cultural Ages span millions of years. Thinking in periods of human history that develop over millions of years is not something that our modern form of education has taught us to do. All the same, the cosmologers of India and those of Yucatan and Mexico have always thought in the context of millions of years. The calendars of the Maya and Aztec have proved to be the most sophisticated and accurate measuring tools ever devised by humans.

The ancients divided the heavens into twelve zones represented by constellation star-pictures of the current Zodiac. So, whether it was the daily revolution of the earth, the yearly progress of the sun, the Cycle of the Precession of the Vernal Equinoxes, or the Galactic Progression of our solar system, the Zodiac always functioned as the one-clock face of the heavenly timepiece. And, the thematic influences behind the twelve houses of the zodiac never change, but always represent a specific and particular nature which comes from the greater universe itself, whether in the shorter or the longer cycles of time.

I know that the question immediately arises, "How can anyone imagine that mankind has historical recall spanning millions of years?" As we said in our original introduction, history does repeat itself within many cycles, and often even in a minimal degree. So that when a regional flood occurred, all the mythology of the Great Cataclysm is recalled and appended to this minor event. Mythology is the product of the constant repetition of numerous cosmic cycles producing the same influences and events, and telling the same stories in many different shades—over and over again. The olden sages and scientists knew the cosmic time of the *real* Ark and the Animals, which was a global event that only happened once within the great Galactic Cycle. But of course, many regional floods occurring time and again served to rekindle the memory of the one great cosmic event. The myth of the Great Flood was piggy-backed upon each significant regional flood. It may be inferred from Albiruni that there is a regular sequence of these regional floods, exactly like eclipses which are also caused by astronomical phenomena, and also cover every region of the globe throughout time.

Therefore, we may now understand that cultural ages and their cultural gods refer to the extremely long periods of the Galactic Cycle as our solar system revolves around the Milky Way Galaxy. With this in mind, let us return to Skytobrachion's account of the Atlantic colony of Hespera on the river Triton in Morocco. This account is preserved by Diodorus Sicilus in his account of the ancient gods, Uranus and Ge (iii.56):

Uranus was their first king who built walled cities and made laws. He subdued much of the earth and since he was a careful observer of the stars he foretold many things which would take place throughout the world. He introduced the year on the basis of the movement of the sun, and the months on that of the moon, and instructed the people about the reoccurring seasons. They proclaimed him to be King of the Universe. To Uranus were born forty-five sons from a number of wives. Eighteen who were called the Titans were by Titaea who was deified and her name changed to Ge. The most renowned of his daughters were Basileia and Rhea (whom some also named Pandora). Basileia was given the appellation of 'Great Mother' and was united in marriage with one of her brothers Hyperion, and from their union were born Helius and Selene. The Titan brothers of Basileia, out of fear for the succession to the kingdom, and through envy put Hyperion to the sword and drowned Helius in the Eridanus. Selene who loved her brother committed suicide. Their mother Basileia thereafter became frenzied and wandered over the land with her hair hanging free, inspired by the noise of kettledrums and cymbals of her followers. The Phrygians also recount her story.

We should appreciate that none of the above events occurred in Morocco. They are cultural memory imported from the far reaches of the Americas side of the Atlantic to the Eastern and African side of this great ocean.

Cronus and Atlas

Sicilus continues with the history reported by Skytobrachion which actually takes place in Morocco, and introduces many of the principals who would later bring Atlantic culture into the Mediterranean regions.

> The kingdom was then divided between Cronus and Atlas. The latter received the regions on the coast of the ocean, and he not only gave the name of Atlantians to his people, but, likewise called the greatest mountain in the land Atlas. He perfected the science of astrology, and was the first to publish to mankind the doctrine of the sphere. He had a son called Hesperus. The seven daughters of Atlas were the Atlantides: Maia (who begot Hermes), Electra, Tygete, Sterope, Merope, Halcyone and Celaeno. These became the first ancestors of a larger part of the human race. The great majority of the most ancient heroes trace their descent back to the Atlantides who are also called the Pleiades and Nymphs.
>
> Cronus, the brother of Atlas, married Rhea and begot the famous Olympian Zeus. Also, in more ancient times there had been another Zeus who was King of Crete, and a brother of Uranus. This Cretan Zeus had ten sons called the Curetes, while Crete was at that time called Idaea, after his spouse. Cronus was the lord of Sicily, Libya and Italy; and was notorious for his impiety and greed. His son, the Olympian Zeus, overthrew him; and became King of the entire world. He was a just ruler, and appropriately honored by

mankind, who gave him the name *Zen*; and acclaimed him god and lord of the universe.

Again, I must say that one can only appreciate the business-like reporting of Skytobrachion, which is brief and to the point. His *Theogony* is perfect and classical Greek. In addition, his information is more explicit as he more clearly identifies Atlas and his son Hesperus, with Morocco.

In cosmology, Aquarius is the house of Cronus/Saturn. Therefore, the geographic longitude of Morocco must also correspond to Aquarius. Time, history, and geography are all coordinated within the Galactic Age of Aquarius, dominated by the brothers, Cronus and Atlas of Morocco.

While Atlas remained in Morocco, Skytobrachion says that Cronus went on to become the lord of Sicily, Libya, and Italy. Some of these areas touch upon the neighboring longitude of Pisces, where the descendents of Cronus and Atlas, and their traditions and sciences, were to settle. Much later on, these colonies and descendents would become the people of Jupiter/Zeus, rightful lord of that Galactic and geographic region of Pisces which does cover the regions of Italy, Sicily, and Libya.

Chapter 3

Morocco and the Golden Apples of the Garden of the Hesperides

Let us take a closer look at the geography of this birthplace of the gods of the Aquarian Culture. This geography still coincides with Aquarius. Now, however, time has moved on and the galactic epoch of our present time has moved on to Aries.

The lands which are now Morocco, Algeria, and Tunisia were called Mauritania by the classical authors. At Strabo's time (25 AD) it was called Mauri or Maurusii, and Massaesyli and Libophoenicia. At the time of the second Punic war (218 BC) the land was called Mauritania and Numidia. The poets and mythographers who used very ancient place names called these Western regions Hesperus, Libya, Western Ethiopia, Triton, Ocean, "on the bounds of ocean," Tartarus, "at the ends of the earth," Hades, and finally, "The Land of Night and Sleep and Dreams."

What we now call the Atlantic Ocean was in ancient times just called Ocean, after the name of this primeval god (*Pauly-Wissowa; Pythias and Posidonios*). Then it was called the Cronian Sea after the god Cronus-Saturn. Afterwards, it was called the Atlantic, after the god Atlas. The sea between Britain and North Spain was called Morinum, and north of Britain was designated as the Hyperborean Sea. The Romans called the Atlantic, the Western or Hesperos Ocean.

Weinstock writes (*Pauly-Wissowa*) that Mauritania is naturally defended by a closed coast seldom broken by bays, while it is guarded to the east by the Atlas Range. The country is extremely fruitful, having supplied Rome with all its wheat. The wine of Lixus is a naturally growing vine brought forth without cultivation. Even before the Berbers and Vandals there were blond Libyans. Hannibal got his elephants from here. It is also noted for its horses which are small, fast, and docile.

Pliny (v.1) reports that Tangiers was founded by the Giant Anteaus with whom Hercules wrestled near his palace in Lixus, 60 miles from Tangiers. This place was also noted as the site of the Garden of the Hesperides, where an arm of the ocean stretches inland to an island on the River Lixus. Also on the other side of Mt. Atlas there are woods and fruit trees filled with the music of flutes, pipes, drums, and cymbals of the Satyrs and the goat-shaped Pans. Here also are the remains of vineyards, and palm groves, and signs of former habitation. The later generations of these peculiar tribes had completely degenerated according to Pliny.

Strabo (17.3.4) says that,

> Maurusia is a fertile country . . . it is surpassing in the size and the number of its trees, and is also productive of everything . . . the rivers are said to contain crocodiles, as also other kinds of animals similar to those in the Nile . . . this country produces a vine so thick it can hardly be encircled by the arms of two men.

Homer, in the *Odyssey* (iv.85) proclaims that in Libya the ewes bear young three times every year.

Regarding the Golden Apples of the Hesperides, Sicilus writes (iii.55) "The island of Hespera was originally a possession of the Libyan Amazons. It was of great size and full of fruit bearing trees and multitudes of flocks."

Pherecydes says that for the wedding of Zeus and Hera, the gods brought presents. Earth (Ge) brought Golden Apples which Hera ordered to be planted in the Garden of the Gods beside Mt. Atlas.

The *Theogony* says, "The Hesperides who guard the rich apples and the trees bearing fruit beyond glorious Ocean."

In the *Homerica* (frag.5) it appears that the Hesperides were the daughters of the goddess, Night. Usually, the Hesperides are the daughters of Atlas, who guard the Golden Apples.

According to the Irish *Stair Ercuil* (xxviii) the four Hesperides were Egle, patron of study; Esper, patron of intelligence; Medusa, of memory; and Aretusa, patron of speech.

There is also mention of a serpent guarding the apples. *Theogony* (330): Ceto and Phorcys bore "the awful snake who guards the apples all of gold in the secret places of the dark earth at its great bounds."

Appollodorus (ii.5) says that the apples were "guarded by an immortal dragon with a hundred heads, offspring of Typhon and Echidna, which spoke with many and divers sorts of voices."

Juba, king of Mauritania, asserts that the Libyans call the citron-lemon, the apple of the Hesperides; and that Hercules brought them to Greece where they are called golden apples.

Athenaeus (ii.82) says that in a part of Greece, Lacedaemon, these Apples of the Hesperides are placed as offerings to the gods; "they are fragrant but not good to eat."

The juice of the lemon preserves books from decay and worm. It is also an antidote to many poisons. The tree was probably regarded sacred for it bears fruit at all seasons of the year. When some are plucked, others are in blossom and others are developing and ripening.

In the Peloponnesus in Greece, Melanion brought golden apples from Aphrodite to win the maiden Atalanta. In Troy, the famous judgment of Paris allotted the prize of the apple to Aphrodite, the foam-born goddess of the ocean.

It would seem that the ancients regarded Morocco and Mauritania as a very fruitful place of origin. The genealogies and mythologies of the inhabitants of Troy and other Greek cities have a direct connection with the ancient Atlantic culture that was preserved in Morocco.

David Hatcher Childress, in his *Lost Cities of Atlantis, Ancient Europe & The Mediterranean* (p. 233), enumerates the following people who believed that Morocco was affiliated with Atlantis: (1) the French geographer E. F. Berlioux, 1874; (2) Gustave Lagneau, 1876; (3) A. F. R. Knotel, 1893; (4) the explorer, E. L. Gentil, 1921; (5) A. L. Rutot; (6) Mario Vivarez; and (7) Otto Silbermann, 1930. Childress (p. 239) also reminds us that the devastating earthquake and tsunami of 1755 which totally destroyed Lisbon, also wrecked havoc upon the entire Atlantic seaboard down to Mauritania, especially the ancient cities of Meknes and Volubilis. This natural catastrophe must finally have eliminated every last vestige of Atlantic cultural relics upon these shores.

As a final word, the possibility of one interpretation of the Golden Apples of the Hesperides is, to my mind, the most simple and pleasing. The Golden Apples are the planets which receive their golden light from the sun. There are seven singing Hesperides equal to the ancient count of the sun, moon, and the visible planets which also were thought to sing like the mythical Sirens, each emitting a special harmonic octave or note. We can see how Atlas, the noted astronomer, came to carry on this astronomical tradition and how his daughters came to be called after the ancient name of the Hesperides. Yet, the true Hesperides belonged to an older astronomical tradition of the world-axis of the serpent tree, when the golden light of the planets was discovered by the daughters who helped dispel the darkness of their ancient mother, the goddess Night. Old Mother Night, the terrible goddess, as she was called. The poets say terrible, because the mere contemplation of her far-off distant era, would send shudders down your spine. Terrible because before her, all was in darkness, she herself was the dawn of enlightenment.

Chapter 4

Atlantic People, Gods, Heroes, and Ethiopians

In today's geography, Ethiopia is a country south of Egypt. In classical times, blacks and people of color were called Ethiopians. The references which we cite here will only relate to the Hesperi or Western Ethiopians of Africa near the Atlantic Ocean.

Homer in the *Odyssey* (i.22) sings, "Poseidon had gone among the far-off Ethiopians—the Ethiopians who dwell sundered in twain, the furthermost of men, some where Hyperion [the sun] sets and some where he rises." The world map of Pomponius Mela (Hapgood, fig.8) places the Hesperii Aethiopes along the greater part of the Atlantic coast of Western Africa.

Strabo (i.16, i.3.26) calls them, "The Ethiopians live at the ends of the earth on the banks of Oceanus." Pausanius (*Attica.33*) comments upon a statue of Nemesis, "In her left hand she holds an apple branch, in her right a cup on which are wrought Ethiopians . . . for the Ethiopians dwell near it [the Ocean] and Ocean is the father of Nemesis."

Dionysus

Herodotus (iii.97) also tells of the long-lived Atlantic Ethiopians who dwell about holy Nysa where Dionysus is the god of their festivals. Sicilus (i.18) says that while Osiris was in Ethiopia, he met the Muses and the Satyr people (companions of Dionysus) who are so proficient in dancing and singing. Clement of Alexandria quotes Orpheus telling of the toys with which the Titans beguiled Dionysus, "Top, wheel and jointed dolls, with beauteous fruit of gold from the clear voiced Hesperides."

Orpheus

The descent of Orpheus into Hades (the West) is well-known. Sicilus (iii.68) reports,

> Orpheus . . . penetrated to the Western parts of Libya as far as the ocean. He also visited Nysa, where the ancient natives of the city relate that Dionysus was reared there, and, after he had learned from the Nyseans of the deeds of this god, one and all, he composed the *Phrygian Poem* as it is called, wherein he made use of the archaic manner both of speech and letters.

The teacher, or brother of Orpheus, according to Apollodorus, was Linus.

Linus

He was the originator of the famous "Linus song" which, according to Herodotus (ii.79), is sung in Egypt, Phoenicia, Cyprus, and elsewhere. The burden of the song is "alas for us." Diogenes Laertius (viii.1.25) says. "So Urania bare Linus, a very lovely son; and him all men who are singers and harpers do bewail at feasts and dances, and as they begin, and as they end, they call on Linus."

Urania is one of the Muses, daughters of Mnemosyne, the sister of Ocean; and the daughter of Uranus. Clement of Alexandria says, "Linus who was skilled in all manner of wisdom." Sicilus relates that he was the first to transfer the Phoenician letters into Greek, to give a name to each character, and to fix its shape. These however, came to be called "Pelasgic"; for they were the first to use them.

Jason and the Argonauts

Strabo cites (i.2.40),

> Mimnermus (625 BC) says that never would Jason . . . have come even to the fair stream of Oceanus . . . to the city of Aeetes where the rays of the swift sun lie in the chamber of gold besides the lips of Oceanus, whither glorious Jason went.

Lycophron in the *Alexandra* (879) writes, "Cast upon the desolate dwelling place of Atlas . . . where Mopsus . . . died [he was the seer of the Argonauts]." Hesiod in the *Catalogue of Women* sings, "Argonauts came through the Ocean to Libya, and so carrying the Argo reached our sea." The Irish *Stair Ercuil* (p. 31) records that the brother of Jason is married to the daughter of the King of Hespera.

The Golden Ram of Phrixius of Colchis is usually placed on the Black Sea. However there appears to be a more ancient Colchis on the Atlantic. Strabo says, "The sanctuary of Phryxus is situated on the confines of Colchis and Iberia [Spain]." In section i.3.21, Strabo relates how these Iberians migrated to regions by the Black Sea. No doubt, they brought their traditions with them.

The connection between the Colchians and the Atlantic is very important because the Colchians were acknowledged to be one of the most ancient of people.

Herodotus says (ii.104), "The Colchians and Egyptians and Ethiopians are the only nations that have from the first practiced circumcision. The Phoenicians and the Syrians of Palestine acknowledge of themselves that they learned the custom from the Egyptians."

Medea, who is the daughter of the King of Colchis, falls in love with Jason. She is regarded as a sorceress who has special knowledge of drugs, potions, and pharmacology. Strabo (i.2.10) criticizes Homer for inventing a blood relationship between this Medea and Circe (another magician) and establishing a residence for them both out by the great ocean.

Yet, Hesiod confirms (*Theogony*, 956), "And Perseis, the daughter of Ocean, bare to unwearying Helios, Circe and Aeetes the king [of Colchis]. And Aeetes . . . took to wife fair-cheeked Idyia, daughter of Ocean, the perfect stream . . . and bare him neat-ankled Medea." Apollodorus in the

Epitome (5.5) reports, "It is said that after death, Achilles consorts with Medea in the Isles of the Blest [the Canary Islands off the coast of Morocco]."

We know that there is a very ancient Atlantic strain among the Greek tribes. It may be useful to use the myth about Jason, the land of Colchis, and King Aeetes, as a test of origin. Those Greeks who affirm that Colchis is in the west, on the shores of the Atlantic, presumably stem from that same region. Those Greeks who attest that Colchis is in the area of the Black Sea, are, no doubt, from that place and of that heritage. I would think that the same rule of origin would also apply to the legend of Andromedea and the sea monster, said to have taken place in the land of the Ethiopians on the Ocean.

Cadmus

Cadmus is the celebrated founder of Thebes in Greece. Along with Linus, he is credited with the introduction of the so-called Phoenician letters to the Greeks. His wife, Harmonia, is a daughter of Electra, a daughter of Atlas. Apollodorus says that after their death, Cadmus and his wife were placed in the Elysian Fields in the West where they were turned into serpents.

Nonnos (13.333) writes,

> Libyans . . . whose home is in the Western clime, the cities of wandering Cadmus near the clouds. For there on a time dwelt Cadmus . . . with his Sithonian bride Harmonia. [Below this account Nonnos mentions Maurusian people, Western Ethiopians, Tritonian Lake and Hesperides] Cadmus . . . paid his footing in the Libyan land by building a hundred cities, and he gave to each lofty walls inaccessible with towers of stone . . . those who dwell in settlements near the moon's birthplace [the new moon rises and first shows herself in the West].

Nonnos clearly mentions Libya, and not Morocco, because he had spoken of the Tritonian Lake of Libya, whose name Triton was borrowed from the original Tritonian Marsh in Morocco. Strabo quite literally gets tired of these confusions and disputes when he exasperatedly writes (I.2.18) about Homer mentioning the river stream of Ocean, the Isles of the Blest,

Ogygia, and the Phaecians: "Now all these incidents are clearly indicated as being placed in fancy in the Atlantic Ocean; but, Polybius [the so-called exemplary historian of Greece] by suppressing them destroys what the poet states in express terms."

Perseus and the Amazons

Apollodorus says that Perseus went to Ethiopia to the court of Cephus and Andromeda to rescue Cassiopeia who was bound to the sea coast for having compared her beauty with the Nereids.

Perseus was also the famous decapitator of Medusa, queen of the Gorgon Amazons. Hesiod in the *Theogony:* "The Gorgons who dwell beyond glorious Ocean in the frontier land towards Night where are the clear voiced Hesperides." The *Cypria* says, "Gorgons, fearful monsters who lived in Sarpedon, a rocky island in the deep eddying Oceanus."

Herodotus remembers (ii.91) that in the time of Perseus that the Gorgon Amazons had risen to power again. Also, in the time of Horus, king of Egypt, there lived a queen of the Amazons named Myrina, who had defeated the tribe of the Gorgon Amazons. Hercules himself had waged war against the Amazons in prior times.

Aphrodite

The Titan generation goddess, Aphrodite, was assuredly born of the foam of the castrated member of her father Uranus. On the Atlantic Ocean, Hesiod in the *Theogony* (850,730) sings, "The Titans under Tartarus who live with Cronus . . . Titan gods . . . at the ends of the huge earth."

Pausanius (iii.23) reports, "The sanctuary of Aphrodite Urania is most holy and it is the most ancient of all sanctuaries of Aphrodite among the Greeks. The goddess herself is represented by an armed image of wood." In the *Golden Ass* by Apuleius, Aphrodite is attended by Nerids and Tritons, "holding a mirror for her to admire herself in."

Demeter

Holy Demeter, the law giver and the grain giver, searches the world for her daughter Persephone, abducted by Hades, the lord of the hosts of the Underworld.

Callimachus (310 BC) in his Hymn VI, *To Demeter* sings, "Hesperus, who alone persuaded Demeter to drink, what time she pursued the unknown tracks of her stolen daughter. Lady, how were thy feet able to carry thee unto the West, unto the Ethiopians and where the Golden Apples are?"

Pausanius (Attica 14) substantiates that the cultivation of grain came from the West: "Concerning Triptolemus who introduced the cultivation of grain to Greece some extent verses of Musaeus, if indeed they are . . . say that Triptolemus was the son of Oceanus and Earth . . . while Choerilus, the Athenian, says he was by . . . Poseidon."

Hades

The appellation Hades may stem from Gades in Spain, just as Tartarus is said to originate from Tartessus in Spain.

Hesiod in the *Theogony* calls Hades the son of Cronus and Rhea (while Apollodorus names him Pluto, the Lord of Hades): "There in front stand the echoing halls of the god of the lower world, strong Hades . . . and there dwells . . . terrible Styx, eldest daughter of back-flowing Ocean."

In the Homeric Hymns, *To Demeter* (ii) it is written, "Dark haired Hades, ruler over the departed . . . Aidoneus, ruler over the dead . . . the ruler of the Many." The poem continues on with Hermes, the descendent of Atlas, driving the golden chariot and the deathless horses of Hades. As well, the poem speaks of the abducted Persephone playing on a meadow with such Western personalities as Electra, Rhodea, Calypso, Pluto, Stzx, Urania, and Pallas.

Pallas Athena

Lastly, there is the great goddess and patron of Athens, Pallas Athena, sprung from the head of Zeus at the River Triton. There is so much to be said about Athena and the mysterious and sacred Palladium, that we will have to defer that pleasure until a later chapter.

Chapter 5

The Transmission of Culture

Part One of proving cultural continuity is simplicity itself. This happens when a colony names its city and river directly after its original homeland. The name of the River Triton originates in Morocco. This name was then carried forward to Libya, and even later to Greece where there are cities founded on rivers named Triton. In modern history, we see this trend in the place names of the colonies in the New World of the Americas and Australia.

Part Two concerns the adherence to a sequential mythology of the same gods covering enormous periods of time. Sometimes the names are changed into different languages. Similar attributes and similar exploits help to identify similar gods even though they have different names among the various nations. The gods Osiris and Dionysus share a great many attributes. The classical authors report that there were three or more appearances of Dionysus over time. This fact alone would convince antiquarians that there could be numerous apparitions of this god under several names, separated by time and nations.

Part Three centers upon the identification of an original homeland. For once a colony transfers the names and mythologies to a new homeland, adoption becomes invention—so long as there is no one remaining to challenge the claim of originality. And this may often be the case in the world, when time has finally destroyed the real place of genesis. Meanwhile, a new time has imbued a sense of permanence in the hearts of the colonists to the extent that the new Tritonian Marsh, or River; is now *unquestionably* the real, original place in the minds of the inhabitants.

Part Four regards historical criticism, which is a very delicate subject. People who read and write history are conservative by definition. As we were told above, even some of the Greek historians, like Polybius, just plain refused to hand down certain specific traditions. In view of all that we have uncovered in respect to a complete context and picture of Atlantic Culture—this makes Polybius's obstinacy look dishonest and just plain ridiculous. Polybius shuns all mysteries and problems because he wishes to establish a simple, teachable format of his own composition. He so arrogantly elevates the teacher above his subject.

Yet, in all fairness, it really seems quite natural for some people to exhibit a perplexed reluctance to report on some of the very ancient and musty histories. Sometimes these histories exhibit so many problems in the realms of age, epoch, and unfamiliar geography, where even the evidence of former human habitation or glory, has totally disappeared or degenerated.

But, heroically, such authors as Homer, Hesiod, Apollodorus, Skytobrachion, Diodorus Sicilus, Strabo, Pausanius, Plutarch, Nonnos, and many others have recognized the element of truth in the histories that they have read. They have therefore reported some of the most interesting stories of human history in the hope that they will serve to illuminate the human condition, which is the greatest of all dramas: composed in part of nature and in part of the divine.

Chapter 6

Egyptian Culture from Morocco, Libya, and the West

The Egyptians had a special reverence for the lands to the west of the Nile. In their cultural heritage, the West represented the far distant past. It also brought to mind the legions and generations of the dead who had created their present culture.

In consequence of these traditions, the Egyptians bury their rulers, who are their demi-gods, on the west bank of the Nile. Their heaven goddess, Hathor, has her head in the West. In the annual ceremony of the renewal of the life of their gods, the Egyptians transfer the shrines of the gods across the Nile as if they were coming from the West, and entering their temples in Egypt from that direction.

The following accounts present evidence that Egyptian culture came from Libya, Morocco, and the regions upon the Atlantic Ocean. We need to remember that the classical poets and historians also referred to the West under the names of Ethiopia, the Underworld, and Hades.

Sicilus (i.97) records,

> The myths which are related about the dalliance of Zeus and

Hera, and of their journey to Ethiopia, Homer got from Egypt: for each year among the Egyptians the shrine of Zeus is carried across the river into Libya, and then brought back some days later, as if the gods were arriving from Ethiopia.

Hesiod says that the river Nile was the son of Ocean. And the grammarian Apollodorus (ii.) traces that Epaphus, of the family of Ocean, married Memphis, the daughter of Nile. They produced a daughter, Libya, after whom the region of Libya was named. This Libya united with the Libyan Poseidon, and one of their grandchildren was Egyptus, who named the land Egypt after himself.

Strabo writes (16.2.35), "The Egyptians were mistaken in representing the Divine Being by the images of beasts and cattle, as were also the Libyans."

Herodotus states (ii.77) that the Egyptians are the healthiest men next to the Libyans. Herodotus also says that the Egyptians only disputed their great antiquity with the Phrygians. Skytobrachion has already told us that the Phrygians and the Atlantians share the mythology of the Great Mother Basileia. Dionysius of Halicarnassus (i.61) says that the descendants of Electra, the daughter of Atlas, came to Phrygia in Asia, and built a temple to the Mother of the Gods; and instituted mysteries and ceremonies which are observed throughout all Phrygia.

Sicilus (i.87) tells us, "In primitive times a hawk brought to the priests in Thebes a book wrapped about with a purple band, which contained written directions concerning the worship of the gods and the honors due them." According to Strabo (17.1.47) the city of Hawks, where the bird is held in high honor, lies opposite to the city of Eileithyia on the Nile. The hawk is accounted the sacred bird of the Hyperborean (a region of the North Atlantic) Apollo, and Eileithyia, the nurse of Apollo. Strabo also reports of a common settlement of Ethiopians and Egyptians above Philae where the Ethiopian Hawk is honored, a bird greater in size than the normal hawk, and far different in its varied plumage.

An essential part of the Egyptian kings' royal regalia was a tail dependent from their backside. Sicilus records (iii.72) that the "first king of Nysa [the birthplace of Dionysus] was Silenius, but his ancestry was unknown to all men because of its antiquity. This man had a tail at the lower part of his back, and his descendants also regularly carried this distinguishing mark because of their participation in his nature." There is also the curious reference of a Seilene speaking to the Phrygian King Midas about the legends of Atlantis. There is a connection between King Midas and an Irish king, in respect to them having ears like that of a horse or donkey.

Herodotus writes (ii.54) that the oracles of Zeus Ammon in Libya, and that of Dodona in Greece, originally came from Thebes in Egypt. This makes it seem as if Ammon was a product of Egypt. Yet, the informants of Herodotus are forced to admit (ii.42) that the Ammonians are colonists from both Egypt and Ethiopia; and speak a language compounded of both nations.

Sicilus, through Skytobrachion, reveals (iii.67) the almost forgotten history of Libya, which is as follows: Ammon the King of Libya lay with a shepherdess, Amaltheia, whom he appointed to be mistress of the Horn of Hesperus, an excellent land full of vines. And of their union they begot the god Dionysius. Skytobrachion relates that this was the first manifestation of Dionysus. The second incarnation of Dionysius was born to Io and Zeus, the King of Egypt. The third revelation of Dionysus came to Zeus and Semele, the daughter of Cadmus, in Greece. The poet Nonnos also follows this threefold manifestation of the god in his history of Dionysus.

Because of the jealousy of his wife Rhea, Ammon is forced to hide Dionysius in the city of Nysa. Sicilus writes of Thymoetes, who wandered in Western Libya as far as Ocean and visited Nysa. He called it the city of Nysa on the River Triton where every kind of fruit tree abounds, along with the wild vine.

Rhea then abandons Ammon for her brother, Cronus, who along with the Titans defeats Ammon. After the war, Ammon is forced to retire to Crete. In order to avenge his father, Dionysius musters an army of Libyans and Amazons under the command of Athena. The good-willed Dionysus grants peace to Cronus, and allows the ascension of the Olympian Zeus to the throne of the gods.

Sicilus (i.96) discloses the following: "Orpheus, for instance, brought from Egypt most of his mystic ceremonies, the orgiastic rites that accompanied his wanderings and his fabulous account of his experiences in Hades. For the rite of Osiris is the same as that of Dionysius; and that of Isis very similar to that of Demeter." Herodotus says (ii.123), "It is believed in Egypt that the rulers of the Underworld are Demeter and Dionysius."

Sicilus continues (i.96),

And the punishments in Hades of the unrighteous, the Fields of the Righteous . . . all these were introduced by Orpheus in imitation of Egyptian funeral customs. Hermes, for instance, the Conductor of Souls, according to the ancient Egyptian custom, brings up the body of the Apis to a certain point and then gives it over to one who wears the mask of Cerberus [the hound of Hades]. And after Orpheus had introduced this notion among the Greeks, Homer followed it when he wrote:

> *Cyllenian Hermes then did summon forth*
> *the Suitors souls, holding his wand in his hand.*

And a little further on he says:

> *They passed Oceanus' streams, the Gleaming*
> *Rock, the Portals of the Sun, the Land of*
> *Dreams; and now they reached the meadows*
> *of Asphodel, where dwell the souls, the*
> *shades of men outworn.*

Sicilus continues,

Now, he calls the river "Oceanus" because in their language the Egyptians speak of the Nile as Oceanus; The Portals of the Sun is the name for the city Heliopolis; and the meadows, the mythical dwelling of the dead is his term for the place near the lake which is called Acherousia, which is near Memphis. And around it are fairest meadows of marsh land and reeds. The same explanation also serves for the statement that the dwelling of the dead is in these regions, since the most and the largest tombs of the Egyptians are situated there.

In addition, Sicilus writes (i.97), "Many other things as well of which mythology tells are still to be found among the Egyptians, the name being still preserved and the custom actually practiced." Here he mentions the 50 daughters of Danaus pouring water into vessels with holes in them. He also tells of Ocnus, the weaver, whose rope is devoured by an ass behind him, as rapidly as he produces it. These are some of the punishments of the unrighteous dead in Hades.

Sicilus continues, "Melampus also, they say, brought from Egypt the rites which the Greeks celebrate in the name of Dionysius; the myths about Cronus, and the War with the Titans, and, in a word, the account of the things which happened to the gods."

Again, Sicilus claims (i.29) that the initiatory rites and mysteries of Demeter of Eleusis were transferred from Egypt by Erechtheus, King of Athens, who himself was of the Egyptian race. This happened on the occasion of bringing a great supply of grain from the Nile when there happened to be a drought in Greece.

The above references indicate, most plainly, the assimilation and cross-assimilation of culture. I think, however, that it must be clear that both Egypt and Greece were drawing traditions from an earlier parent culture, located in the West. For Hephaestus is regarded as the most ancient god by the Egyptians themselves. Below are some remarks concerning the context and antiquity of Hephaestus.

Pausanius (*Arcadia*, 41.5) writes that Eurymone, the daughter of Ocean, received Hephaestus, as did Thetis, the Nereid, according to Homer in the *Iliad*.

Apollodorus (*Epitome*, ii.8) writes, "When Pelops had reached the Ocean, and been cleansed by Hephaestus."

Ancient Libya

The predominance of Libya belonged to an age long before the rise of Egypt, and at a time when the Sahara Desert had not as yet been created by the wild ride of Phaeton who drove his father's sun chariot too close to the earth.

There is some testimony and maps which show that North Africa was once a half river, half ocean marshland of many islands, connected in the south to the Atlantic Ocean. There is, of course, evidence to verify that this land was once covered in part by water. Later as the geography changed, the civilizations located there built elaborate and lengthy systems of aqueducts to preserve their land.

Stephen S. Mehler, in *The Land of Osiris,* evokes the ancient Khemit folk culture of Egypt, whose ancestors remembered when the Nile flowed on the western side of the Pyramids. This work also details many of the mysterious aqueducts and smaller water channels on the plateau of Giza.

David Hatcher Childress, in *Lost Cities & Ancient Mysteries of Africa & Arabia,* cites some early explorer's testimony about these regions. He writes about Count Byron De Prorok, *In Quest of Lost Worlds;* who tells of his journey from Algeiers to the Haggar Mountains, "Through the depression to Gabes salt lakes that were perhaps at one time part of the inland sea, and similarly are to be found in other parts of Northern Africa . . . possibly the Tritons . . . sailed on the open water here." Count Byron continues, "Drawings showed also rhinoceros and hippopotamus which were long vanished from the region . . . a jungle when the drawings were made." He continues, "The pharaohs were fighting the Libyans whose territory once stretched from the Atlantic to the Nile . . . a race that has almost disappeared because the elements have dried up their continent."

Childress also cites L. Taylor Hansen's *The Ancient Atlantic* who reports,

> The Sahara was once held by the curve of the Atlas range from the Gulf of Gabes to the mountains south of dry Lake Chad . . . only after the sudden sinking of the southern arm of the Atlas Mountains did the Niger river break through these southern mountains, and tear its way out to the Atlantic . . . the giant lake had made an island out of the Ahaggar Mountains and the Air Mountains.

Hopefully, there will be a renewed interest in investigating these Libyan regions which must hold many of the keys to the great cultural context that inspired the world prior to the ages that gave rise to the excellence of Egypt.

PART IV:

THE HEAVEN-HOLDERS
AND THE EARTH-HOLDERS

Introduction

Atlas is shown holding the sphere of the heavens upon his shoulders. He is portrayed like this because he was one of the first astronomers to name the stars and contemplate their movements. The homeland of Atlas was Morocco. In reverence to his memory, the mountains and the ocean of this region bear his name.

Greek and Egyptian mythology places the origin of the gods in the West, on the shores of the Atlantic Ocean and in the homeland of Atlas. His contributions to astronomy and cartography are immense. This is why Atlas was called not only the *Heaven-Holder*, but also the *Earth-Holder*. Yet, Atlas was but the heir to a long scientific tradition that existed upon the Atlantic. The West is the ancient home of gods, heroes, religion, astronomy, and science.

An important part of the story of Atlas is that he is relieved of his burden of the celestial sphere by Hercules. The interpretation of this relief is quite simply—the transmission of culture from one epoch and place to another. Namely, that the discoveries of Atlas were carried forward by

Hercules. This transmission also applies to the god Poseidon of Libya who is also referred to as an "Earth-Holder."

Another epithet of Poseidon is "Earth-Shaker." In the Egyptian astronomical pictures, the heavens are always supported by various deities, including Geb, who is identified with Cronus. All of these deities are personified as Heaven-Holders or Earth-Holders, a distinction which we hope to clarify as we proceed.

In ancient thought, the Heaven-Holders and Earth-Holders presented the concept of possessing the highest scientific knowledge. This knowledge was a great treasure of mankind, and a cache of sacred information that had been carried forward from the past, and would be carefully transmitted in the future.

These signs, names, and symbols became a special arcane code which transcended all ages of mankind. Even in our modern European tradition emperors, kings, and queens, and even the Christ-child are shown holding the globe of the terrestrial sphere as Earth-Holders.

In some contexts, it would appear that the *Heaven-Holders* are the masters of science, culture, and religion. And, that, on the other hand, the *Earth-Holders* are the masters of politics, civilization, and the world.

A part of our study is to shed light upon the different meanings of these two concepts. They have been used as symbols of a secret culture of knowledge and political power underlying and directing the framework of culture and civilization. It is possible that there are two clandestine agendas at work. And it is quite natural that these dual powers have been in contention since the beginning of all time.

But, before we may continue with this interesting topic, we need to learn more about Atlas and the other Earth and Heaven-Holders.

First, we would like to examine other gods who were Heaven-Supporters in order to see if these gods fit into this mold of gifted scientists, inspired philosophers, and prophets.

Ocean

The god Ocean is said to support and surround the world in the form of oceanic water. Ocean water was regarded as the source of biological life. Also, this Oceanic water was thought to be the inspiration of the sciences. This was because the tides were the first vehicle to demonstrate the connection between events here on earth and the positions of the moon and stars of heaven. Ocean was also regarded as the supporter of the Heavenly Stream or Heavenly Ocean. This is none other than our galaxy, that highway of the stars known as the Milky Way. This god was therefore the ocean, upon which the heavenly barks of the Egyptians sail.

It should be apparent that Ocean was the first astrologer to connect the rhythm of the tides to astronomical phenomena. In his honor, the seas of the world were called oceans. Some mythographers, however, do not regard him as the first of the gods. This is because Ocean is also said to have been a brother of Iapetus. Yet, Iapetus marries a daughter of Ocean which demonstrates that Ocean was of a previous generation. In proof of this conundrum we find that the mythographers admit that when the Titan generation attacked their father, Uranus, Ocean was not among them. Apollodorus (i.1.4) says, "And they all but Ocean, attacked him." Therefore, it is quite certain that the god, Ocean, belongs to the generation prior to Uranus.

Pausanius in his *Arcadia* (41.5) tells us that Hephaestus, the oldest god of the Egyptians, took to wife, Eurynome, the daughter of Ocean. Nonnos writes (41.175), "Ocean, first messenger of the laws." And very curiously, Nonnos makes Ocean to be the sire of the New Savior, instead of Dionysius, who is the actual hero of Nonnos's entire work. Hesiod in his *Theogony* (886) also confirms that a new "King of gods and men" is to be born of a daughter of Ocean. In some mystic fellowships; the god Ocean in his guise of the Milky Way Galaxy, could be accepted as the symbol of the Great Spirit.

Ocean, and a variation called *Pontus* are the earliest of the gods to be linked to the tradition of the Heaven-Holders. There was also a son of Uranus, named in honor of Ocean. All the later sea and ocean gods adopted the traditions of Ocean and his personal symbol, the trident: These gods were Nereus, Triton, Poseidon, and Neptune.

In art, Ocean is depicted with a long, wet beard, and curly hair tangled with water plants, with oars and tridents in his grasp. On the shields of Achilles and Hercules, he is the stream which encircles the earth. Sometimes, he is shown with crab claws or astride a sea crab. In his company are dolphins, seashell trumpets, oars, anchors, and a torch. His masks depict him with large, melancholy eyes, and water spewing from his open mouth.

Uranus

In mythology, Uranus is called Earth-Embracer and Heaven-Holder. The Latin *Caelus*, or Sky, is identified with Uranus. The same identification applies to the Phoenician, Akmon Akmonides, the Thunder-hammer.

According to E. Wust (*Pauly-Wissowa*): the god or goddess, Night, begat Phanes; and together they produced Uranus and Ge, the Earth. In Orphic tradition, Chaos took the form of an egg and begot Phanes. By another view, Chaos united with Eros, who is Love. Sometimes, Ge is called the mother, or even the grandmother of Uranus. In this context, Akmon the son of Ge, is called the father of Uranus.

As was said above, a Homeric fragment places Ocean and Tethys directly after Chaos; and therefore, before Uranus. Uranus and Ge are said to have produced the Hundred-handed, the Titans, Moires, the Cyclopes, and the fountain nymphs. Other wives of Uranus are Hestia, by whom he begot Demeter. By the goddess Day, he produced Aphrodite and the ithyphallic Hermes. Uranus also took Night and Titan as wives.

In principle, Uranus is the Sky in union with the Earth. Upon their separation, plants, animals, and men are engendered. Some say that the separation of Heaven and Earth was turned into the legend of the castration of Uranus by his son, Cronus. The Egyptians, however, regard the earth as a male god, *Geb* or *Keb*. He has an adulterous union with Nut, the heaven goddess, who lies over and upon the earth. And Shu, her husband, tries to prevent this union.

It seems apparent that Uranus absorbed the cosmology of Ocean. One version has it that Uranus brought together the waters of Ocean and Ge for the purpose of creation. Uranus became the heavenly waters upon which the sun, moon, planets, and stars navigated in their celestial barks. The Greeks say that Uranus too often joined with Ge, until she became saturated, groaning with the weight of these unions. She became dissatisfied with any future concourse with the heavenly waters. Thereupon, Cronus castrated Uranus. In the Egyptian view, Shu constantly interferes with the union of his wife, Nut, and the earth god, Geb. It is Shu who cautions them to separate and return back to their own spheres, so that the universe may not become dissolved through their constant attachment, and that harmony may be preserved.

The philosophy of Uranus proposes that the harmony and equilibrium of the universe is Love. Yet, the union of elementary forces produces strife, which accounts for the motion of the cosmic cycles. These ideas of love, union, and separation were revived in classical times by Empedocles and Heraclites.

Pythagoras called Uranus by the name *Cosmos*. Uranus is the father of Memory, who is the mother of the Muses who inspire scientists, inventors, artists, and poets. Nonnos writes (38.31), "Urania, the Muse who knows the round circuit of the stars."

Uranus is undoubtedly of Atlantic origin. Skytobrachion directly calls him king and god of Atlantic Mauritania. His issue are connected with the classical West: Atlas, Basileia, Eros, Hermes, Iapetos, the later Ocean, Pallas, Pan, and many others. Of his blood and seed were born Aphrodite, the Erinyes, Giants, Phaiaken, and Silenien. And it is Pausanius who declares that one of the oldest images in Greece is that of Aphrodite Urania, she who appears armed like one of the Amazons of the West.

In art, Uranus is shown much like Ocean. He is bearded, naked, with a flowing cloak held in a bow over his head, in emulation of the heavenly stream, or vault of the heavens.

These then are the Earth-Heaven-Holders that came prior to Atlas. In knowing about these forefathers, we are better equipped to understand Atlas and his achievements by understanding the traditions that came before him.

Chapter 1

Atlas of Morocco, Paradigm of all Earth and Heaven-Holders

In the 16th century, the famed Flemish geographer and mapmaker, Gerardus Mercator, placed a picture of Atlas holding the globe upon the front-page of his collection of maps. All subsequent collections of maps were forever called after the name of Atlas. Mercator's taste was not dictated by quaintness, but founded upon the tradition that Atlas was the first great cartographer to use astronomy as the basis of global measurement.

Mercator was probably well aware of the famous ancient statue of Atlas, posed as the Heaven-Holder, in the Royal Museum at Naples. This statue is entirely of marble, and thought to date from about 300 BC. It is the oldest extant celestial globe in the world.

Homer in the *Odyssey* (i.52) sings, "Atlas of baneful mind who knows the depths of every sea, and himself holds the tall pillars which keep earth and heaven apart." The Oracle of Delphi echoes this tradition (*Herodotus*, i.43) by proclaiming, "I can count the sands, and I can measure the ocean, I have ears for the silent, and I know what the dumb-man meaneth."

Pausanius in *Attica* (33) records, "For the Nasamones, whom Herodotus calls the Atlantes, and those who profess to know the measurements of the earth, named the Lixitae, are the Libyans who live farthest close to Mt. Atlas." The Lixus is that river in Morocco upon which the palace of Antaeus the Giant was located, with whom Hercules, another Earth-Holder, wrestled and fought.

In order to know the measurements of the earth and its geography, one needs to know astronomy. Siculus reports (iv.27), "For Atlas had worked out the science of astrology to a degree surpassing others and had ingeniously discovered the spherical nature of the stars, and for this reason was generally believed to be bearing the entire firmament upon his shoulders." Pliny relates (ii.6) that Anaximander of Miletus discovered the obliquity of the zodiac, admitting, "The firmament itself having been explained long before by Atlas."

Hesiod in the *Theogony* (507) sings, "Now Iapetus took to wife the neat-ankled maid Clymene, daughter of Ocean . . . and she bare him a stout-hearted son, Atlas." Apollodorus (i.2) writes, Atlas "who bears the heavens on his shoulders is the son of Iapetus and Asia, an Oceanid." Whatever the case, because Iapetus is called a son of Uranus and/or a son of a daughter of Ocean, Atlas inherits the traditions of these former Heaven-Holders.

Wernike in his article in *Pauly-Wissowa* says that some variant sources say that the father of Atlas is Aether, Uranus, Iapetus, Poseidon, or Hesperos. Atlas, himself is variously called a Giant or a Titan. The *Stair Ercuil* reports that Atlas taught the art of memory, and Memory is a daughter of Uranus. Atlas's brothers are the great intellectuals Prometheus, Epimetheus, and Menoitios.

Plato in the *Critias* (120b) says that the kings of Atlantis conceded the leadership to the royal branch of Atlas. Skytobrachion has already told us that Atlas and his brother, Cronus, divided the world between them. Plato also remarks that Gaderius, the king of Gades in Spain, was a younger brother of Atlas. Variant sources say that the wife of Atlas was: the Oceanid, Pleione or Aithra; or Hesperis, Calypso, or Selene, the moon.

Without a doubt, Atlas is one of the great patriarchs of antiquity—especially through his celebrated daughters, the Pleiades. They were also called the Nymphs or Atlantides; who, according to Sicilus, fostered a great part of mankind and several of the heroes. Hellanikos affirms that Atlas is the ancestor of the old tribes of the Greek Peloponnesus, Boeothia, Troy, Italy, Cyrene, and of most of the ancient noble houses. Wernike says that the Arcadians and the Hyperboreans of the North Atlantic especially claim kinship to Atlas.

This comment by Hellanikos is most important, because we seem to get the impression that the Greeks are a young and new people who got all their education, sciences, and philosophy from the Egyptians. The Greek philosophers are generally reported to have traveled to Egypt, as if going there to attend universities of higher education. This is substantially true of the classical Greeks from 500 BC onward, but we should realize that a strong ancient Atlantic tradition always existed among certain Greeks, Trojans, and Italians.

To resume, Atlas is thought to be the father of the Hesperides who guard the Golden Apples of the Garden of Paradise. One of these Hesperides, Pasiphae, is the mother of the noted god of Libya and Egypt, Ammon. The number of tribes and people connected to the daughters of the patriarch, Atlas, constitutes a separate study in itself as they are too numerous to mention here.

Wernike says that in mythology Atlas usually carries the heavens or Olympus on his head, hands, or on his shoulders or neck. Later he was shown holding the zodiac upon a round shield. Sometimes he carries the earth, or both the earth and the heavens. In later myth, Atlas turns the earth's axis upon his shoulders. Occasionally, he is said to lean against the pillars which keep the heavens floating over and apart from the earth. He was sometimes thought of as the world axis, or the horizon. Much later, it was even suggested that Atlas carried the heavens, not of his own free will; but rather, by the constraint of the later god Zeus. This is the same Zeus who punished and bound Prometheus, the brother of Atlas, for revealing the art of fire to mankind.

In this context of punishment; Atlas is delighted to be relieved of the burden of the heavens by the next Heaven-Holder, who is Hercules on his mission, looking for the Apples of the Hesperides. As we noted before, the Golden Apples may be a code name for the sun, moon, and planets, so it is apparent that Hercules came in search of astronomical knowledge. Naturally, it is an easy task for Atlas to retrieve the Golden Apples from his own daughters. Wernike says that Atlas is also credited with being the founder of music and mathematics. Nonnos (13.360) sings, "Libyan Atlas awoke a tune of the heavenly harp."

It is beyond question that Atlas is connected with the Atlantic Ocean and Mt. Atlas in Morocco, which both bear his name. Hesiod in the *Theogony* sings, "And Atlas through hard constraint upholds the wide heaven . . . standing at the borders of the earth before the clear-voiced Hesperides . . . there stands the awful home of murky Night." In art, Atlas is shown in the company of the Hesperides who give water to the twelve-headed snake who guards the tree of Paradise, and the Golden Apples.

Homer styles Atlas as "*oloofronos*," of deep, dark, baneful mind; cunning, clever, and aloof. These adjectives seem to belong to the era of Aquarius and his brother, Cronus. Caesar in his *African War* tries to teach his troops, "to recognize the tricks, traps and stratagems of the enemy." The enemy is the North Africans who are unfavorably compared to the valorous and straightforward Gauls, whose simple tactics were easier to deal with.

In art, Atlas is often depicted with animal ears. The Egyptians contrived this sort of symbolism into an extreme form of ideal iconography conveying subtle and shaded meaning. It is noteworthy that the very ancient Phrygians cherished their tale of King Midas of the donkey ears. In Ireland, there is a hero of a specific tribe connected with the Fomorian navigators who was said to have had horse's ears. Indeed, the African Fomorians are often defamed as having animal ears.

In art, Atlas is also shown in the company of Athena, the Satyrs of Mt. Atlas, the goddess Nike, and, also, the Sphinx. Most important, Atlas is portrayed like the previous Earth-Holders naked, like Ocean, with a long, curly, tangled beard and hair. In resemblance to Uranus, Atlas occasionally wears the Heavenly *Star-Mantle*, embroidered with a multitude of stars, in the form of a cape, robe, or a shawl. He holds the scepter of the ruler of the universe.

The epoch of Atlas and his brother, Cronus, is referred to as the Golden Age of mankind. Babrius, in his prologue to the *Aesopic Fables*, reports,

> Now in the Golden Age, not only men, but all the other living creatures had the power of speech . . . even the pine tree talked, and the leaves of the laurel. The fish swimming about in the sea chatted with the friendly sailor . . . the sparrows conversed with the farmer . . . and good fellowship prevailed between gods and mortals.

Such tranquility in the world could only have been achieved during a period of truly elevated science and philosophy. For Peace is the work of Justice, *Pax opus Justicia*. And justice and compassion are the fruit of understanding and reason.

What we actually know about Atlas—the extent of his science and cosmology—is really very little. All we can really say is that he definitely lived in Morocco; and he is undoubtedly associated with the tradition of the Earth-Heaven-Holders. There is no doubt that the descendants of Atlas were numerous, and that they spread the tradition of Atlas throughout the entire Mediterranean, the Near East, as well as the Atlantic seaboard far into northern Europe and Scandinavia.

We can, however, assume and interpolate a veritable tapestry of facts and history by simply following this tradition of the Earth-Holders through Hercules and Poseidon unto Egypt. I, therefore, believe that the gods and goddesses who support the Circular Zodiac of Dendera will tell us all about the cosmological beliefs of Atlas. Because, what the Dendera stone represents is the cosmic science carried forward by Ocean, Uranus, Atlas, Poseidon, and Hercules.

Chapter 2

The Pleiades, Daughters of Atlas

We can learn more about Atlas through his famous daughters, the Pleiades. These maidens are also called the Atlantides, Nymphs, Vergiliae, and occasionally alluded to as the Hesperides, who guard the Golden Apples.

Sicilus writes (iii.60),

> Atlas had seven daughters called the Atlantides . . . these daughters lay with the most renowned heroes and gods, and thus became the first ancestors of the larger part of the race of human beings, giving birth to those who because of their high achievements, came to be called gods and heroes . . . who became the founders in some instances of nations and in other cases of cities. Consequently, not only among certain barbarians, but among the Greeks as well, the great majority of the most ancient heroes trace their descent back to the Atlantides. These daughters were also distinguished for their chastity, and after their death attained immortal honor among men, by whom they were enthroned in the heavens and endowed with the appellation of Pleiades.

Apollodorus reports (iii.10) the Arcadian tradition that the Pleiades were born of Atlas and Pleione, the daughter of Ocean.

The names of these Atlantides-Pleiades were:

Maia: The founder of the Greek Arcadians. She and Zeus produced the famous inventor and scientist, Hermes/Mercury.

Electra: She and Zeus were the parents of Dardanos and Iasion, the ancestors of the famous Trojans. Hesiod calls her dark-faced. Her name was carried on by a daughter of Agamemnon and Danaus. In extreme antiquity the name Electra was held by a daughter of Ocean, who was the mother of Iris and the Harpies.

Taygete: She and Zeus had Lacedaemon and Hellan, and thereby became mother of the famous Spartans.

Sterope also called **Asterope:** The mother or wife of Oenomaus of Pisa in Greece, whose daughter was Hippodamia. Pelops, a friend of Poseidon, won Hippodamia and subjugated the entire Peloponessus. Sterope is also a more ancient name of the mother of the Sirens, whom some interpret to be the planets of our solar system.

Celaeno: She lay with Poseidon and produced Lycus, whose name is associated with the strange rituals and sacrifices of the werewolf, and those tribes that take their family name from their mother. More anciently, Celaeno is a name associated with the brother of Atlas; Prometheus, with whom she had Lycus and Chimaireus. Later in history, the name Celaeno is used by a daughter of Danaus, who also has a nephew called Lycus. This Danaus is the son of Belus, king of Egypt, son of Posiedon and Libya. Danaus is the famed ruler of Argos in Greece, where his daughters unite with the sons of his brother, Egyptus.

Merope: She is the wife of Sisyphos, who is punished in Hades in the fruitless effort of rolling a stone up an unconquerable hill.

One of the seven sisters of Sisyphos, who was one of seven brothers, is called Ogygia, the ancient name of Ireland. We will report on the strong tradition surrounding the number seven when we arrive at Irish history. Meropian men are spoken of as inhabitants of the city of Cos in Asia Minor. Tantalus is also tormented in Hades. And he is the grandfather of Sisyphos.

Alcyone: Poseidon also took her as a wife, and they had two sons, among whose children were another Lycus, Zethus, and Amphion, who again had seven daughters and seven sons. Alcyone also had a daughter, Aethusa, who associated with Apollo.

Again, though we have not gleaned any astronomical/cosmological information about the science of Atlas, we are not surprised to hear that Atlas was the progenitor of Hermes, the most famous of all scientists and intellectuals.

I also think that the cultural tradition of the wolf and the number seven belong to Atlas. And we will keep following this thread of tradition where it leads us through Libya, Egypt, the Peloponnesus of Greece, and on to Troy—from where it directs us to Rome.

The Pleiades are said to have been transformed into doves, and then later into the seven-star cluster in the constellation of Taurus, in honor of their supreme wisdom. Taurus is the exaltation of the moon which draws upon the tides of the ocean. As acceptable sacrifices to the gods, bulls and horses had to have the markings of the Pleiades cluster on their bodies. The Pleiades are mentioned as attendants of the huntress, Artemis, who is an aspect of the moon goddess. Some have said that Selene, the moon, was one of the wives of Atlas.

Teukros and Manilius disagree as to their exact astronomical position and their relative brightness in the sky. This may suggest that this star group has undergone some changes of position in the past. Astrologically, their influence is benevolent, and they produce devotees of Venus, and the wine god, Bacchus. More importantly, they seem to generate the number seven. In Brittany and Ireland we have the tradition of the Seven Saints. In Ephesus there is the legend of the Seven Sleepers. Ephesus is especially holy to Our Lady, but in ancient times it was founded by the Libyan Amazons who established the first cult and statue to Artemis, the huntress by the moon.

In ancient times hunting and fishing were conducted according to special times within the seasons, solar and planetary aspects, and phases of the moon.

The musical lyre of Hermes was made by him with seven strings.

The ancients believed that each particular planet produced a specific harmonic wavelength as they transited through the sky. The clear-voice singing Hesperides/Pleiades may be an indication of this belief. The Hesperides give water to the twelve-headed snake on the Tree of Life. This may refer to the heavenly water of Ocean inspiring the twelve signs of the zodiac with power and influence. Some pictures of Gemini depict a man and woman under the Tree of Life. Naturally, Gemini and Taurus are adjoining neighbors.

Finally, the tradition of the Pleiades makes us regard the importance of women in respect to the continuity and transfer of culture and tradition. The homeland of Atlas in Morocco produced great veneration for female deities. Some mythologists even speak of Ge and Night as having given birth to their husbands—an unusual affirmation of matriarchal society. Morocco was also the homeland of the great female warriors and groups called the Gorgons, Amazons, Furies, and Fates, and many other female deities.

Above Morocco and in the same longitude of Aquarius, we also find deep devotion to ancient and modern mother goddesses in Portugal, Spain, France, England, and Ireland.

Chapter 3

Hermes, Son of Maia, Grandson of Atlas

Sicilus records (i.16),

> It was by Hermes, for instance, according to the Egyptians, that the common language of mankind was first articulated, and that many objects which were still nameless, received an appellation, that the alphabet was invented, and that the ordinances regarding the honors and offerings due to the gods were duly established. He was the first also to observe the orderly arrangement of the stars, and the harmony of the musical sounds and their nature, to establish a wrestling school, and to give thought to the rhythmical movement of the human body and its proper development. He also made a lyre . . . The Greeks also were taught by him how to expound their thoughts . . . The olive tree also, they claim, was his discovery, not Athena's, as the Greeks say.

Theodor Hopfner, in his commentary on Plutarch's *Isis and Osiris,* says that the Egyptians claim that their holy and scientific books originate from Hermes. In the *Aegyptiaca,* Manetho relates that his information about the antiquity and the reigns of the Dynasties stems from Hermes Trismegistus, the Good Spirit called Agathodaemon, who is the son of the second Hermes. The Agathodaemon translated the traditions from stones remaining after the flood, which had been inscribed by Thoth, the primitive Hermes, who lived before the time of Cronus and Atlas.

Ptolemy and the astrologers explain that the influence of the planet Hermes/Mercury is cooperative and subservient, and amplifying the power of those with whom he is associated. Hermes is therefore the Vizier, the guide, teacher, and protector of kings, all of whom he serves. He is, as well, the guardian spirit of tradition and the sciences. He is carpenter, mason, artificer, architect, teacher, doctor, and judge. Hermes leads Hera, Athena, and Aphrodite to the judgment of Paris. In Egypt, he is the advocate of Horus in the disputes over his father's kingdom.

Cosmologically, Hermes communicates the active and rational intelligence of the universe to our world. On the other hand, the moon is said to communicate the passive intelligence of true feelings and correct intuition; and the set plan of biological development to the world. The rational Hermes has a special sympathy and connection with the intuitive moon, and her exaltation in Taurus; where his aunts, the Pleiades, also reside.

In Egyptian art and philosophy, Hermes is the wise companion of the moon. He is often portrayed sitting in the orb of the moon. He is also called the god of sport, games, and luck bringing. We have already related the story by Plutarch that Hermes reconciled the calendar, and that he had to sit down at a game-board with the moon goddess and win parts of days from her. Hermes's sacred name among the Egyptians is *Osirgariack-Noumafi*, which specifically means the waxing moon from the time of new moon to full moon. During this period, the generative light of the moon promotes the development of life and plants from the embryonic state. Anciently, Hermes is portrayed as *ithyphallic*, because the changes of the moon phase of light activate menstruation and sexual lust. Later, Hermes is shown as a garden god, assisting the germination of plants. In the same sense, he encourages animal fecundity, and he is called the god of cattle, the lord of herds, and even the father of the progenic goat-footed Pan, who is regarded as the father of all nature.

God of cattle seems to be an ancient notion of Hermes's special relationship with the moon and her sign of Taurus, the bull. Hopfner relates that in the conflict with Seth, Isis is decapitated. Hermes replaces her lost head with a horned-cow's head. Moon goddesses are forever portrayed with the moon's orb, and/or with the horn's of Taurus somewhere in their entablature. Hermes is sometimes called the son of Isis, and sometimes he appears as her father and teacher. Isis, herself, embodies the dual cosmic function of Hermes: she is thought to be the moon, conveyor of passive intelligence. Also, Isis is thought of in the role of Athena/Neith, the determined, rational intelligence.

In the tradition of Morocco and the West, the moon rises in the west, from the ocean, the land of Elysium, Hades, and the land of the past, and also the Land of the Ever-Living Ones. In this connection with the moon, Hermes is the *psychepompos*, the conductor of the souls, and special envoy to Hades/Pluto. Homer in the *Odyssey* (24) sings, "Hermes, the savior, led them down the dank ways. Past the streams of Ocean they went, past the rock Leucas, past the portals of the sun and the land of dreams, and quickly came to the meads of asphodel, where the spirits dwell, the shades of men out-worn." The Egyptians also show Hermes as a Judge in the Underworld, and the master of the scales of justice, upon which the heart of the deceased person is weighed against the light feather of truth.

Apollodorus writes (i.6) concerning the battle of the Giants, "And Hermes, wearing the helmet of Hades." This helmet seems to have been a dog-headed mask meant to represent Cerberus, the guardian of the Underworld. Hopfner (ii., p. 9) writes that Hermes is called dog, because he is fecund, watchful, untiring, devoted, knowing, and because of his keen senses. The Egyptian god, Anubis, is dog-headed, or, more correctly, jackal-headed, and sometimes confused with the wolf-headed god Upuat. He is patron of embalming, and his priests wear the dog-mask. The Egyptian representation of Hermes is ibis-headed, but as the herald of the dead souls he is shown as dog-headed and is called Hermanubis according to Hopfner. In walking, the ibis appears to form a perfect triangle with the ground. This perfect equilateral triangle is the symbol of occult wisdom.

In his *Sphaera*, Boll tells us that in more ancient times the sign of Taurus was the sign of the Dog. And dogs were the companions of the huntress, Artemis, who is connected with this zodiac sign. In Ireland there are numerous megalithic graves upon high mountains called dog's-graves. Mercury/Hermes's sympathy to the moon's generative and intuitive reason is unquestionable. The secret of the Helmet of Hades, which makes the wearer invisible, may be connected with the waning and decreasing light of the moon, when she is nearly invisible to sight, though the body of the moon is still in the heavens.

The Library of Apollodorus, *The Homeric Hymn to Hermes,* Hesiod's *Theogony* and *Astronomy* all agree, "The Pleiades . . . whom glorious Atlas begot . . . in the mountain of Cyllene, Maia bare Hermes." Manilius traces the history of astronomy in his *Astronomica,* and relates, "You, God of Cyllene, are the first founder of this great and holy science." Cyllene is in Arcadia in Greece, which was apparently one of the greatest strongholds of original Atlantic culture. In Egypt, the Good Daemon was called the man from Hermau, the city of Hermes. So it could be conjectured that Cyllene and Hermopolis may most probably have been colonies from the Atlantic.

All the stories about Hermes connect him to an Atlantic and Oceanic origin. Homer says that Hermes leads the souls past the streams of ocean. Hermes fabricated the lyre of seven strings from the shell of a sea tortoise. In mythology, it is Aphrodite, the ocean-born goddess, and Hermes who combine to produce the Hermaphrodite, whose name is Atlantios.

Mount Atlas in Morocco is famed as the habitat of the Satyrs and the Pans. Hermes is the father of Pan. Apollodorus reports (ii.4) that under the guidance of Hermes and Athena, Perseus was conveyed to the daughters of Phorcus, sisters of the Gorgons, who possessed the cap of Hades and the winged sandals, "And having received also from Hermes an adamantine sickle, he flew to the ocean and caught the Gorgons asleep." Hermes and Athena are chosen as guides because they are Western deities and familiar with their homeland. Afterwards, Hermes restores the cap of Hades, the sandals and wallet to the Phorcides. Also (iii.4), after the birth of Dionysus, Zeus gives him to the safekeeping of Hermes, who conveyed him to the Nymphs of "Nysa of Asia." Asia is an Oceanid, and wife of Iapetus, the father of Atlas.

There is a wealth of testimony to the effect that Hermes belongs to the most ancient group of gods. This is because he is called the father of science, invention, and writing. He is the father of Pan, whom the Egyptians regard as the oldest of the gods. Hopfner says that some believe that Hermes is the father of Isis, while other assert she is the daughter of Prometheus. These distinguish between Prometheus, the discoverer of wisdom and prophecy; and Hermes, the author of the art of writing and speech. Hesiod in *Works and Days* says that Hermes put speech into the first woman. In myth, Prometheus is generally accounted to have given the gift of fire to mankind. While *The Homeric Hymns to Hermes* state, "For it was Hermes who first invented fire-sticks and fire." Apollodorus records (i.7), "Prometheus molded men out of water and earth." Hesiod, however, says that it was Hephaestus who was the first to mix earth and water to produce mankind. Hephaestus is the first god of the Egyptians. Gisinger and Herter in *Pauly-Wissowa* remark that the tradition of Ocean was later absorbed under the name of Prometheus.

The impression that anyone would receive from the above testimonials is that Hermes became a catchall for most of the great achievements of mankind. He is called by many names: Agathodaemon, Thoth, Hermes, Mercury, Cadmilus, Cadmos, Lug, and abundant other epithets. I would believe that he was the first astrologer/astronomer/philosopher to make the connection between the moon and the tides of the ocean. Because he is so intimately connected with the moon in myth, I would further think that Hermes also conceived the relationship between the moon and its power to draw upon the underground springs of water, which enliven the magic associated with all ancient megalithic monuments. This is especially true when the moon is in aspects with the sun and the planets. In this sense, Hermes may also be seen in his character as a magician.

Hermes is the cosmological messenger who associates and brings together the power of the heavenly ocean of our galaxy with the oceans and arterial waters of our own world. The sperm and seeds of all possible creations lie dormant within the earth from giants to dinosaurs to butterflies. It is Hermes who communicates the correct cosmic time of specific generations to the earth.

In astrology, Hermes is the assistant, the messenger, the guide and counselor of all forces that he becomes associated with. In unfavorable aspect, he produces thieves, cheats, and miscreants as in the story of Hermes stealing the cattle of Apollo. The zodiac signs of the planet Mercury are the Celestial Virgin, Virgo, and the Tree of Paradise, Gemini.

Hermes/Thoth is the inventor of the demotic and the sacred forms of writing. Because he replaces the lost head of Isis with a cow's head; it may be that he introduced totem and shaman practices from the Atlantic to Libya, and then to Egypt. Following the inspiration of the Schwaller de Lubcizs's, it would seem that Hermes not only is credited with the institution of the Hieroglyphs; but, he must be the creator of the nuances of symbolism and the symbolique which are connected with these sacred hieroglyphic signs which intone a variety of philosophical meaning.

Hermes is artisan, builder, and architect. Above all he is a cosmologer. For, Diogenes Laertius writes that, "Linus composed a poem describing the creation of the world, the courses of the sun and moon; and the growth of animals and plants." Linus, of course, is the son of Hermes and the Muse Urania, "who knows the round circuit of the heavens." Hermes is a descendent of Atlas of Morocco. It cannot be doubted that Hermes is of Atlantic origin, because all of the mythological accounts connect him to these regions.

Chapter 4

Poseidon: Earth-Holder and Earth-Shaker

We have talked about the very ancient tradition of the Heaven-Holders and the Earth-Holders who have transmitted culture, science, and religion over extraordinary long periods of time. It is our belief that mythology carefully chronicles the great cosmic periods to which these Heaven-Holders and Earth-Holders belong:

> First, there was Ocean who ruled the Galactic Age of Libra.
> Then, Uranus dominated the Galactic Age of Scorpio.
> Then, Helios was the inspiration of Sagittarius.
> Then, Agathodaemon-Thoth ruled the Age of Capricorn.
> Then, Atlas and Cronus ruled the Galactic Age of Aquarius.
> Finally, Poseidon, Pluto, and Zeus ruled the Galactic Age of Pisces.

The appearance of the Messiah and his bloody crucifixion heralds the New Age of Aries, which imparts a new cosmic theme to the world. We are attempting to decipher what the ancients are telling us about their scientific discoveries concerning their system of connecting cosmic cycles of galactic ages with history.

Above, we noticed that sometimes; the rulers of these Great Galactic Ages come in pairs of brothers, such as Atlas and Cronus. But, only one of them was officially granted the mantel of the Heaven-Holder or Earth-Holder.

The main ruler of the Galactic Age of Pisces always appears to be Zeus/Jupiter. But, it is his brother, Poseidon, the god of the sea, to whom mythology grants the title of the Earth-Heaven-Holder

Poseidon is generally considered to be the son of Cronus and Rhea He is most generally connected with the geography of Libya which suffered a tremendous natural calamity that turned a once fruitful area into a desert. This may be the explanation of why the Egyptian Zeus became the prominent god in mythology. Poseidon is also the direct progenitor of the people who transmitted culture from Libya to Egypt, Greece, and the Middle-East.

Apollodorus (ii.i.4) tells us that Poseidon and Libya had twin sons, Agenor and Belus. Agenor departed to Phoenicia, and became the ancestor of a great stock of people. Belus reigned over Egypt and had the famous twin sons, Egyptus and Danaus, who had numerous issue, who founded and ruled over many cities and nations.

Poseidon's wife, Libya, was the daughter of Epaphus and Memphis. Epaphus's mother was the cow-shaped Io, daughter of Inachus, a son of Ocean and Tethys. Apollodorus (i.4) also records other unions of Poseidon, "Poseidon wedded Amphitrite, daughter of Ocean, and there were born to him Triton and Rhode."

Poseidon also has a direct connection with Atlas, when he consorts with his daughters, Celaeno and Alcyone, two of the famous Pleiades.

Hesiod in his *Theogony* (i.15) directly calls him, "Poseidon the earth-holder who shakes the earth." Siculus (xv.49.4) also says that authority over earthquakes belongs to Poseidon. Frazer, the translator of Apollodorus, comments that among some people there exists the idea of a giant supporting the weight of the earth. An earthquake occurs when he rolls over, or shifts the burden to another shoulder. Apollodorus also records that Poseidon has power over springs, and that he sent a flood over Western Ethiopia, and a flood over Troy. He also produced a sea on the Acropolis at Athens, and afterward flooded Attica.

There are numerous instances that connect the name Poseidon with science, astronomy, and cosmology. Museaus, from whom we get the name museum, was the grandson of Poseidon. Diogenes Laertius says that this Museaus of Athens was the first to compose a genealogy of the gods, to construct a sphere, and to maintain that all things proceed from unity, and are again resolved into unity.

Poseidon also succeeded to the ownership of the oracle at Delphi, whose priestess proclaimed that she could count the sands and measure the ocean. We have reported that the famous cosmological poem, upon which Plato's *Timeaus* was based, was first composed by Linus, son of Hermes and Urania. There is a variant version of his pedigree in the *Contest of Homer and Hesiod* (311) which claims that Linus is the son of Apollo and Aethusa, daughter of Poseidon.

One of the keys to recognizing people and nations associated with the traditions of Ocean, and later with Poseidon, is the worship and reverence of horses and bulls. The European and Britannic Celts sacrificed horses to their sea god by plunging them over cliffs. The very early Spanish and Moroccans, the Phoenicians, and later the Vikings, ornamented the prows of their ships with horse heads. The Spanish instituted the running of the bulls, and the ceremonial bullfights. The Cretans, as well, had their elaborate gymnastic displays, arching their bodies over the backs of bulls.

The *Homeric Hymn to Poseidon* (xx.11) sings, "A two-fold office the gods allotted you, O Shaker of the Earth, to be a tamer of horses and a savior of ships. Hail, Poseidon, Holder of the Earth." Poseidon and Medusa produce the winged horse, Pegasus. He and Demeter produce the horse, Areion. Plato reports that equestrian contests were held on Atlantis. In the contest over Athens: Athena brought the olive tree as a gift, while Poseidon offered a horse.

In regard to bulls, Apollodorus (iii.1.3) records that Minos was of the family of Poseidon and Libya. In a dispute over the kingdom of Crete, and to prove that he was the rightful heir, he prayed to Poseidon to make a bull appear from the depths of the sea as a sign. The animal was so wonderful that Minos decided to retain it, and sacrifice an ordinary bull to Poseidon. This substitution made Poseidon very angry, and, according to one version, he then transformed his sacred bull into the savage beast called the Minotaur, the bull-headed man.

Poseidon is called the builder of Troy. He is also an artificer, inventor, and a god of medicine. Apollodorus relates (*Epitome*) that Poseidon gave Pelops a "winged chariot, such that even when it ran through the sea, the axles were not wet." In *The Returns* it says, "The famous Earth-Shaker gave both of them gifts . . . to heal all kinds of wounds . . . full and perfect knowledge to tell hidden diseases and cure desperate sickness."

In the *Contest of Homer and Hesiod* it is related that both of these great poets trace their descent from Apollo and Aethusa, daughter of Poseidon. Furthermore, Poseidon is lord of Helicon, the abode of the Muses, who bathe themselves in the Horse's Spring.

Poseidon, as the inheritor of the tradition of the Heavenly Ocean, has the power of *metamorphosis* into all forms and elements. The *Odyssey* (iv.385) speaks of Proteus, "who knows the depths of every sea," and as the servant of Poseidon can "assume all manner of shapes of all things that move upon the earth and of water, and of wondrous blazing fire."

The names Ocean and Poseidon are often confused and used interchangeably. The poet Nonnos is often guilty of this practice. Plato actually makes Poseidon, instead of Ocean, the lord of Atlantis, and a precursor of Atlas. This fault of Plato is a shame, and utterly out of context of all accepted sequence of mythology. Apollodorus (iii.12) frankly admits that it is not known whether the river Asopus is the son of Ocean, or Poseidon. This type of confusion actually demonstrates and affirms how faithfully and beautifully Poseidon carries on the tradition of Ocean.

The most important fact about Poseidon is that he is almost exclusively associated with Libya. He carries forward many of the arts and sciences of Hermes. We will need another chapter to look more closely at this amazing character of so many compounded attributes and personalities.

The famous contest over Attica between Poseidon and Athena is more easily understood if we remember to relate Poseidon to Libya. What the people of Attica are saying is that they are now rejecting the long-term influence of Libya, whose time and power is passing on. They favor the more current culture of Egypt, represented by Athena-Neith of the Greco-friendly city of Sais in Egypt. After Athena wins, Greece began its Egyptian Renaissance—a period when every Greek scientist, philosopher, and historian visited the regions of the Nile.

Chapter 5

More Poseidon and Horse Culture

We need to cover a few more points about the epoch of Poseidon. We will see that Poseidon *and* Hercules both share in the cultural transmission of the Age of Galactic Pisces. The simplest solution is that Poseidon is the Earth-Heaven-Holder of Libya, which unfortunately became a desert. Hercules is the Earth-Heaven-Holder of Egypt, which survived the devastation of that region only through the miracle of the ever-flowing Nile.

Again, we need to reaffirm that the mythographers append much of the lore of the earlier Earth-Holders onto the name of Poseidon.

Apollodorus says (i.2.1) that Zeus, Poseidon, and Pluto fought against Cronus and the Titan generation and divided their kingdoms among themselves: "To Zeus was allotted the dominion of the heavens, to Poseidon the dominion of the sea, to Pluto the dominion in Hades."

Mythology is not fun, it is not cute; it is an important scientific and historical document relating to cosmic cycles. What Apollodorus has written above is inaccurate and historically destructive. He has failed in the mythographer's duty to translate time periods, geography, and persons into symbolic poetry, which can be remembered for all time.

The real meaning of the above quotation is as follows: The residence of Zeus is in Egypt, Greece, and the Eastern Mediterranean. The domain of Poseidon is in Libya, which has been destroyed in great part. Poseidon and Libya characterize the old naval culture and empire of the Atlantic. Most of the old traditions fit well upon the shoulders of Poseidon. Zeus and Egypt do not conform to the oceanic and naval character of the past. Finally, Pluto is the lord of the far distant and dead past in Morocco and the West.

Herodotus writes (ii.50), "Alone of all nations the Libyans have had among them the name of Poseidon from the first, and they have ever honored this god." This quote is one of the foundation stones to the penetration of the mystery of mythology—namely, the firm equation of the name of Poseidon with the geography of Libya.

Procopius (*Buildings*, 7.vi.1) states, "And the land on the left of the Nile bears the name of Libya as far as the Ocean." Homer in the *Odyssey* (i.20) sings, "Poseidon had gone among the far-off Ethiopians." Apollodorus (iii.15) says that Poseidon conveyed his son, Emolpus, to Ethiopia to be cared for by his daughter, whom he had by Amphitrite, an Oceanid. Apollodorus also relates that Antaeus (ii.5), the governor of Morocco, is a son of Poseidon. Hesiod in the *Theogony* (732) sings that the Titan gods are confined "in a dank place where are the ends of the huge earth. And they may not go out, for Poseidon fixed gates of bronze upon it." Hesiod also sings (275) that Poseidon lay with Medusa, "one of the Gorgons who dwell beyond Ocean towards Night in the land of the Hesperides."

This particular report by Hesiod, and similar references, continually make me think that Night and the original Hesperides were located farther out in the Atlantic—and that their myth was completely taken over and adopted by the ancient Moroccans. Also, we often hear the poets refer to Nix or Night, Echidna, Calypso, and all extremely ancient western personalities as terrible, frightening, dank, and dark. This is because they belong to such olden ages that they are hoary with the patina and cobwebs of history, making the very process of recalling their names to mind a quite chilling experience.

There seems to have been contention between Zeus of Egypt and Poseidon of Libya. Sicilus says (iii.73) that Dionysius, son of King Ammon of Libya, established Zeus as King of Egypt. Yet, Herodotus (ii.43) asserts that the Egyptians deny any knowledge of the name of Poseidon.

Apollodorus says (ii.13) that Poseidon and Zeus, his other co-regent of the world, were rivals for the hand of the illustrious Nereid, Thetis, who was professed to be the maiden who was ordained to produce The New Lord of Heaven. But, neither of the two suitors were able to win her, as the honor went to the more ancient god, Ocean.

The family of Poseidon was as illustrious as any of the descendents of Zeus. The offspring of Poseidon inhabited Attica, Athens, Delphi, Argos, Sicily, Troy, Rome, and Rhodes. Minos of Crete was Poseidon's ally and also his father-in-law because Poseidon consorted with Minos's daughter, Euryale. Apollodorus (ii.v.10) says that the sons of Poseidon were in Liguria between France and Italy. Poseidon unites with the family of Boreas (the North Wind). A similar communication occurs when the Hyperborean Apollo joins with a daughter of Poseidon. This once again affirms a connection between Libya and the North Atlantic regions.

Poseidon is noted as a master builder or *mechanikos,* because he built the walls of Troy. The great Cyclopean walls of ancient Athens, Tiryns, and Mycenae were historically attributed to the Pelasgians. According to Apollodorus, Pelasgus is of the family of Ocean, through his mother, Niobe. Herodotus suggests (ii.50) the connection between the Pelasgians and Poseidon in a round about fashion saying, "Poseidon of whom the Pelasgians learnt the knowledge of from the Libyans." In the history of their own islands; the Sardinians and the Balearic Islanders affirm that their megalithic Nuragica were built by the Libyans.

We are familiar with the exquisite wrestling scenes depicted on some of the temple walls of Egypt. Apollodorus (ii.v.11) tells of "Anteaus, son of Poseidon, who used to kill strangers by forcing them to wrestle." Also (ii.v. 10), "Eryx, King of the Elymi in Sicily, son of Poseidon, challenged Heracles to a wrestling bout." And (ii.v.9), "Polygonus and Telegonus, sons of Proteus, son of Poseidon, were killed in a wrestling match by Hercules." Odysseus wrestled with this same Proteus. Circumcision, personal health, and hygiene are said to have been promoted by the Libyans as part of their tradition and culture.

Again we have some additional remarks concerning the Horse Culture of the ancient Atlantic. Morocco and Libya were forever famous for fast horses and the equestrian agility of their riders. Caesar in his *African War* describes the equestrian tactics of the Numidians, who directed their horses without bridles as many ancient people did. Plato tells of the horse races on

Atlantis in honor of Poseidon. Fischer, in *Weltwenden,* declares that the horse culture spread throughout Europe. St. Boniface discouraged the eating of horsemeat, which he declared unclean. He also decried the ritualistic offering of horses, which were thrown from cliffs into the ocean.

Strabo relates (5.3.2) that Romulus invited the Sabine to attend a "horse race sacred to Poseidon, the rite is still today performed." On this occasion the famous rape of the Sabine women took place.

We may remember as well that when the Greeks laid down the long siege of Troy, they employed a special stratagem to gain entrance to the walls which Poseidon had built. The Greek scheme was to offer them the famous Wooden Horse. And, of course, if the inhabitants were truly a people of Poseidon, they could not reject this wondrous gift because the horse is sacred to their god, Poseidon. This is an especially significant myth because every element is full of meaning, design, and symbolism once we know the code.

The ancient inhabitants of Venice, the Eneti, bred a famous stock of horses which they sacrificed to Diomedes. We are familiar with the world-renowned bronze horses which stand over the portal of the Church of San Marco in Venice. These were so admired that Napoleon stole them. Frazer records (*Apollodorus,* p. 34, 297) that the descendants of the Phoenician Cadmus held the hereditary priesthood of Poseidon on the Island of Rhodes, where every year the Rhodians threw a chariot and four horses into the sea for the use of the sun god. The *doge* of Venice ritualistically betrothed himself and his city to the sea each year, by throwing a most valuable ring into the waves. This seems to echo the ritual of the Rhodians, famous navigators of antiquity.

The horse-culture tradition, though steadfastly connected with Poseidon, must assuredly reach far back into the epoch of Ocean himself. For, in the *Epic Cycle* (6) it says, "Cronus took the shape of a horse and lay with Philyra, the daughter of Ocean. Through this cause, Chiron was born a centaur." This Chiron was a famous cosmologers who is immortalized in the zodiac as the sign of Sagittarius, the horse-man.

E. M. Whishaw, in her *Atlantis in Spain* (ch.xvii), recounts Strabo who tells us that Libyan kings carefully managed their stud farms which produced 100,000 colts annually. Strabo also mentions Eudoxus who found the prow of a ship, which had been wrecked coming from the west, with a horse carved on it. At the market place, certain pilots recognized it as being from

Gades. Apparently lesser traders had small vessels which they called "horses" from the figures of that animal borne on the prow, in which they went fishing as far away as the River Lixus in Morocco.

Whishaw continues to say that Libyan chariots are referred to again and again in Egyptain records and by the classical writers. The booty taken from the Libyan Prince Meshwesh by Ramses III in about 1000 BC included a hundred chariots. The four-horse drawn battle chariot came from Libya. The entire Libyan contingent serving King Xerxes were on chariots. Cyrene in Libya was their celebrated chariot center where women manned the reins. A Neolithic burial near Seville proves that the Tartessians had chariots like the Libyans. Again there is the celebrated myth that Lusitania was the place where the west wind, Zephyr, impregnated the mare, Harpya Podarge, grazing by the ocean. This produced the very swift and graceful horses of Achilles.

In conclusion, we must reiterate that the name Poseidon is forever connected with Libya. And, naturally, the lore of Poseidon is also found in those places that the Libyans conquered; like Sardinia and Spain. Poseidon belongs to the same generation as Zeus during the cosmic Age of Pisces. More so than Zeus of Egypt, Poseidon adopted the nautical traditions of the god Ocean and Atlas of Morocco. The Libyans called their famous marsh the Tritonian Marsh, copying this name directly from the Tritonian Marsh of Atlantic Morocco.

Chapter 6

Hercules, The last Earth-Holder of the Classical Period

Sicilus (iii. 74) asserts that there were *three* great men who bore the name Hercules/Heracles: "The most ancient Heracles . . . had been born in Egypt, had subdued with arms a large part of the inhabited world, and had set up the pillar which is in Libya." Herodotus confirms (ii.43) that the name Heracles came to Greece from Egypt where he is a very ancient god and one of the original eight gods. Herodotus continues to say that there is an ancient temple to Hercules at the Phoenician city of Tyre, whose citizens pay him extravagant honors. Starbo also confirms (16.2.23).

The second Hercules, according to Strabo, was one of the Idaean Dactyls of the island of Crete. He was a noted wizard and a general, and it was he who established the Olympic Games. Some myths say that Cronus and Zeus wrestled at these first games.

The third Hercules was the son of Alcmene and Zeus. He was born before the Trojan War and visited a large part of the inhabited world. It was he who set up the pillar in Europe. This particular god's name is *Heracles* as distinct from the two Hercules before him. Herodotus painstakingly rehearses (ii.43, 91,145) that the ancestry of this Heracles definitely stems from Egypt.

Some variants report that Hercules was a son of Uranus (*Pauly-Wissowa*), while the *Stair Ercuil* concludes that he was the son of nature or Pan, son of Uranus or Hermes. Whatever the truth of the matter is, there is no question about the fact that all three Hercules trace back to a former Earth-Holder.

Apollodorus (ii.5.11) says that Hercules relieved Atlas of the burden of the sphere. The sources all agree that Hercules received the sciences from Atlas. Sicilus relates (iv.27),

> Atlas instructed him quite freely in the knowledge of astrology
> . . . he had brought to the Greeks the doctrine of the sphere . . . he
> gained great fame, as if he had taken over the burden of the
> firmament which Atlas had borne, since men intimated in this
> enigmatic way what had actually taken place.

The very unusual document of Irish literature called the *Stair Ercuil* relates that Hercules "lacked none of the accomplishments of kingship except that he was not versed in the arts," and therefore he went to Atlas, "a great master in the seven elegant liberal arts, and that he taught the *ars memorative,* that is, the art of memory to everyone in general." This book says that Hercules took away the books of Atlas, and that he fought the Hydra of Lerna whose seven human heads Seneca had interpreted as the seven liberal arts.

The *Stair Ercuil* continues to say that all the scholars praised Hercules, who went to Athens and Lycia where he taught what he had learned. Hercules also learned and practiced the magical arts in a subterranean cave in Salamanca and Catalonia, but Atlas foretold him by means of astrology that Hercules would not complete the building of Seville. Hercules gave

Spain to his son Hispan. In Egypt, Hercules killed Busiris, the king whose scribes practiced astrology. The Egyptians offered Hercules the kingdom, which he refused. But, he did establish proper law and good customs in that country, which he left in charge of those who would maintain them.

Hercules stems from the ancestry and tradition of the Atlantic, and he faithfully transmits that heritage. Yet the mythographers agree that Hercules and his descendants are the enemies of Poseidon, his sons, and allies. Again, simply put, Hercules, the Egyptian, is a national enemy of Poseidon, the Libyan. Yet, both share the same cultural and scientific heritage. Apollodorus (ii.5) relates that Heracles was cleansed and initiated into the mysteries of Demeter of Eleusis by Eumolpus, son of Poseidon and Chione, daughter of Boreas of the Northern Atlantic.

Again we should review the story of the contest for Attica between Poseidon, with his gift of the horse; and Athena, with her gift of the olive tree. The choice of Athena could be seen as a selection of an agrarian culture over the sea-trading culture of the horse-headed vessels of Poseidon. In a manner, this is true because in the later time Libya's splendid resources were dried up into desert, while the Egypt of Athena of Sais always prospered as an agrarian culture.

Therefore, within the mythology of this period there exists a definite conflict, namely: "Who is the real Earth-Heaven-Holder?" Many of the reports favor Poseidon because of his naval heritage of the Atlantic. Other accounts praise Hercules because of the early Egyptian traditions of Ra, Shu, Tefnut, and Geb.

Cosmologically, Hercules is identified with numerous heavenly aspects which confuse, rather than illuminate, his character. The Greeks call Mars, the Star of Hercules. Plutarch in *Isis and Osiris* says that the Egyptians claim that Hercules sits in the sun and accompanies its revolutions. Hopfner in his commentary on Plutarch, *Uber Isis und Osiris* (ii., p. 186), says that in Egyptian Thebes there is a temple of Chons, the moon god, called the temple of Hercules.

Hopfner writes that the Egyptians equate Hercules with Seth, who is the enemy of Osiris, just as in Greek tradition where Hercules does not get along with the issue of Poseidon. Osiris is the god of the moon; the Nile and the heavenly waters of Ocean. Osiris is also the god of the West where the moon rises. Hopfner says (ii., p. 18, 159) that Hercules/Seth is said to consort with Astarte, with whom he produced Hierosolymos and Judaios. Therefore Hercules is associated with the people to the east of Egypt in the direction of the rising sun. Consequently, it seems as if myth has not yet truly distilled the character and influence of Hercules.

The advance of civilizations and political history follows the direction of the Cycle of the Precession of the Vernal Equinoxes. The images of this type of history are vibrant and near at hand, because they are but a few thousand years old. However, the ability to perceive the advance of culture requires an intellect which can recognize merit and character over immense periods of time. I think that myth is subject to extraordinarily long periods of refined and redefined consideration by the cosmologers. This is because they are adverse to characterize a tradition which is still in the process of historical development. I believe they had not formulated the final cultural impact of Hercules.

Possibly the best identification of Hercules/Seth is that Hopfner (i., p. 22, 166) reports that he is called the Lord of Su, or Shu. This Shu is depicted with Ra and Tefnut, supporting the celestial globe of the circular zodiac of Dendera. In the tomb of King Sethos I, in the Valley of the Kings (*Egypt*, plate 220), Shu, in the place of the constellation Hercules, is shown holding the earth's axis upon his shoulders. In the same tomb, Shu is depicted supporting the divine celestial cow whose body is covered with stars and the journey of the sun's bark. Also depicted are eight spirits as symbols of the supporters of the pillars of heaven, surrounding the four legs of the heavenly cow. Similar scenes of Shu as Heaven-Holder appear in the tombs of Tutankhamen, and Ramses the First and Second (*Egypt*, p. 483).

The Heavenly Cow, Hathor of Dendera, is associated with the zodiac sign Taurus. We have already spoken of the special association of Atlas and his daughters, the Pleiades, with the sign of Taurus. Hathor means "the house of Horus" who was originally a sky god. On the throne of King Sesostris (*Egypt*, plate 88), Horus and Seth are shown symbolically uniting Upper and Lower Egypt. In ancient art Hathor, one of the oldest Egyptian deities, is depicted with a human face, but with the ears and horns of a cow. Curiously, as we noticed before, this type of animal cosmetic adornment is typical of Atlas and most of the ancient Atlantic people.

Just like Atlas, Hathor has seven virgin daughters. Hopfner (i., p. 37) relates that these are the patronesses of music and dance, and that they prophesy the fate of newborn children. The Seven Hathoren are the guardians of the four pillars of heaven, and they are represented as snake-headed. We should remember that the seven singing Pleiades/Hesperides guard the sacred snake which hangs upon the Tree of Paradise. And we will recall that this tree is often regarded as the heaven-supporting pillar. Finally, Hathor is also associated with the patron goddess of the ancient Phoenician city of Byblos. This city is also deeply connected with the myth of Osiris.

In the form of a simplified overview, it may be said that the Egyptian Hercules, like the Libyan Poseidon, transmits the cosmological sciences of the former cultural age of Atlas. Hercules and Poseidon both belong to the cultural age of Zeus and the geographic regions that correspond to Galactic Pisces.

PART V:

HERITAGE OF THE EARTH-HOLDER, AND THE SECRET CULTURE

Introduction

Why have we spent so long on the subject of the Earth-Heaven-Holders? The answer is that we wished to establish that there was a formal recognizable path for the transmission of culture, science, and religion. The ancients called this hierarchical path by the name of Earth-Holder and Heaven-Holder. And if we wish to rediscover the thoughts of ancient people, we need to be versed in their philosophy. Their worldview was that heavenly forms are transferred through cosmic cycles to our entire world in general, and to regions of the globe in particular as they are designated by time.

Furthermore, because the sub-cycles revolve more rapidly they repeat themselves more frequently, allowing important themes to be rehearsed many times within the slower progress of the greater cosmic cycles.

For convenience, we have used the term Earth-Holder and Heaven-Holder interchangeably. But, in essence, the former means: the person who controls the political power in the world, while Heaven-Holder means the one who controls science and religion. Many times these may be embodied within the same person, because it often requires great power to influence other nations, as well as to safeguard and to transmit information and tradition.

The ancient worldview was expressed in their mythological code of a sequence of gods and their cultural ages, which are related to specific regions of the globe, which in turn are related to specific astronomical time periods. This is the foundation of their scientific code which is like the introduction to a Shakespearean play in the succinct historical definition of Person, Place, and Time.

I wonder if we would be surprised to find out that the role and heritage of the Earth-Holder had been passed down to our own modern day and age? If this were true, then we must wonder about the reason for continuing this tradition. Are there still some people in this world that are safeguarding a secret culture?

There is no doubt that very ancient traditions have been brought forward to our times. In art, the infant Jesus is often depicted holding the globe in his hand; just like the ancient Earth-Holders.

Procopius, in his *Buildings* (7.i.2), describes an equestrian statue of the 6th century Emperor Justinian,

> Upon this horse is mounted a colossal bronze figure of the Emperor. And the figure is habited like Achilles, that is, the costume he wears is known by that name . . . and in his left hand he holds a globe, by which the sculptor signifies that the whole earth and sea are subject to him, yet he has neither sword nor spear nor any other weapon, but a cross stands upon the globe which he carries, the emblem by which he alone has obtained both his Empire and his victory in war.

Dewing, the translator of Procopius, comments that the Emperor considered himself to be the vice-regent of God on earth, akin to the pagan tradition that the king is like a god among men. Justinian himself encouraged the revival of ancient Imperial symbolism like the Achilles costume, which had been worn during the reign of the usurper Basiliscus (475–476 AD). Pliny says that semi-nude statues holding a spear are called Achillean.

Above we have reviewed that the horse is a symbol of Ocean and Poseidon. This animal, down through all history, has proved to be the ultimate military advantage—from Scythian horsemen to Conquistadors. In the case of the statue of Justinian, the globe and the horse is a double symbol of the Earth-Holder. In his epoch it was considered immodest to depict a living or historical person as naked. Because of the traditions of Ocean, artisans only chose the equestrian statue for the very highest and rarest of personages.

The globe which the Holy Roman Emperor carried was always alluded to as the "Reich's Apple" or the "Empire Apple." This is perhaps a curious reference to the Apples of the Hesperides. For an excellent review of Imperial symbolism one may consult L. P. L'Orange's *Iconography of the Cosmic Kingship*, the title of which has more to say than is written in most books.

The significance of Justinian's Achilles's costume is apparent: Homer in the *Iliad* (xviii., p. 368, p. 617) tells how Thetis, the Nereid, went to the house of Hephaestus to commission the shield of Achilles. Hephaestus recites how he had worked in the Kingdom of Ocean, during the time he was allied to Eurynome, the daughter of Ocean. On the shield he depicted the Pleiades and Hyades, Orion, the son of Poseidon, and the northern constellation of the Bear. Around the rim of the shield he depicted the great river of Ocean.

The tradition of the Earth-Holder lives on through Charlemagne down to the Queens of England, Elizabeth and Victoria, who have been portrayed holding the globe. In the next chapter we will investigate some very curious traditions of the Holy Roman Church, which apparently stem from this ancient cultural heritage.

It must be appreciated that the concept of the Earth-Holder is not a simple one. It is the sign of a worldview and a cosmology which proclaims: *On earth, as it is in heaven.*

Earth-Holder is an image that guarantees that the philosophy of politics is united under one banner with culture, science and religion. It is a token of the Golden Age when all was united under one worldly authority.

Chapter 1

Pontifex Maximus

The equestrian statue of Justinian demonstrates that the symbolism of the Earth-Holder was used in the Imperial regalia. We would now like to examine the ancient heritage of the Pope and the city of Rome. We feel that there is some evidence that extremely ancient traditions are designedly being carried forward, and not just symbolically, but by formal promulgation.

Around the year 1000 AD, Albiruni wrote that there were four cities of the patriarchs in Christendom: Constantinople, Rome, Alexandria, and Antiochia. These cities were called the Thrones. In the course of time and events, Rome ascended to the primacy of the Thrones.

The Roman *Codex Juris Canonici,* Canon 218 says that the Roman Pontifex is the successor to Peter. He enjoys not only the first honor, but has the supreme authority over the Universal Church in matters of faith, morals, usages, and law throughout the globe. Section 2 says that he is independent of human authority. Canon 219 elucidates that the Romanus Pontifex has supreme powers of jurisdiction, and that once he is legitimately elected, he rules by Divine Right.

The *Synopsis Theologiae Dogmaticae* (687, 688) says that the Apostle Peter founded the Church of Rome and was proclaimed to be a special friend of

Christ, who singled him out for the primacy saying, "you are Simon, son of Jona, called Peter [Rock], and on this rock I will build my church."

The variety of traditions and ancient canons required Gratian to compile a *Concordia* of discordant canons in 1150 AD. Finally, the *Dogmaticae* (594) records that the standard of the Catholic faith is the word of God, or scripture, or tradition as interpreted by the infallible authority of the Church.

We would like to note that the papacy holds the globe in its grasp. In so-called spiritual matters, it occasionally transcends the cultural and legal norms of independent nations. It does this by Infallible and Divine Right— granted by God Himself. It should be further noted that what began as the office of the Patriarch of Rome is never mentioned in Canon Law, but rather, he is referred to as the "Successor of Peter" and "Romanus Pontifex."

Plutarch writes in *Numa* (9) that the Office of the High Priest of Roman Pontifex was instituted by King Numa. The Roman historian Dionysius Halicarnassus writes (ii.63) of the great law-giver, Numa, "That all these rites which he found established by Romulus, either in custom or in law, he left untouched, looking upon them all as established in the best possible manner."

In actual fact, the office of Pontifex is older than both Numa and Romulus (750 BC), the founder of Rome. For, after the Trojan War, the defeated Aeneas took flight to Italy, bringing with him the sacred Dowry of Atlas. Here, Aeneas founded the city of Lavinium, named after his wife, the daughter of Latinus, son of Calypso, who was a daughter of Atlas or Circe.

There occurred a dispute over the rightful kingship between Iulus, the grandson of Aeneas, and Silvius, who had been reared by Lavinia and Tyrrhenus. Silvius won the kingship, but Iulus received another distinction. Dionysius Halicarnassus (i.70) informs us that,

> Upon Iulus was conferred, instead of the sovereignty, a certain sacred authority and honor preferable to the royal dignity, both for security and ease of life, and this prerogative was enjoyed even to my day by his posterity, who were called Julii after him. This house became the greatest, and at the same time, the most illustrious of any we know of.

It may be inferred that this sacred authority is the office of the Pontifex Maximus which was held by both Julian Emperors: Julius Caesar and Augustus. We might notice that most of the Imperial forms, and the very designation of *Caesar* and *Kaiser*, stem from these Julians.

Dionysius Halicarnassus describes (ii.73),

> Those who held the highest priesthood and the greatest power among the Romans. These from one of the duties they perform, namely, the repairing of the wooden bridge, are in their own language called *pontifices*. But they have jurisdiction over the most weighty matters. For they are the judges in all religious causes ... they make laws for the observance of any religious rites . . . they are the expounders and interpreters of everything relating to the worship of the gods and demons; and if they find that any disobey their orders, they inflict punishment upon them ... they are not liable to any prosecution or punishment, nor are they accountable to the senate or to the people, at least concerning religious matters . . . when one of them dies, another is appointed in his place, being chosen, not by the people, but by the Pontifices themselves.

The Pontifex Maximus is the chief of the Pontifices. Plutarch writes (*Numa*, 9) that they supervise the care and worship of the perpetual fire ministered to by the Vestal Virgins. The fire itself had to be made by lighting a pure and unpolluted flame from the rays of the sun, usually by means of concave metal mirrors. I believe the Easter fire is created under this formula in our present day.

The name Vesta or Hestia belongs to the earth goddess. Herodotus (ii.50) says that this name came from the Pelasgians, who according to Apollodorus stem from the god Ocean. The Vestal Virgins are also responsible for the safe-keeping of the Dowry of Atlas. Dionysius Halicarnassus (i.69) says,

> That the holy objects brought into Italy by Aeneas were the images of the Great Gods ... and the Palladium, famous in legend, which they say is kept by the Holy Virgins in the Temple of Vesta . . . and there may also be other objects besides these which are kept secret from us who are not initiated.

We will investiage the Palladium in a following chapter.

Plutarch writes in *Numa* (9) that the Pontifices have the duty of expounding and interpreting divine will, and preventing any departure from established custom. According to Dionysius Halicarnassus (i.68) Dardanus had been commanded to worship the ancestral gods and to guard the Palladium. St. Patrick's acknowledgment and validation of the ancient laws of Ireland clearly shows the Roman Church's attitude toward preexisting usages, as confirmed by Canon 23. For the philosophy of the Church argues that at no time has God allowed mankind to be destitute of the guidance of the Holy Spirit.

The Roman Church has always spoken out against abortion. Josephus in his *Against Apion* (ii.202) recites the Hebrew custom, that "the law orders all the offspring to be brought up and forbids women either to cause abortion or to make away with the fetus ... because she destroys a soul and diminishes the race." This proscription is also found among the mandates of the Atlantic Hyperborean Apollo who originated the Hippocratic oath, which states, "I swear by Apollo ... I will not give to a woman a pessary to cause abortion."

Like a true Heaven-Holder, the Roman Pontiff performs the office of a cosmologer in the regulation of the official calendar of the world. Asimov says (p. 22, p. 49, p. 109, p. 137) that Meton of Athens published the formula of the nineteen-year lunar cycle about 440 BC. This cycle is used by the Hebrews and by Christians, who use it to calculate the Passover and the Feast of Easter. The Roman calendar was in the charge of the Pontifices. Julius Caesar, in his office of Pontifex Maximus, reformed the calendar of Meton in 46 BC, using the ideas of Sosigenes and the Alexandrian astronomers. Afterwards, Pope Sixtus IV enlisted the advice of Regiomontanus to reform the Julian calendar. Finally, Pope Gregory VIII reformed the calendar which is used today throughout the greater part of the business world, except where religious ritual proscribes another usage.

The Metonic cycle originates from the Atlantic Hyperborean Apollo. Siculus relates (ii.47) that Apollo comes every nineteen years to dance on a certain Atlantic island: "The period in which the return of the stars to the same place in the heavens is accomplished; and for this reason the nineteen year period is called by the Greeks the year of Meton." The festival of Apollo took place from the Vernal Equinox until the rising of the Pleiades, the daughters of Atlas. Some theorists have surmised that this sacred dancing place was Stonehenge.

It is clear that the Pope, or Pontifex Maximus, is the keeper of very ancient traditions. He is a cosmologer, he is independent of human authority; and his influence is worldwide. He rules by Divine Right and his judgments are infallible. The connection of his office with the heritage of Atlas is remarkable and indisputable.

Chapter 2

The Dowry of the Palladium

We are obliged to tell the reader that we are not going to find out *exactly* what the Palladium is, or what it signifies. Yet, what I do find most interesting is that there were so many people involved over such an enormous period of time who were solely concerned about the Palladium's preservation!

The Palladium originates on the river Triton in Morocco. Then a daughter of Ocean, or Atlas, brought it to Arcadia in Greece. From there it came to Samothrace. The Flood of Deucalion then occurred in these regions. Therefore, and in consequence, the Palladium was carried to Troy. This is the land of Mysia, Caria, and the ancient Phrygians who are so ancient that they actually dispute their priority with the Egyptians. After the Trojan War, the Palladium was safely transferred to its new home in Rome.

Apollodorus tells us (iii.12),

> The story of the Palladium is as follows: They say that when Athena was born she was brought up by Triton, who had a daughter Pallas, and that both girls practiced the arts of war, but that once on a time they fell out; and when Pallas was about to strike a blow,

Zeus in fear interposed the aegis; and Pallas, being startled, looked up, and so fell wounded by Athena. And being exceedingly grieved for her, Athena had a wooden image made in her likeness, and wrapped the aegis, which she had feared, about the breast of it, and set it up beside Zeus and honored it. But afterwards Electra, at the time of her violation, took refuge at the image, and Zeus threw the Palladium along with Ate into the Illian country; and Ilus built a temple for it, and honored it. Such is the legend of the Palladium.

Ilus was the son of Dardanus, a son of Electra who was a daughter of Atlas. Apollodorus continues (iii.12.3),

> Ilus went to Phrygia, and finding games held there by the king, he was victorious in wrestling. As a prize . . . the king . . . gave him also a dappled cow and bade him found a city wherever the animal should lie down...and when she was come to what was called the hill of Phrygian Ate, she lay down; There Ilus built a city and called it Ilium [Troy].

It will be recalled that wrestling and the constellation of Taurus (bull and heavenly cow) are connected with the culture of Ocean and the Earth-Holders like Atlas.

Dionysius Halicarnassus (i.68) relates a slightly different version involving,

> Charyse, the daughter of Pallas, when she was married to Dardanus by whom she had two sons . . . and these succeeded Atlas in the kingdom, reigned for some time in Arcadia. Charyse brought for her dowry, the gifts of Athena, that is the Palladia and the sacred symbols of the Great Gods.

Here, Dionysius Halicarnassus preserves the same traditional movement from Arcadia, to Thrace, to Troy, and finally to Rome. Then an oracle is quoted which says,

> In the town thou buildest, worship undying fond to gods ancestral; guard them, sacrifice, adore with choirs. For while these

holy things in thy land remain, god's daughter's gifts of old, bestow upon thy spouse, secure from harm thy city shall abide forevermore. Dardanus, accordingly, left the statues in the city which he founded . . . looking upon them as sent from heaven . . . Aeneas . . . took out of the sanctuary the images of the Great Gods and the Palladium . . . brought them into Italy . . . the Palladium, famous in legend, which they say is kept by the holy virgins in the temple of Vesta, where the perpetual fire is also preserved.

Dionysius Halicarnassus further affirms that he found evidence of holy things known *only* to the pontiffs and Vestal Virgins. These matters were not legal to be revealed to the public. The historian does mention the Salii, who during the festival of Minerva/Athena, sing and dance in praise of the gods of war. In their procession they wear bucklers and even publicly expose one buckler which is called Heaven-fallen. "No buckler of that shape had ever before been known among the Italians" (ii.71).

Apollodorus (iii.12) described the "Palladium, fallen from heaven . . . It was three cubits in height, its feet joined together; in its right hand it held a spear aloft, and in the other a distaff and spindle." Frazer reports that Clement of Alexandria says that the Palladium was made out of the bones of Pelops, who is of the family of Ocean and Tethys. Also, Pherecydes says that the Palladia refers to a "shape not made with hands" and explains the name as meaning, "to throw or cast." There is the tradition that the image fell through the half-completed roof of the temple that Ilus was building, and that it dropped straight into the very place of the sacred sanctuary.

Heirlooms of great antiquity have their special sanctity in their very age, and from where and from whom they came. They are holy in memory, not necessarily because of what they represent. These keepsakes may be quite simple mementoes, but of an extreme heritage, or pertaining to extraordinary events of the past. Therefore, they may be quite insignificant in their appearance.

The Hebrews had their Ark of the Covenant, the Moslems their heaven-fallen Kaaba Stone, said to have been given to Abraham by the arch-angel Gabriel. The Christians have their fragments of the True Cross, the Turin Shroud, and other relics. The classical world had its relics of Osiris of the Egyptians, and the toys that Dionysius played with as a child, which were preserved at Eleusis. All these dowries provide a respectful connection with the past, which in turn promotes the hope for carrying on their tradition in the future. They are usually accompanied by the formula: So long as these ancient objects are respected and cared for by you, your city will be preserved and protected.

We can easily imagine the mystery of the Great Gods, and who they were, for we have done nothing but talk about them throughout the above pages. The Palladium was possibly a meteor of a curious, human-like shape which was accessorized with a spear, distaff, and spindle.

Whether the Palladium contained the wooden image of Pallas, wrapped in the aegis of Zeus; will, perhaps, never be known. What is remarkable is the persistence with which these relics were preserved. They were held sacred over an immense period of time. They were transferred over great distances, as they journeyed from the Atlantic Ocean to Arcadia, to Samothrace and Troy, and finally arrived at Rome.

Chapter 3

The Pallium and Ceremonial Robes

The Pallium is a large, square piece of wool or silk used as a mantle. It must properly extend so far as to cover the feet. The Roman Church inherited its usage from the Romans, who appropriated it from the Greeks. For the Romans, the Pallium was a token meaning *friends of Greek culture.* Later it became a sign of social standing. In Greece it was worn by actors, but especially by the philosophers, because an essential part of the concept of the Pallium is that it betokens wisdom. Aesclepius himself wore this garment, as did his followers.

The Roman toga was worn as a token of an official capacity, while the Pallium denoted learning, or art. It was used by the medical profession, musicians, poets, rhetoricians, sophists, and teachers. Yet, the Pallium was also worn by the Emperors Augustus, Tiberius, Hadrian, and the Caesars. Cato wore one instead of the toga.

Christ and his apostles wore the Pallium. In art it is a symbol of Christ enthroned as master and teacher. In the 6th century, the Pallium was adopted as the mantle of the Popes, and used by them to distinguish their Metropolitan bishops and archbishops. The Church admits that the Pallium comes from ancient tradition, and prescribes that its use be only liturgical, and not carried outside the church or in processions.

While the Pallium is an essential sign of a Roman archbishop, it is conferred more particularly upon his metropolitan seat, and is not transferable by the archbishop should he be removed from that place.

Most of the above information comes from the article of R. Kreis v. Schaewen in *Pauly-Wissowa*. He continues to say that in art it was depicted as large, and having many folds. In later usage it was reduced to a small piece, or strip around the shoulders, worn over another mantle, and ornamented with a cross.

Special garments and ceremonial robes naturally distinguish the status of an individual. But, we should notice that the Popes use the Pallium as a token of their far-reaching authority throughout the globe. In essence, the Pope bestows the Pallium upon a geographic place, and a city. Because, as was said the bishop who receives the Pallium cannot take it with him to another city. It is not transferable. Keating writes (p. 336, p. 517) that in 1152, the Roman Cardinal Johannes Paprion made a voyage to Ireland, bringing four capes called Pallium for the four archbishops of Ireland. It will be noticed that the bishops did not travel to Rome to be invested there with this new distinction. But rather, each Pallium was brought to the city and palace of each bishop.

In my mind, the Pallium represents the all-encompassing global authority of the Earth-Holder. The Pallium should not be confused with the Star Mantle of the Heaven-Holder. For, as its name implies, it is covered all over with stars. The Star Mantle is spoken of in classical literature. Certain images of the Blessed Virgin are clothed in a mantle studded with stars as a token of the heavens. Our Lady of Guadalupe is depicted wearing one of these, and by her feet are the horns of Taurus, the exaltation of the moon, and a certain sign of the moon goddess. It has always fascinated me why this New World image is represented in traditional Atlantic symbolism and form?

The Roman Church uses a wide variety of special cloths in its rites and liturgical services. In the rite of the initiation and consecration of the holy nuns the initiates must lie prostrate in front of the altar, and are covered over with a blanket. In this fashion they become the sacred brides of Christ.

Special garments are an outward sign of the innermost beliefs, ideals, and traditions of the wearer. Plutarch explains in his *Isis and Osiris* (352) that Isis, discloses the divine mysteries to those who truly and justly have the name of *bearers of the sacred vessels* and *wearers of the sacred robes.* These are those who within their own soul, as though within a casket, bear the sacred writings about the gods . . . for this reason, too, the fact that the deceased votaries of Isis are decked with these garments is a sign that these sacred writings accompany them (italics mine).

Ceremonial costumes denoting Divine authority have been used politically to mollify the wrath of conquerors. Keating reports that Simon, the High Priest of the Jews, dressed himself in his pontifical robes to assuage Alexander who had resolved to level Jerusalem to the ground. Pope Alexander did the same with Attila and Pope Benedict used the same stratagem when confronting the Goth, Fotilias, who, in turn, withdrew his forces out of Italy.

We have discussed how the traditions of the Heavenly Ocean were adopted by Uranus, who holds the heavenly mantle in a bow over his head. This symbolism was preserved throughout Europe and the Mediterranean world. Spanuth in his *Atlantis of the North* (p. 74) tells of the Blue Star Mantle of Emperor Henry II preserved at Bamberg, embroidered in gold upon blue silk, and depicting the sun, moon and stars. Similar symbolic garments were worn by the generals of Alexander who divided his world empire. These Star Mantles were also worn by the Kings of ancient Rome, and later by Julius and Augustus Caesar. Blue ceremonial robes are mentioned by Plato in connection with Atlantis, and have been found in an old Nordic sacred place in Schleswig-Holstein. Similar robes are connected with the Hyperborean Apollo, and are also said to have been worn by the god Odin.

Homer sings in the *Odyssey* (vii.259), "With my tears would I wet the immortal raiment which Calypso gave me . . . and she sent me on my way . . . clad in immortal raiment." Nonnos writes (xl.577), "Heracles clad Dionysius in a starry robe." Apollodorus (ii.4.11) and Sicilus (iv.14) relate that each one of the gods honored Hercules with appropriate gifts, while Athena presented him with a robe.

Dummler differentiates between the *Aegis* and the *Peplon*, or mantle of Athena at Sais. The Aegis is thought to be a goat skin which covers the wooden or stone, heaven-fallen image of Pallas Athena. The Thunder god was said to throw things by means of a goatskin sling.

Herodotus reports on the origin of the Aegis (iv.189),

> It would seem that the robe and aegis of the images of Athena
> were copied by the Greeks from the Libyan Women: for save that
> the dress of Libyan women is leathern, and that the tassels of their
> goatskin corselets are not snakes, but made of thongs of hides, in
> all else their equipment is the same. Nay, the very name betrays that
> the raiment of the statues of Pallas have come from Libya; for
> Libyan women wear hairless, tasseled goatskins over their dress,
> colored with madder, and the Greeks have changed the name of
> these goatskins into their *Aegis*. Furthermore, to my thinking the
> ceremonial chant first took its rise in Libya; for the women of that
> country chant very tunefully.

Athena is truly the equilateral triangle of arcane wisdom. She wears the
three robes of life: the protective goatskin of the Aegis, which symbolizes
the necessity of wars and change; the Peplon of hidden wisdom, which
must also signify the astronomical Star Mantle—which serves as a token of
all the other sciences; and the Pallium, the symbol of authority, and the
delegation and transmission of power and tradition.

It is markedly apparent that Athena is the main figure in the tradition
of the Palladium. As well, the mythology surrounding Athena intimately
connects her with the heritage of the divine and secular vestments.
Therefore, it seems appropriate to examine the legend of Athena in the
following chapter.

Chapter 4

Athena and Pallas

Athena is the most ancient all-transcending, all-encompassing cultural goddess. She is related to fire and water, male and female, virgin and mother, war and peace, cunning and intellect; and to nearly every locality of the Mediterranean from Morocco, to Libya, to Egypt, to Greece, and to Rome.

All this is no wonder, because Clement of Alexandria (ii.24) and Cicero in his *De Natura Deorum* (iii.23) say that there have been five incarnations of Athena throughout history.

The first Athena is said to be the daughter of Hephaestus, and to have produced Apollo. She is the patron of handicrafts, artisans, smiths, potters, woodworkers, wagon builders, and domestic industry such as weaving and spinning.

The second Athena is the daughter of Neilus, son of Ocean. She is worshipped in the Egyptian city of Sais. Plutarch writes in his *Isis and Osiris* (354), "In Sais the statue of Athena, whom they believe to be Isis, bore the inscription, *'I am all that has been, and is, and shall be, and never a mortal has lifted my mantle [Peplon].'"* It is her initiates who are the wearers of the sacred robes.

The third appearance of Athena was the daughter of Cronus, and it is she who is the inventor of the arts of war. Cicero considers her to have been a daughter of the Cretan Zeus, a brother of Uranus. In a fight with Ares she put on the dog-headed cap of Hades.

The fourth incarnation of Athena was a daughter of Olympian Zeus or Zeus Ammon. This Athena was called *Koria* or *Coryphasia,* after her mother who was a daughter of Ocean. It was she who invented the four-horsed chariot. Herodotus (iv.189) says, "It is from the Libyans that the Greeks have learnt to drive four-horse chariots."

Libya is one of the homes of the Amazons and the Phoenicians. The ancient Phoenicians, at a much later time, resettled the area from which they had originated. Here they established the new city of Carthage. Lycophron in his *Alexandra* (657) calls Athena a Phoenician goddess. Sicilus says (iii.71) that Athena was the ideal of the Amazons. And indeed, the shield of Athena was decorated with Amazons and Giants. The Gorgon Medusa dared to vie with Athena in beauty. Athena enlists Perseus to vanquish Medusa, and afterwards receives her dreadful head to ornament her shield.

Nonnos (8.345) styles her, "Libyan Athena"; and Pausanius relates in his *Attica* (14.6) that the Libyans say that Athena is the daughter of Poseidon and Lake Tritonis. Hesiod says Athena was a daughter of Poseidon and Amphitrite, a daughter of Ocean. Athena is also called horse goddess because of her father, Poseidon. The Wooden Horse of Troy was dedicated to Athena, goddess of wisdom and strategy.

Under the heading of this fourth appearance must also be mentioned the famous Athena born to Zeus and the wisest of the goddesses, Metis, daughter of Ocean. After intercourse, Zeus swallowed Metis because it was professed that she would deliver the New Lord of Heaven. Prometheus, Hephaestus, or Hermes then smote the head of Zeus at the River Triton; and from his head Athena appeared fully armed. This is the Athena associated with the sign of Aries, the head of the zodiac. Teukros says that Athena appears in the first decan of Aries. In art she is shown holding a ram.

According to Cicero and Clement, the fifth incarnation of Athena is the daughter of the Giant Pallas and Titanis, daughter of Ocean. Because her father, Pallas, attempted to violate her maidenhood, Athena slew him and made the protective aegis out of his skin. She is portrayed with wings on her ankles, and she is said to have taken part in the slaughter of the Giants. This is the famous Pallas Athena.

These are the generations of Athena. Now let us examine the ancient name Pallas, which also appears as the name of a Titan who marries Styx, the daughter of Ocean. Athena created the Palladium in honor of her nurse whom she had accidentally killed. This nurse, Pallas, was the daughter of Triton. And Triton and Rhode were the issue of Poseidon and Amphitrite, daughter of Ocean.

We know that Athens is called after Athena, and that the city was founded on the river called Triton, in memory of Lake Triton in Libya. And this Libyan Triton received its name in recollection of the Tritonian Marsh in Morocco. The early king Pandion of Athens also called his son, Pallas. So, it must be considered that Pallas is a very ancient name connected with the heritage of Ocean, which was passed down over a very long time. King Lycaon of Arcadia also called his son, Pallas.

The Pallium and Palladium seem to stem from one of the earliest traditions of recorded human culture. Most intriguing of all is that there is a final piece of evidence that shows the Pallium's connection with the sea and the waters of the ocean. The Pallium is usually made from wool or silk. But, Procopius in his *Buildings* (iii.1.18) tells of another material for ceremonial robes which comes from ocean waters. There were certain mantles only to be worn by the Roman Emperor and the Persian King. However, the Armenian satraps received them as symbols of office from the Roman Emperor:

> It is worthwhile to describe these insignia, for they will never again be seen by man. There is a cloak made of wool, not such as is produced by sheep, but gathered from the sea. Pinnos [a bivalve which grows a silky beard], the creature is called on which this wool grows.

We will continue with a further chapter on Athena and Pallas to glean more detail, and to explore further information about this great cultural goddess.

Chapter 5

Athena of Many Names

Four daughters and a son of Ocean are mentioned as the parents of Athena: Amphitrite, Titanis, Metis, Coryphasia, and Nile.

We have seen how naturally Poseidon adopts the concept and tradition of Ocean. He is also called the father of one of the incarnations of Athena. Callimachus too sings of the *Bath of Pallas* concerning the women of Pelasgia, Achaia, Argos, Thebes, and Helicon, who every year took their image of Athena to their river to wash, in memory of the time when Athena bathed herself and her horses in the springs of Ocean after the Battle of the Giants. Athena was born on the Moroccan river in the Tritonian Marsh on the Atlantic Ocean. From this original homeland her tradition was carried throughout the Mediterranean world.

Hephaestus, Cronus, Zeus, and Pallas are each spoken of as a father of Athena. Atlas and his brother Prometheus, and Hermes, the grandson of Atlas, are said to have assisted at the birth of Athena. Electra, the daughter of Atlas, had possession of the safe-keeping of the dowry of the Palladium.

Dummler tells (*Pauly-Wissowa*) that Athena was begotten of the Light, the father of gods and men. The Titan Themis gave Athena the Aegis before her birth, and Athena came into the world fully clothed and with a loud cry, whereupon the Earth and Sea answered her in reverence and the sun stood still. The statements *born of the Light, and the sun standing still,* seem to suggest that Athena may have been a true incarnation of the will of God, and an important revelation of the far distant past.

Shouting and roaring is the name of *Athena Enkelados.* Sometimes she is depicted throwing a thunderbolt, instead of a spear. In this guise, she may be seen as the daughter of Zeus, the loud thunderer, who received the lightning bolts from the Cyclopes, sons of Uranus and Ge. Yet, Hephaestus is also a god who has the thunder bolts. And as well "loud booming and roaring" are also epithets of the great and ancient god, Ocean. The Homeric Hymns, *To Athena* (xi) say, "Dread is she, and with Ares, she loves deeds of war, the sack of cities and the shouting and the battle."

Athena is connected with clothes. In the *Theogony* (570), Hesiod relates that the gods created woman to torment men as the price of the gift of fire. "Athena clothed this first woman with silvery raiment, and down from her head she spread a broidered veil."

Athena is called *glaukopis,* which some translators have rendered as gray or blue eyed. Voss correctly relates that *glauk-opis* means owl-headed or owl-eyed, after her totem bird. The owl is a creature of the moonlit night, proverbial for its wisdom, just as the moon is the agent of intelligence and inspiration. Flocks of owls are a sign of victory in war. These are also the token of *Athena Polias,* the city goddess, because owls live in the battered and broken town walls.

Nonnos (v.67) describes the founding of Greek Thebes by the Phoenician Cadmus, "First to the western clime he allotted the Onaian Gate to *Mene Glaukopidi* . . . because the moon herself, bull-shaped . . . being triform is Tritonis Athena." Siculus relates (iii.53.6) that the most sacred city on the Island of Hespera in the Tritonian Marsh was called Mene. The moon goddesses, like Selene, Artemis, and Diana, are accounted chaste and virgin. And, it is Athena who presides over the ritual bride-bath of virtuous maidens.

In Arcadia, *Athena Alea* is the goddess of warm water springs. Dummler remarks that the trident and horse of Poseidon and Athena are an ancient sign for wells. The geometricians dedicated the equilateral triangle to Athena, as the symbol of occult wisdom.

She is *Trito-genia,* born on the river Triton. Athena is the guardian of Dionysius in the city of Nysa. It is she who protects him from the jealousy of the Titans. In her temple at Athens, a sacred and propitious snake was housed. The Aegis shield of Athena is surrounded by serpents. The Wooden Horse is built by Athena's contriving and instruction. The councilor, Laocoon, and his son are overwhelmed by two serpents when they try to warm the Trojans of this trick.

Numerous health properties are ascribed to the olive, the sacred tree of Athena, who is also called *Hygieia*. The olive is called Moria, or fate, and any one who felled an olive would surely die. The Moria were born in the West, daughters of the goddess Night. They are Clotho, Lachesis, and Atropos, who spin the thread of life, measure it, and cut it off. The goddess Athena is also depicted with the spindle, as a twofold sign of domestic industry as well as fate.

It is apparent that Athena is among the most ancient of cultural goddesses. She is militant and military, yet kind and domestic. She is intelligent and health conscious. She is matron of cool springs and chaste maidens. She is also connected with the end of all things, death, and fate. She is truly Athena *of the many names*. When a deity has so many and conflicting attributes it is a sure sign of fathomless antiquity.

We have spent a lot of time establishing Athena's connection with the ancient West on the ocean coastlands of Morocco. This is important, because so many living and historical traditions are associated with Athena: namely, the Palladium, the Pallium, the Peplon, and Aegis.

This connection of Athena with the ancient traditions of the Atlantic Ocean is vital to our theme. It represents another chapter in our demonstration that Culture follows the directional flow of the Galactic Cycle from the West to the East.

It is now time to proceed to the cosmological section of our work. We have established that the ancients had discovered the Galactic Cycle, which they described in terms of their mythological sequence of the gods which developed in the far West and slowly moved toward the East.

Now that we have established this groundwork, it will enable us to more easily understand the mysteries of ancient astrology and cosmology. This is because the cycle of our movement around the center of our Milky Way Galaxy was a principle element of their ancient sciences. Without realizing that the ancients knew about Galactic Movement, their words and their works appear to be nonsensical. Once we credit them with this discovery, we must be in awe of their achievement.

PART VI:

ASTROLOGY, THE LANGUAGE OF COSMOLOGY

Introduction

When I was a student of philosophy and classical studies at the University of San Francisco, I was determined to read each and every classical work in their library.

One of the books that I came across was Ptolemy's *Tetrabiblios,* which is about classical astrology. I applied these precepts of classical astrology to many interesting and diverse topics: the day of the Battle of Waterloo; the cause of a child's debilitating gastroenteritis; the possibility of a racehorse's chance of winning a third *Arc de Triumph;* earthquake prediction; and many other peculiar topics. Astrology became my great interest. I patiently rode this hobbyhorse for about 15 years. Sometimes my results were gratifying, but just as often they were disappointing. Success and failure were so evenly matched that it really seemed pointless to continue on with this pursuit.

Failure is the greatest of all teachers. The lack of success instantly strikes at the heart, and is powerfully grounded within the soul. In this way, failure opens the blind eyes of understanding.

With all this in mind, I praise the day that Ptolemy's work came into my hands, because it taught me what astrology really meant, and from where it originated. Without an understanding of astrology, no one can appreciate the worldview of the ancients, and no one can ever hope to master their myths or their cosmology.

We continue to say that the ancient people thought cosmologically. Their philosophy was built upon a foundation of astronomy, and how they interpreted heaven's impact upon human history. We have already recounted the story of Cronus and Rhea, in which Hermes had to win portions of days from the moon goddess so that a time period could be created in which Rhea could give birth.

It is clear to everyone that this story combines elements of fairytale, myth, history, religion, astronomy, astrology, and cosmology. All these elements are woven around the instance of the scientific calculation of the year in order to promote accurate calendar reform.

In the mind of the ancient people the heavens were of the utmost importance, because the stars kept them in touch with God. The vault of the stars not only allowed them communication with the pantheon of local, ancestral, and regional revelations, but also, the stars gave them access to the God of the Universe.

This absolutely vital connection of people and the stars is beautifully proved by some of the Native North American Indians. At the time that we encountered them, their lives appeared to be nomadic and centered upon following the migrations of buffalo. Yet, one of their most special ceremonial sites for purification, worship, and herb gathering was the Bighorn Medicine Wheel at 9,642 feet in altitude, upon Medicine Mountain, Wyoming. Adjacent to this religious site were altars and ceremonial sweat-houses as a part of the complex devoted to the Sun Dance conducted at the time of the solstices. During 1972–1974, Dr. John Eddy discovered that the Bighorn Medicine Wheel's spokes were aligned to the equinoxes and the solstices. The 80-foot diameter wheel also charted the heliactic risings of major stars like Aldebaran, Rigel, Sirius, and also tracked the movement of the moon along its 28 day cycle. Eddy's astronomical studies and many other worldwide investigations were precipitated by the research conducted by G. S. Hawkins in the late 1960's. This work showed that Stonehenge was an accurate lunar, solar, and stellar computation instrument.

There are about 150 of these wheels, many with 28 spokes, located in Canada and North America. These observatories, Chaco Canyon, and the works of the Maya and Aztec all present documents written in stone and architecture that must convince us that we will never know the ancient mind unless we get to know their cosmology. These ancient and divers people, from wandering hunters to farmers and city dwellers, were not all interested in astronomy by chance. Astronomy was the road to their religion, which in turn, gave purpose and direction to their lives.

Astrology, The Key to Cosmology

We will investigate what astrology can and cannot achieve. But, what is more important for our subject is the understanding that astrology is based solely upon ancient cosmology. Once we realize this fact, we can interpolate the most hidden and arcane knowledge. Ancient cosmological knowledge was the product of research, reassessment, and transmission over incredible reaches of time.

The highest and most august findings concerning our universe were encoded and hidden within the common practices of a fortune-teller's art.

Once again, the ancients had disguised their most noble thoughts within a cocoon of demotic, or popular astrology, in order to hide the real truth of their highest cosmological theories. This outer wrapping has its own specific purpose. It conveniently serves to safeguard the real science by insuring its preservation and transmission through the agency of popular culture.

Though the trappings of astrology look suspect, we need to proceed like a careful archaeologist by carefully dusting off the debris and bringing the real evidence to light. Much of the information of astrology is the product of extremely long periods of scientific observation, and, we do not wish to discard valuable scientific observations just because we cannot immediately fathom the idiom through which this information has come down to us.

How long a period of observation do you think that it took the Egyptians to figure out that the double-star Sirius has a recognizable regular period that could be used to equate with the solar year? Realizing that 1,461 years is this regular period of the Sirius (Sothic) cycle, how many of these periods did it take to come up with this equation? Of course, the scientific observer is hoping that there are no wars, or social or natural upheavals, to disturb his observatory, records, city, or nation. There just doesn't seem to be enough time and stability to figure this all out by observation.

Just how long is long-term observation? We know that the people of Chaco Canyon in the southwest United States used the 19 year Metonic Cycle of the moon. Their cities and landmarks were disposed to demarcate the rising of the moon in relation to other villages. Further, landmarks were specifically laid out in the landscape to show off different positional risings, moving between north and south, within this 19 year cycle. One really has trouble wondering just how long it took to recognize, record, and finally engineer such an elaborate design.

Furthermore, let us consider the extreme accuracy of the Mayan calendar which is based upon the movements of the planet Venus. For the Mayan, the end-time of one of their important cycles is June 6, 2012. On this day Venus crosses in front of the sun; from our perspective here on the earth. How could the Mayan calculate this particular date so far in the distant future with such precision?

According to Berman (*Old Farmer's Almanac*, 2004), transits across the face of the sun by Venus occur in pairs 105.5 and 121.5 years apart. The last transits occurred in December 1874 and 1882. The current transits are no longer in December, but now change to June 8, 2004 and June 6, 2012. The next pair will revert back to December transits. The 2004 transit will not be seen west of the Rocky Mountains, but mostly in Europe and Asia. The 2012 transit will be visible from most of North America.

My questions to the reader are: Considering that there are twin transits, eight years apart, which reoccur over 105.5 years apart, which are not necessarily visible in your locality; and alternating between June and December—"How long do you think it would take an observer, focusing their total attention and energies toward watching Venus, to even think out the possibility of discovering an important regular cycle?" Also, after recognizing the possibility of this cycle, "How long would it take to determine its absolute regularity and prove its dependability as a calendarical principle which could accurately determine fixed dates in the far distant future?"

It should be noted that the Mayan end-cycle date of 2012 is interpretative. Yet, since the interpreters correctly forecasted the Sixth Sun Eclipse date of July 11, 1991, which included silver celestial apparitions, we will follow their lead for now!

The constellation of Taurus, the Pleiades, and other astronomical groupings are among the cave paintings of Alta Mira in France. Cosmology has been a part of human culture forever. Therefore, we will not dismiss astrology from the body of human knowledge just because we do not understand its meaning at this particular time.

Chapter 1

Origin of Astrology: The Moon, Tides, and the Ocean

A strology means *the logic of the stars*. This science was discovered on the shores of the ocean by observing that the moon was directly responsible for the ebb and flow of the tides. Once you learn an important fact about a great thing like the ocean, you push yourself to discover more information.

Once this step was taken toward the first observation of natural phenomena, the path was opened to the revelation of all the other sciences. Looking up at the sun, moon, and the stars could teach you a lot about what was going on down below.

The first scientists discovered the repetitive cycles of the earth, sun, moon, and the planets. They discovered that all cycles emulate the seasons by following the natural order of Moist–Hot–Dry–Cold. The scientists further learned that the moon draws not only upon the tides, but also upon the subterranean streams and the blood and water content of all living creatures, including man. All the things that they discovered were natural physical laws. When we speak about the logic of the stars we mean only that which applies to astronomical movement, physics, and that which can be scientifically and repeatedly demonstrated under similar conditions. This and only this, is what astrology has ever meant, or will ever mean. We will have to disabuse ourselves of the idea that astrology is about compiling personal horoscopes, which fortune-telling pursuit is anathema in astrology.

A Word About Fate

The cosmologers did not recognize cause and effect, for the reason that everything is a part of the universe. Astronomical cycles are just a part of the cosmos along with the other cycles. We are not fatalistic astrologers because we get up in the morning to go to work, that's just how our bodies have adjusted to the daily astronomical cycle of night and day because of the spinning of our planet. Again, we are not fatalists because we go to the beach during the summer time, that's just when the yearly astronomical cycle usually allows the most heat to reach the northern latitudes.

Our planet is probably the farthest removed from the center of the universe. Therefore, at the lowest and most common level of a species, individuals (a-political) are able to enjoy freedom of choice. It is at this level that change, mutation, and development is possible within a self-contained cosmic system where everything is a part of everything. This is what permits nature to develop. Also, since we are so far away from God, the cosmologers are dedicated to establish communication with the Divine. Therefore, we must fully appreciate and respect every instance of the Revelation of the Divine Spirit. We ourselves are free because our bodies are not around long enough to become engulfed by the cycles of time and fate. Also, our intelligence is so versatile and fast moving that it can transcend all of time and fate.

Finally, astrology is not a sorcerer's science; it is the logic of astronomical phenomena and cycles. There is the famous example of Christopher Columbus warning the governor of Cuba to delay the sailing of the treasure-laden fleet returning to Spain. Columbus based his prediction upon the meteorological conditions of the relationships of the sun, moon, and planets at that time of the month. As it turned out, the entire fleet was lost due to the advent of outrageous storms. This again demonstrates that intimate cosmological knowledge is allied with maritime cultures and the navigational arts.

What Large Numbers You Have?

Ancient astrology provides us with some reasonably large numbers of periods of years which seem to reflect their knowledge of the Precessional Cycle.

The modern astronomer Jeans says that the earth is not quite globular, but rather orange-shaped and bulging a bit at its equator. The sun's gravitational pull on this bulge slowly but continually changes the direction in which the earth's axis points in space. The result is that the pole of the heavens, that region of the sky to which the earth's axis points, moves around the sky in a circle which takes 25,800 years to complete. This phenomenon is known as Precession. Furthermore, Bradley discovered that the earth's axis underwent small periodic shifts due to the changes in the direction of the gravitational attraction of the moon. In addition, the perturbations of the moon, discovered by La Grange, might also affect the axis of the earth.

In ancient times, any community who was interested in astrology would of necessity have encountered the shifting seasonal pattern of their holy days after a period as short as 500 years, and thereby discovered the Cycle of Precession. That is to say, determining that the Spring Equinox moves through the twelve houses of the zodiac over time is very basic astronomy.

The modern estimate for the Precession of the Vernal Equinoxes is based upon the observations of Hipparchus (190 BC) who figured a period of 26,700 years to complete a revolution of all the signs of the zodiac. The present scientific estimate for the Cycle of the Precession of the Vernal Equinoxes is about 25,720 and also 25,920 years which equals 432 sixty-year cycles of Jupiter. The same figure is also divisible by 360 which gives us the holy number 72, which also divides into 432.

The Mayan Cycle of the Pleiades (from the sacred Tzolk'in calendar) has a period of 26,000 years (www.crystalinks.com). This figure is the 52-year Pleiades period multiplied by 500 which equals 26,000 years. This period is also broken down into five stages of 5,200 years. The latest Mayan calendar is based upon one of these minor stages, namely: 3114 BC plus 2012 AD equal almost 5,200 (5,126) years (www.thewildrose.net).

Manetho in his *Aegyptica* says that Egyptian history includes the rule of the gods, demi-gods, and spirits of the dead which comprised 24,925 years. Diogenes Laertius doubles this figure by saying that Hephaestus, the first god, ruled 48,863 years before Alexander the Great. What is important here is that Manetho and Diogenes Laertius have related the Precessional Cycle to the history of Egypt. Ptolemy gave a figure of 36,000 years relying upon Chaldean and Egyptian estimates of the Great World Year, which Plato also followed. Pseudo-Manetho records that the sum total of all the 30 Egyptian dynasties comprises 36,525 years. If this period is broken up or divided 25 times into periods of 1,461 Sothic periods of the cycle of the star Sirius, it reveals a full Cycle of Precession. Soviet archaeologists at Aswan dam discovered records of Sothic cycles for this period of 36,525 years. The star Sirius is the only fixed star with an invariable cycle of 365.25 days, coinciding to the true length of our year.

Really Big Numbers

Most people are not aware that the ancient cosmologers had discovered the cycles that express the spinning or directional movement of our galaxy within the universe. Most historians have imagined that the immense numbers of the ancient scientists were to be explained as multiples of the Precessional Cycle. Perhaps some of them were, but when we learn that the ancients calculated in terms of many millions and up to billions of years, we must consider that they had discovered something that even we have not as yet learned to comprehend.

Not only did the ancients calculate cycles in terms of millions and up to billions of years, they kept records of the changing constellation images which are a consequence of our galaxy spinning on its axis and moving through the universe. Galactic Movement changes our earth's perspective of star groups. Boll has told us that the Babylonian Star Catalogues kept records of ancient constellations which had moved and changed their shape and thereby disappeared from the sky altogether. Obviously the stars do not disappear, only our perspective of them changes as well as their own incidental movement. This displacement of the heavens is confirmed by Nonnos in his *Dionysica* who tells several stories about how the zodiac star-pictures and other constellations have moved out of their positions.

In 1927, the Dutch astronomer, Oort demonstrated that our galaxy was rotating about its center, which lies in the direction of our perspective toward Sagittarius. The American radio engineer, Lansky (b. 1905) discovered a constant radio source in the direction of Sagittarius, which supported the contention of Shapley and Oort that the center of the galaxy lay in the direction of Sagittarius.

While we are just at the threshold of gathering information about our galaxy, the ancients were well acquainted with its movements and cycles. Boll has spent some time directing our attention to the fact that of all the zodiac signs, Sagittarius is the most detailed and intricately developed. It is said that this sign depicts Chiron, one of the primeval founders of astronomy. The Circular Stone Zodiac shows Gemini and Sagittarius directly above the rectangles on each side of this zodiac which are covered with the zigzag symbols representing water which in this case stands for the heavenly ocean, or the Milky Way galaxy. Indeed, any observer of the night sky will see that the zodiac crosses the circular stream of the Milky Way in only two places, that of Gemini and Sagittarius. Figuring out that one of these two signs is in the general direction of our perspective toward the center of our galaxy is not that difficult a mental conjecture. Estimating the precise degree of that position is beyond observation.

There are two major problems in astronomical observation. One of these is astronomical refraction caused by the density of our atmosphere which makes a star appear higher in the sky than its actual geometric altitude. The second problem of observation relates to time and distance. The distance across the Milky Way Galaxy is said to be about 100,000 light years, which means that the light that we see indicates where those stars were 100,000 years ago.

Our sun is only one of hundreds of billions of stars that are in the bounds of our galaxy alone. And this galaxy is but one of more than 100 billion galaxies in the universe. Oort supposed that our sun completed a revolution around the galactic center in about 200,000,000 years. Estimates of other astronomers are between 40 and 250 million years. We will see that the ancients speculated in these terms of extreme periods of time.

Diodorus Sicilus (ii.31.9) records that Chaldean observations extended over a period of 473,000 years. Boll-Bezold-Gundel (p. 25, p. 99) have even found a source that gives a period of 720,000 years of observation. Eisler (p. 159) and also, Bouche-Leclerq report that the Chaldeans and later the Babylonians theorized greater cycles in periods of 36,000; 72,000; 720,000 to 1,440,000 years.

Cycles encompassing millions of years are common in the ancient astronomy of India. Richard L. Thompson in his *Mysteries of the Sacred Universe* says that Albiruni reports that *Surya-siddhanta,* an emissary of the sun god, communicated ancient cosmology to an enlightened being named Maya, over 2 million years ago. Furthermore (p. 305), another ancient astronomer named Munjal is cited as saying that there are 199,669 revolutions of the Precession of the Vernal Equinoxes of the zodiac in a *kalpa* of 4,320,000,000 years.

Mary Miller in *The Gods and Symbols of Ancient Mexico and the Maya* writes concerning the calendar, "Mesoamerican calendars tracked the solar year, lunar year, Venus cycle, and other perceivable phenomena as well as supernatural and ritual cycles whose fundamental bases remain unknown." The Maya have produced the most accurate calendar system of our historical ages, by relying upon observable phenomena. We do not understand their "supernatural and ritual" cycles because we are only becoming reacquainted with galactic observation.

Some researchers have compared the unique astronomy of the Americas with the Vedic astronomy of India. We just spoke about the Mayan end-date-cycle of 2012 AD. This particular cycle is only a portion of another cycle within greater majestic cycles. Most of us are only superficially familiar with segments of a few of the Mayan cycles. Yet, in actuality, the Maya have 20 different calendar systems which deal in cycles of 102 thousand, 2 million, 41 million, 840 million, to 16.4 billion years (www.thewildrose.net).

The Mayan have no difficulty dealing with galactic perception or the enormous time periods involved in galactic computation. In fact they derive their astrology from the nature of the Milky Way in terms of 13 different galactic energies. These are sent as light frequencies from the central sun cluster of our galaxy. The Maya say that the earth has been a part of the Galactic Cycle seven times already during a period of 16.4 billion years.

It is quite apparent that the religious and cosmological texts of Mesoamerica that were destroyed constitute an irreplaceable gap in our scientific astronomical knowledge that may never be replaced. This is true because the knowledge of galactic cycles is not available through observation, but it is the delicate product of cultural transmission by intelligent, inspired, and holy people.

History of Astrology

As a matter of information, let us review the historical and mythological basis of our own astronomical heritage.

Bouche-Leclercq says (pp. 575–577) that according to the mythographers, the honor of introducing the science of astronomy or astrology, as it was called, belongs to Atlas, the father of the Pleiades and Hyades. Atlas was the son, or grandson, of Uranus. Other astronomers also mentioned are: Atlas's brother, Prometheus, the creator and educator of the human species; and the Centaur Chiron, who is characterized in the zodiac as the constellation of Sagittarius. His home is said to have been Mt. Pelion in Magnesia in northern Greece.

The Egyptians and Chaldeans dispute which of them was the first nation to advance the science of astronomy. The Western Ethiopians claim to be the oldest of them all, because Atlas was a son of the country of ancient Libya, and his children and disciples enlightened the Egyptians, Chaldeans, Phrygians, and Phoenicians.

Clement claims that Atlas was a Phrygian astronomer, and St. Augustine regarded Atlas as a contemporary of Moses. The Egyptians claim that this science was revealed to them by Hermes, and later by Asclepios, Nechepso, and Petosiris. It may be remembered that Hermes is the grandson of Atlas. The Roman, Manilius (i.30) says that Hermes was the first founder of this great and holy science of astronomy.

The Phoenician, Heracles-Melqart, god of Tyre, is a disciple of Atlas, and he appropriated the name of the Pillars of Atlas to himself. Nonnos (xl.367) calls him "Starclad Hercules, lord of fire, prince of the universe . . . city holder of Tyre."

Prometheus, the brother of Atlas, is said to have had an astronomical observatory in the Caucasus Mountains on the borders of Assyria, which Bouche-Leclercq considers near enough to Chaldea to have been an influence. The Chaldeans and Babylonians, themselves, claim that Istar/Venus instructed Hermes in astronomy. Pliny (6.121) says that the Babylonian Jupiter-Belus discovered astronomy, while Seneca (vii.3) reports that Berosos translated the doctrines of Belus. In myth, Belus is the son of Poseidon of Libya, who according to Siculus (i.28) sent colonies to Babylon where they introduced astronomy.

Bouche-Leclercq (pp. 53–55) gives the priority for the invention of astronomy to the Egyptians, because of their magnificent zodiacs of

Dendera, Esneh, and Akhim, and the multiplicity of their astronomical texts. Furthermore, the Egyptians were more sophisticated in regulating their calendar by the star Sirius, while the Chaldeans still employed the lunar calendar.

Again, he says that the Chaldeans give the preponderant astrological influence to the planets, without great distinction to the powers of the constellations and the zodiac. In the 3rd century BC, Manethon expressed the Egyptian astronomical teachings, while Berosos expounded those of the Chaldean. It so happened that the ruler Antiochus Soter preferred the teachings of Berosos, which he propagated and published. This led to a general vogue toward the Chaldean ideas which supplanted Egyptian astronomy in the public favor for a time. Bouche-Leclercq says that the Alexandrian Jews attributed their cosmology to the Chaldeans, to the detriment of the Egyptians, Phoenicians, and Carians. Unfortunately, this authority does not mention the Persian sage, Zoroaster, the source of the prophecy of the Three Wise Men.

However, Franz Boll in his *Sphaera* says that historically it is impossible to determine whether the constellation pictures are of Eastern or Western origin. He says that Newton's chronological system was based on the assumption that the sphaera was invented by Chiron in 936 BC to guide the Argonauts in search of the Golden Fleece. In 1775, the astronomer Bailly proposed that the sphaera was invented by the Persians in 3200 BC, while Dupuis credited the Egyptians as the originators 13,000–18,000 years ago when the Vernal Equinox was in Libra. In 1875, Gustav Schlegel's *Uranographic Chionoise* proclaimed that the sphaera of the constellations of the heavens was introduced in China in 14,000 BC.

Above, we read that the Western Ethiopians claimed that in astronomy, they held a more ancient tradition than even the Egyptians and the Chaldeans. One of the finest examples of cultural-scientific transmission is among the Dogon of Chad and the Sudan, just at the southern extreme of the Sahara Desert, and in the region of olden Western Ethiopia. In 1907, French missionaries came in contact with these people and discovered that they were aware that Sirius was a double star.

Some have attempted to discredit the astronomy of the Dogon, saying that the double nature of Sirius was described by Bessell as early as 1844. Yet the Dogon accurately describe the elliptical orbit of the smaller Sirius b, and go so far as to celebrate its cycle at the proper moment every 50 years. Furthermore, they know of the rings of Saturn and tell of the four major moons of Jupiter. In the 1940s, Dr. Marcel Griaule studied these people in detail. It is quite apparent that astronomy is a part of their cultural heritage.

Chapter 2

Water, Fire, Air, and Earth Within the Cosmological Cycles

The ancients were astounded by the magnificence of nature. They took great pleasure in contemplating the magic, accord, and balance of the elements. These seemed to be arranged in a definite order of cycles in order to temper the harsh effects of any one element acting exclusively on its own. These basic elements, natures, humors, or concepts are characterized as: Moist, Hot, Dry, and Cold. They corresponded directly to the elementary natures of Water, Fire, Air, and Earth.

Previously, we discussed that the ancients often wrapped their most sophisticated concepts within a cocoon of popular meaning in order to guarantee the preservation of these concepts.

Anyone who was forced to take a course in philosophy as part of their general education is familiar with the early Greek philosophers who championed any one of the four elemental natures: There was Thales who poses that Water is the most fundamental. Anaximenes spoke about Air, and Heracleitos regarded Fire as the first principle of all things. Anaxagoras added Earth as a secondary element to water. As we said before, these early philosophers visited Egypt as part of their general education. Naturally, when they got to Egypt they were not escorted directly into the most holy sanctuaries of the Inner Temples. This would have been inappropriate and preposterous. These foreign students were entertained by the philosophers of the Porticoes of the Outer Temple. There in long discourses, the novice Greeks were presented with many of the important concepts of geometry, astronomy, physics, and other important natural sciences. Perhaps even some religious, mythological, and historical subjects were discussed, depending upon the intellectual sagacity of the visitor.

We should not imagine that the Inner Temple was like a bank vault full of wisdom, where the visitor could freely avail of tangible sacred knowledge. We have been led to believe that the Inner Temple was only for the initiated and the secret societies like the Rosicrucian's and Templars. These ideas are all wrong. The Inner Temple is a state of mind and a level of spiritual development. It is an attitude and a direction of life that is cut off from, and above, the paltry concerns of personal existence, community, and nation. Schwaller de Lubciz in his *Sacred Science* (p. 98) so beautifully expresses, "While the revelation of Horus is reserved for the intimate teaching of the temple, for those who have renounced the illusions of this earth."

The Inner Temple is the natural law in combination with the higher workings of the spirit. Because in every attempt to formulate a Unified Field Theory, the difficulty arises that the various elements, in whatever combination, will never be sufficient to express the spiritual reality motivating life.

At first, a scientific system called the "the laws of Moist, Hot, Dry, and Cold" sounds impossibly childish. *Yet, everything that we observe in nature, and its cycles, follows the sequence of this law.* All of the following obey this law: the day, the lunation's of the moon, the seasons of the year, all the higher cosmic cycles, the sequence of human, animal, vegetative life, and aging.

The ancients saw that the tilted axis of the earth produced the seasons. There was Moisture in the spring-time, Heat in summer, Dryness in autumn, and Cold in winter. So that the effects of these seasons might not prove to be overpowering on the delicate growth and balance of nature, the ancients appreciated that the cycles of the Moon, during each and every season, served to mitigate the predominant humor of that season. Thus, the New Moon to the First Quarter produced Moisture; the First Quarter until Full Moon generated Heat; the phases from Full Moon to Last Quarter were productive of Dryness; and the Last Quarter till New Moon was a period of Cold.

To further temper this gentle accordance of annual seasons and the effects of the moon, the ancients judged that the daily spinning of the earth also contributed to the harmony by eliciting dew and Moisture at sunrise to noon, whence Heat was generated till sundown, and then a period of Dryness prevailed to midnight, after which Cold predominated till daybreak came once again.

The duration and strength of the cycles seems to present a law of balance and accord. Namely, the shorter cycles, like the daily spinning of the earth are strong and immediate in effect, but short in duration. The longer and majestic cycles are farther removed and gentler in their effects, but persisting over great periods of time.

Balance and counter-balance is to be encountered everywhere. These cyclical systems of controlling the excessive power of any one element, is indeed why life is possible on our earth. It is no less marvelous that our planet is at the precise distance from the sun to enjoy its warmth, and no further away from it that it could be frozen in space. Again, it seems wonderful that the orb of the moon should just cover the face of the sun at eclipse.

There are countless galaxies in the universe, and some of them contain solar systems with planets. Yet, *Earth is unique.* The universe has been created to allow life in what seems to be an insignificant corner of a realm of countless possibilities. Our Earth is the *most holy* and *sacred* of all material places.

Astronomers who are looking for life in the universe first look for a solar system that has a large Jupiter-like planet; at a similar distance from its star. This is because without the gravitational mass of Jupiter, our earth would be openly bombarded by meteors and space debris which would soon destroy the delicate balance of our life-supporting paradise.

There are infinitesimal factors that permit the inception of life here on earth. The factors that allow life to go forward are the continuing and repetitive cosmic cycles. Within this system segments of time are created analogous to the weather and climate in our atmosphere. Moisture continues only for so long, until it actually draws Heat to the space it occupies. Heat endures only so long until drought and Dryness fills its space. Then the Dryness comes to its climax, a factor which then actually draws the Cold, which afterwards attracts Moisture to the place that it occupies. The cycle repeats and repeats itself, because every action has a direct and inescapable consequence. The system becomes an entity unto itself. It has life and breathes, and has palpitations of its heart.

From these laws the concept of Macrocosm and Microcosm is born. Therefore, we should say that the universe is a system of consequent, continuing, and repetitive cycles, which weave and interweave a pattern of life.

Every movement and action has a necessary consequence. And if the cycles are mutually balanced, so that one effect never overwhelms another, the pattern of consequences continues on and on. If, however an effect is too monstrous and overpowering, it will destroy the system of sympathetic cycles and cause the finality of this cosmic context within the universe.

In addition to the cycles of day, month, and year, there are numerous tempering influences of the other cycles: namely those of solar and lunar eclipses, the perigee appearances of the other planets, who in conjunction and in aspect with one another, predicate their own particular humors upon the above mentioned cycles of nature. I would think that all this aforementioned was public and common knowledge to all educated ancient people. This was the groundwork and foundation of their religious celebrations.

The Cosmological Cycles

The first sacred cycle is the Precessional Cycle. Because of the slow gyration of the earth's axis as it spins around the sun, the Vernal Equinox falls backward along the sun's apparent yearly course through the zodiac. (Technically, the Precession of the Equinoxes is understood as being due to the gravity couple of the sun and moon acting on the oblate shape of the rotating earth. It is not due to the "wobbling of the earth's axis" but it is the wobbling of the earth's axis of rotation, as in a precessing gyroscope or simple top, according to Professor P. A. Wayman of the Dublin Institute for Advanced Studies). The first day of Spring occurred 2,005 years ago when the sun was in the first point of the sign of Aries. During those 2,005 years the Vernal Equinox has moved through all of Pisces, and is approaching Aquarius, and will enter that sign about 2160 AD. The authors of *The Message of the Sphinx* (1996) make the case that the Sphinx in Egypt was originally lion-headed, and celebrated a time when the Vernal Equinox was in the sign of Leo, at the period between 10,800–8640 BC.

Schwaller de Lubicz (p. 177) relates that Precession is divided into periods of twelve months, each with a duration of about 2,160 years. Furthermore, each month is subdivided into three decans of 720 years. The length of the period of the Precessional Cycle, as with all things astronomical, varies over time. Below are some general figures for recent historical epochs:

		Elementary Nature
Virgo	12,960–10,800 BC	Air and Dry
Leo	10,800–8640 BC	Fire and Hot
Cancer	8640–6480 BC	Water and Moist
Gemini	6480–4320 BC	Earth and Cold
Taurus	4320–2160 BC	Air and Dry
Aries	2160 BC–0	Fire and Hot
Pisces	0–2160 AD	Water and Moist
Aquarius	2160–4320 AD	Earth and Cold

(Please note: these effects are subject to other higher cycles which further determine the genuine climatological result. These higher cycles will be discussed later.)

During these time periods, the entire globe was subject to the astronomical influences of this sacred cycle. In 1961, Schwaller de Lubicz was one of the first investigators to credibly speak about the historical and cult connections of the Cycle of Precession. He speaks (p. 176) of Virgo, which could have motivated the attribution of Sirius to Isis. And further (p. 177),

> Thus it is that Pharonic prehistory was dominated by the Twins [Gemini], Shu and Tefnut . . . as representing the two crowns of the Empire, and the double capitals of the North and South Kingdom . . . From the Middle Empire to the beginning of the Christian era, we see the domination of the Ram [Aries], under the predominance of Amon . . . that the generating fire is 'extracted' . . . by the grace of Thoth, master of Hermopolis.

The Precessional Cycle engenders the same four humors upon the lower cycles. But, it does this in reverse order: namely, Cold, followed by Dry, Hot, and then Moist. In this way a contrary theme of balance is introduced.

In our comprehension of time the Precessional Cycle, moving through the twelve months, or houses of the zodiac, lasts for a quite long period of about 25,920 years. Since it is a part of the harmonious and balancing cycles, most of its effects are gentle and kind. Yet, we will later realize, that some of its effects can be quite dramatic when it works in alliance with one of the superior majestic cycles. Occurrences such as minor ice ages, changes in sea level, and the creation of deserts through drought are some of the consequences.

The Galactic Cycle

The Galactic Cycle is one of the majestic cycles with a period that is of extreme duration. Its influence is superior to the Precessional Cycle. As the sun travels with its accompanying planetary system, it completes an orbit of its home galaxy, the Milky Way. This extreme revolution also goes through a twelve-station cycle repeating the natures of the four elements: Moist, Hot, Dry, and Cold. The flow of this cycle is in the same sequence of seasons as the annual cycle of the year. This trip around the center of the Milky Way Galaxy takes about 40 to 200 million years to complete

The ancient cosmologers created an astro-historical system called mythology to record the progress, the time periods, and events of this great cycle. Ancient mythology is the historical record of the solar system and our earth going around the galaxy. References to this great cycle are rare and somewhat obscure. Heath (vii.) quotes Aetius, who says that Xenophanes (570 BC) maintains that the sun goes forward ad infinitum. Heath (xiv.) speaks about Oenopides of Chios, who cites Aristotle's *Meterologica*, wherein he says that the Pythagoreans held that the sun at one time moved in the Milky Way.

The Cycle of the Universe

While our solar system is located in one of the arms of the galaxy which is spinning upon its axis—*the entire Milky Way Galaxy itself is moving within a Cycle of the Universe.* For less confusion, we have simply called this cycle Universal Season, because it is used in the reckoning of greater climatic periods.

Some Footnotes to Cycles

The ancients appreciated that the male nature corresponds to the Diurnal Cycle, because each day, food and sustenance must be provided for the family. The female nature corresponds to the Annual Cycle, because of the need to plan for the seasonal survival of the family by successful domestic economy, and the preservation of food over the course of the year. The male nature is in turn represented by the Precessional Cycle, because of the drive to create cities and empires, and great works of architecture. Lastly, the female nature is linked to the Galactic Cycle because it concerns itself with the long-term preservation of culture, science, and religion. It is for this reason that the divine feminine nature has been so highly regarded among all peoples as the ultimate bearer of culture.

We should also remember that all of the great cultures and civilizations which exhibited advanced technological concepts also exhibited an extremely refined religious consciousness. With the ancients, religion and science walk hand in hand. In the Ancient Worldview the revelations of sages, prophets, and demi-gods define time and places of geography. Namely, the place and cosmic time, when and where, one of these divine messengers comes forward, becomes the most important of scientific facts. These facts are necessary to correlate cosmic time and global position. Thereby, religion and science ultimately become partners.

The cosmological-scientific religion is best represented in the pantheon of Egyptian gods, heroes, demi-gods, and spirits. They represented specific periods within the many cosmic cycles which we have described above. Without any doubt, the Egyptians and all Atlantic colonists believed in One Supreme God. This pantheon of demi-gods and manifestations was the descriptive tool of their science. In the same manner as we use the Periodic Table of Elements to describe the constitution of matter; the ancient people used gods and heroes to characterize and anthropomorphize time periods.

In one sense, the ancients ascended to a higher level of comprehending nature. For in their naturalized elementary table, they described how matter acts in relation to time and the many cycles of the cosmos.

Astronomical Determination of Precession

We have noted how simple it is for any observer, who has a wide vista, to determine with great accuracy the time of the winter and summer solstice, and the days of equal length. All you need to do is to fix a central point on a firmly positioned flat-topped rock. Then mark a point from the center in the direction where the sun reaches its furthest rising south; and also its furthest setting place south, during the year. From these most southward points, the sun will begin to move northward again along the horizon until the summer solstice rising, and summer solstice setting.

By bisecting the winter and summer solstice rising and setting lines, the observer will have determined the rising and setting of the sun at the equinoxes. After several generations, people might begin to notice that the equinoctial and solstical positions are beginning to be represented against a new backdrop of stars and constellations of the zodiac. Therefore, the Precessional Cycle of the Vernal Equinoxes was to be discovered early in the history of astronomical observation.

Chapter 3

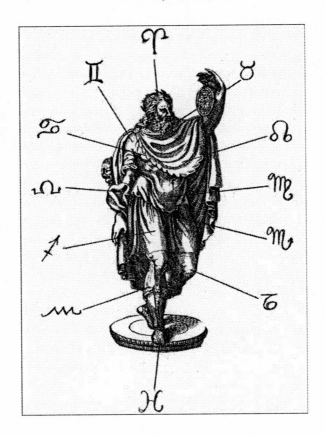

Microcosm and the Cosmic Body

The ancients considered that the world was a microcosm—a mirror image of the universe. The world contained and reflected everything that was present in the cosmos as a whole. It was a tiny, yet precise, model of the larger universe, which is the macrocosm. The ancients pondered upon the uniqueness of life, and the multiplicity of interrelated and coordinated conditions that had to be in place for life to be formed, nourished, and perpetuated. The Ancient Worldview realized that it takes an entire universe to produce life in one little corner of its realm.

Humans, men and women, are the last word and epitome of life on this planet. They, themselves, are the microcosm of the life of the world. Therefore, humans are also the microcosm of the entire universe. Alcmaeon (500 BC), the disciple of Pythagoras, held the view that the human body was a microcosm, reflecting in small the universe, or macrocosm.

After long periods of astronomical observation, the first scientists attempted to relate the lunar cycle to the annular cycle of the sun during the course of the year. They also found out that the summer and winter solstice, and spring and autumnal equinox appear against a backdrop of new stars because of the Precession of the Vernal Equinox. There were many more things happening in the sky than was first assumed. None of the apparent cycles fulfilled themselves in nice, round numbers of fixed periods. The reason for this was that each cycle was operating within a larger cycle which was again in turn under another larger cycle, and so on. Therefore, they guessed and approximated that the annular cycle of the year, exclusive of other forces, was about 360 days in length. This system, of dividing the circle of the heavens into 360 degrees, provided a mathematical system based on the number six: the sexigesimal system, which proved to be readily divisible into whole round numbers by all of the other numbers, 1 through 12, except 7 and 11.

The ancients then divided the circle of the heavens into twelve fixed fields or zones. Within each of these fields they conceptualized star pictures, or constellations. They created relationships between the star groups by using imagined images based upon their history and mythology. This proved to be a convenient way of finding locations and positions in celestial geography.

It provided another advantage; namely, the constellation pictures provided a grid that was used to determine if any of the stars within these groups were moving. We have frequently mentioned that Franz Boll reported upon the Babylonian Star Catalogues of ancient constellation pictures which were no longer to be recognized in the heavens. This idea was supported by Nonnos in his *Dionysiaca* (II.650). Nonnos devotes several portions of his work to the changes in the positions of the star pictures in the sky: "For

Helios replaced the manned Lion, who had moved out of the path of the zodiac, beside the Maiden who holds the corn-ear; Selene took the Crab, now crawling over the forehead of the heavenly Lion, and drew him back opposite cold Capricorn, and fixed him there."

Our human bodies were thought to be the microcosm of the macrocosm of the universe that creates them. Therefore, the universe was thought to have the form of a human body, which was then divided into twelve parts. Sextus Empericus (V.22) tells us of the,

> Chaldeans who have referred each part of the human body to one of the signs as sympathizing therewith; thus they call the head -the Ram, the neck -the Bull, the shoulders -the Twins, the breast -the Crab, the sides -the Lion, the buttocks -the Virgin, the flanks -the Scales, the pudenda and womb -the Scorpion, the thighs -the Archer, the knees -Capricorn, the shins -Aquarius, the feet -the Fishes (italics mine).

Other sources, like Ptolemy and Manilius, report that the heart pertains to Leo; and the womb and intestines come under the auspices of Virgo.

It appears that this system of corporeal affinity was universal. For we notice the images of Buddha with his immense belly, supposedly signifying fruitfulness. In reality, the sacred artist is showing that Buddha gets his high philosophical nature from the region of Virgo, the lower belly, which is the sign of Hermes/Mercury/Thoth. The convolutions of souterrains, labyrinths, and mazes are also related to the intestines and womb. Virgo is the zodiac sign of intuition, and the intelligence which we call "gut feeling." The mythographers say that Zeus sewed up Dionysius in the womb of his thigh. They are relating that this incident occurred during a cosmic period of Sagittarius. In this same respect, a sacred ithyphallic figure would show a relationship to the cosmic period of Scorpio.

The identification of parts of the body with the zodiac is best shown in the Egyptian astronomical images where Hathor, the heaven goddess, is curving her long body above the earth. Naturally, segments of her body contain the stars and the constellations of the zodiac. Myths involving parts of the body and deities are a sure allusion to the cosmic time periods of a specific zodiac sign. Schwaller de Lubicz in his *The Temples of Karnak* (p. 29) tells of the supreme antiquity of the High God Atum, saying that he was born of the Heavenly Ocean in such ancient times that it was even earlier than the time,

> *"before the Eye of Horus had been put out,*
> *before Seth's testes were severed."*

Strabo (15.1) writes concerning the ambassadors sent from India to Caesar, "The gifts consisted of the Hermes, a man who was born without arms, whom I myself have seen." The arms of the cosmic body belong to the sign of Gemini, the lunar house of the wisdom of Hermes/Mercury. Several of the Egyptian gods are represented with their arms hidden, such as the god Ptah (*Brit. Mus.25261*).

Once again, to demonstrate that this system was universal and global, we refer to the following: Dick Teresi in his *Lost Discoveries* (p. 75) writes,

> The second god rests a hand on the back of the first, with a scroll containing bar and dot numerals streaming from his armpit . . . his armpit represents math . . . The significance of numbers emanating from the armpit, a common image in Mayan art, remains unclear.

As above, the arms and shoulders are related to Hermes/Mercury, inventor of numerals and math.

It is very difficult for us to understand an astrological system which produces manifestations which are contrary to what they mean to represent. I am speaking, of course, of the sacred images of Hermes without arms. In the 36 decan manifestations which accompany the zodiac constellations of Dendera, the image under Aries, representing the head is the one without a head. We will see, as we progress, that cosmic influences often generate contrarieties, in their constant effort to balance the many influences of nature.

Again we refer to the heaven goddess, Nut, arched over the globe of the earth. In the *Egyptian Astronomical Texts* (ii.67–82), it is recorded that Nut, the heaven goddess, is called the "sow who eats her piglets" because she swallows the stars and the sun in the West, where her head and mouth reside. Her husband, the earth god, Geb, is angry with her for destroying everything. But the sun and stars travel through the twelve stations of her body during the night: hand, lip, tooth, breast, gallbladder, intestines, vulva, and thigh. The opening of her thighs allows the rebirth of the sun in the East.

Relating to our theme of the cosmic cycles, it must be recognized that the vulva of the heaven goddess, which permits the sun to be reborn, is directly by the sign of Aries on the circular zodiac of Dendera. Therefore, this part of her body means *now*, beginning and birth. It is now the cosmic time of Aries, which is called the head of the universe. So, the Dendera image betokens *born of the head*, which is Aries. This very same image and symbolism is identical to the myth of Athena, who was born of the head of Zeus.

Harmony and the Discordant Elements

Seneca (vii.27) states that "all the harmony of this universe is formed out of discordant elements." Plato, in the *Timeaus* (55), considered "the universe to be essentially one . . . but as for kinds . . . let us assign them severally to fire and earth and water and air." Seneca (iii.14) says,

> The Egyptians established four elements, then formed a pair from each one. They considered the atmosphere male where it was windy, female where it is cloudy and inactive. They call the sea masculine water, all other water is feminine. They call fire masculine where a flame burns, and feminine where it glows, but is harmless to touch. They call male the firmer earth, such as rocks and crags. They assign the term female to our soil that is tractable for cultivation.

The Egyptians wish to consider different qualities in the stages and changes in the four elementary natures. For, like the seasons of the year, the moisture of Spring seems to engender the heat of Summer, and so on. The discordant elements are powerful and pure at the zenith and culmination of their cycle. After this culmination, they seem to taper off, and become productive of a totally different nature. This is a reflection of the overall harmony of nature. Or, to put it into the scientific terms of *La Chatelier's Principle* (1850 AD), "Every change of one of the factors of an equilibrium brings about a rearrangement of the system in such a direction as to minimize the original change" (Azimov).

Therefore we should appreciate that the universe may be envisaged as a great human body. This body communicates its nature to its various parts through the many heavenly cycles of time. The influences of moisture, heat, drought, and cold are carefully balanced through the synchronization of many cosmic cycles. Miraculously, a context of nature is achieved where both stability and change can co-exist.

Chapter 4

Earth, Planets, and the Thema Mundi

We have explored the idea that our globe is a microcosm of the universe. But, we also need to speak about the earth as a part of the solar system of the sun and the other planets.

Whenever the ancients talk about the earth as the *center* of the universe, they are relating that the earth, the sun, and the planets are one entity within the universe. The ancients are describing our solar system operating within our galaxy, described from our perspective here upon the earth.

Let us look at some of the misrepresentations of ancient narratives, reported out of their context, and how they have influenced our historical view. I remember reading a school text that said that *early man thought that the earth was flat, and that the sun revolved around this pancake*. We have all graduated from this view. Yet, we still do not credit antiquity with a complete and scientific cosmological knowledge.

Misunderstanding

We have shown that the Greek scientific tradition stems from their Atlantic connection and heritage. But, in terms of our history, the classical

Greek scientific interest originates from their Egyptian Renaissance. This time period was when it became fashionable for the Greeks to visit Egypt. Few of these Greeks ever penetrated the dark mysteries of the Inner Temple. They were allowed contact with the philosophical porches of the Outer Temples of Egypt. The educational process of these Outer Temple philosophers is admirably described by Isha Schwaller de Lubicz in her *Her-Bak*.

The teachings of these Egyptian philosophers were confined to a basic introduction to the life sciences. They guarded the doors of the temples, and on occasion would recommend promising students for more advanced studies. Therefore, our understanding of Greek and Egyptian science, as reported by the Greeks, is confined to many basic statements and primary philosophical concepts. These introductory lessons, by definition, often neglected to present the ramifications of the context to which they applied.

Heath says, "There is not the slightest doubt that Aristarchus (310–230 BC) was the first to put forward the heliocentric hypothesis." Aristarchus proposed that "the fixed stars and the sun remain unmoved, that the earth revolves about the sun in the circumference of a circle, the sun lying in the middle of the orbit."

Asimov (p. 36) tells us, "Copernicus (1473 AD) seems to have known of Aristarchus's views, mentioning them in a passage that he later eliminated, as though not wishing to compromise his own originality." Heath also points out that Seleucus (150 BC) supported the heliocentric theory. Furthermore, Copernicus was accused of being a Pythagorean heretic because of his views. Pythagoras was perhaps one of the few Greeks to have been admitted into the Inner Temple of higher cosmological knowledge. Copernicus's so-called discovery was even predated by Nicholas of Cusa who announced the heliocentric theory in Europe as early as 1401 AD.

Stegeman in his *Astrologie unt Universal Geschichte* reveals that the Alexandrine poet Nonnos (5th century AD) repeatedly endorses the heliocentric view. Nonnos (41.345) writes, "Helios, central navel of the seven traveling planets." Nonnos also brought forth the curious cosmo-chronological system of the ancients which linked religion, history, and astronomy.

Seneca (vii.25) also repudiates the notion of real retrograde motion of the planets, which is necessary to geocentric theory:

You are wrong if you judge that any star either stops or alters its orbit. It is not possible for celestial bodies to stand still or turn away. They all move forward. Once they are set in motion, they advance. The end of their orbital motion will be the same as their own end.

The Planets

We need to understand that the planets of the solar system are all part of the microcosm of the earth, when the ancients are speaking of universal influences. At other times the movements of the planets are interpreted from the context of what we see from the earth.

Seneca (vii.3) notes,

> This observation of celestial bodies has been brought into Greece and is new. Eudoxus was the first one to bring knowledge of these orbits from Egypt into Greece . . . Later Conon . . . collected the eclipses of the sun recorded by the Egyptians . . . Apollonius of Myrrdus . . . says that the Chaldeans place comets in the category of planets and have determined their orbits.

Eisler (p. 170) says that the Babylonians called the planets *"the little goats,"* because of their capricious movements. The Egyptians called them the *"little sons of Horu,"* indicating that they received their illumination from their father, the sun god. The Chaldeans called these wanderers *"the messengers or angels"* which announce the will of the universe to the nations of the earth (italics mine).

I think that it is quite beautiful and correct to call the planets "the messengers and angels," because they transmit and balance the energies of the many cycles influencing our earth. It is well-known to science that the size of Jupiter protects our globe by deflecting space objects away from the earth. The planets also serve as transmitters within the great web of communication throughout the universe.

As our solar system circles the center of our galaxy, the sun and its planets undergo many changes. The planets themselves exhibit notable eccentricities in their orbits, axial inclinations, speeds, revolutions, variations in their size, and in every aspect of their mechanics.

Some of these irregularities have been noticed in the past. Heath quotes Anaxagoras as proclaiming that the axis of the earth was originally perpendicular, and has only been displaced through time to its present inclination. Empedocles (484 BC) reported that the revolution of the heavens, which is now 24 hours, was formerly equal to 10 months, and at a later period seven times the current rate.

Strabo (17.1.36) says, "We must not take it for granted, first that the earth is not always so constant that it is always of this or that size." Albiruni (p. 202) reports, "In the time of Jam, the population increased at such a rate that the earth could no longer contain them; therefore God made the earth thrice as large as it had been before." These scraps of information demonstrate that the ancients recognized change and mutability as a part of the nature of the universe.

The Thema Mundi

Our galaxy is a part of the greater universe. It is therefore traveling forward in a direction, and it is also spinning on its own galactic axis. These are two very important movements which change our galaxy's perspective toward the center of the universe in two important ways. Each of these two movements represents a cosmic cycle that eventually affects life here on the earth. The axial spinning of our galaxy we have called Galactic Progression, and a variety of terms like Movement, Position, and Revolution. The total directional movement of our galaxy within the universe, we have called Universal Season.

Every form of astrology is based upon the two types of movement of our galaxy in relation to the universe. This is because all astrology is based only upon the universe, and it is through our galaxy that we are put into contact with the universe. Our galaxy's changing perspective becomes the foundation of the astrology of cosmic cycles down to the lowliest form called planetary astrology.

In order to represent the movement called Universal Season, the ancient cosmologers opposed Aries and Taurus with their heads averted away from each other. And to underscore their intention and meaning, the ancients made Aries the exaltation of the sun, and Taurus the exaltation of the moon. The cosmologers explained that our world came into being when our galaxy was located in the perspective of Taurus which marked the advent of Universal Spring. It was in this epoch that life first formed in the oceans of our planet. We are now far removed from this time, having gone through summer and autumn; we are now in the winter of the Cycle of the Universal Season.

As we said above, the second great movement that our galaxy experiences as it travels through the universe is that it spins upon its own galactic axis, thereby changing our solar system's perspective toward the universe. We called this cycle Galactic Progression, Movement, or Revolution. The ancient cosmologers spoke about this cycle in their philosophy of the Thema Mundi, or the theme of the world.

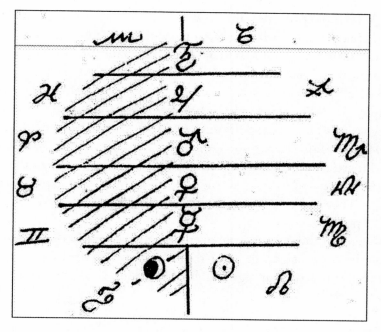

According to the Thema Mundi, the circle of the signs of the zodiac is divided into two half circles by a line between Cancer and Leo, which are the signs of the moon and the sun. The region from Cancer to Aquarius is dark like the night and represents the cycle of Cold to Moist. The other half circle from Leo to Capricorn is full of light like the day and represents the cycle of Heat and Dryness.

Because night and day are analogous to winter, spring, summer, and autumn; these seasons represent the Thema Mundi, the theme of the world—the great day or the great year that the world goes through. Therefore, the cosmologers represented Galactic Progression by dividing the circle of the zodiac into two halves of night and day.

Again, as we said, the astrology of the cosmic cycles, planetary astrology, and each and every other form of astrology is founded upon the Thema Mundi and the Universal Season, both of which clearly represent our only possible relationship to the universe. Therefore, whenever we see a zodiac we must appreciate that a zodiac represents our perspective looking through those constellations as a means of viewing every possible cosmic cycle: from the day, to the year, to precession, and to the highest of all the cycles.

The cosmologers say that Aries is the lunar house of the planet Mars, the depression of Saturn, the exaltation of the sun, and a member of the triangle of Jupiter and the sun. As well, Aries is located on the night side of the Thema Mundi, yet it is called a masculine and diurnal sign, beholding and equinoctial. We should understand from all this that the zodiac conveys a multiplicity of meanings.

Basically, however, it all comes down to the fundamental natural laws of Moist–Hot–Dry–Cold and the physics of astronomical relationships of cycles, heavenly bodies, and the universe. Therefore, because of the planetary position of Mars relative to our solar system, his nature corresponds to Hot. The relative position of Mars in the zodiac and to the other planets, and the totality of all the cosmic cycles, results in an equation of pure physics. There is no magic, no mysticism just physical laws expressed in relative position.

Whenever the planets, sun, or moon appear against the background of any of the zodiac signs, they serve to communicate their own natures plus the relationship of that sign to all the natures of all the cycles that the zodiac represents.

Review

All power originates within the primeval cycle of the entire universe. The universe itself is rotating, transforming, and developing. Therefore, even the universe goes through the seasonal changes from spring, to summer, to fall, and to winter—*from moist to hot, to dry to cold*. Within the seasons of the universe, our Milky Way Galaxy is traveling and spinning around on its own axis, and thereby experiencing its own cycle of Moist–Hot–Dry–Cold which resemble the cycles of the day and the seasons of the year.

Eisler (p. 192) says that this Theme of the World, or *Thema Mundi*, was revealed to Hermes, Anubis, and Imhotep. According to Josephus, Adam, the first man, was acquainted with this theme. Also, Berossus copied the *Thema Mundi* from Belus, the Chaldean.

The picture of the aversion of the heads of Aries and Taurus is depicted on the Stone Circular Zodiac of Dendera. This was the cosmologer's representation of the Cycle of the Universal Seasons.

This Janus-like posture of the two signs looking over their shoulders and away from each is very rare in astronomical representation. There is one other constellation with head-averted-over-shoulder which appears directly 180 degrees away and in opposition to Aries and Taurus.

The cosmologers represented that our Milky Way Galaxy was, in the universal perspective, relative to the line dividing Pisces and Aries. The birth canal of the giant Hathor goddess is exactly opposite to Aries/Pisces, and the Egyptians always portray the rising sun as if it were born of the birth canal of the goddess Hathor.

Therefore, the cosmologers who designed the Circular Zodiac of Dendera are telling us that our Milky Way Galaxy is in the position of Aries/Pisces, and also at the time before the midpoint of Universal Winter in Aries/Taurus. It is apparent that the cosmologers are saying that the planets derive their influence from no other source than the present position of the Milky Way Galaxy relative to the entire universe. In concurrence, Mayan astronomy derives all energy only from the universe.

In conclusion, the Thema Mundi of the astrologers is, in reality, the Thema Universal of the cosmologers. Whether it is the planets, the Precessional Cycle, the Galactic Cycle, or any other astronomical phenomena, they all derive their power and influence only and directly from the universe.

Ptolemy and the Astrologers

It would be interesting to review some of the misconceptions about astrology and cosmology which were due to Ptolemy, whom we must always respect as a faithful transmitter of science, but who sometimes did not totally research his subject by looking for instances of ancient knowledge.

Ptolemy makes a statement which totally confused the astrologers. In his *Tetrabiblios* (i.22) he writes,

> From our previous demonstrations, we observe that their natures, powers, and familiarities [of the planets] take their cause from the solstice and equinoctial starting places, and from no other source. For, if other starting places are assumed, we shall either be compelled no longer to use the natures of the signs for prognostication, or, if we use them, to be in error, since the spaces of the zodiac which implant their powers in the planets would then pass over to others and become alienated.

Following Ptolemy's direction—the astrologers would have to get together every 2,160 years (when the Precession of the Vernal Equinoxes moves to a new sign) in order to redefine the source of the powers of the planets. This issue became such a problem that the ephemeredes of the astrologers just flat-out pretended that Precession stopped at Aries, as if it were an old clock that no one had bothered to wind up!

Previously, (i.11) Ptolemy had defined the solstice, equinoctial, solid, and bicorporal signs of the zodiac, without alluding to the problem of the movement of the Precession of the Vernal Equinoxes. Nor does he comment on this factor in (i.10), "On the effects of the Seasons," where he says,

> Although there is no natural beginning of the zodiac, since it is a circle, they assume that the sign which begins with the Vernal Equinox, that of Aries, is the starting point of them all, making the excessive moisture of the spring the first part of the zodiac as though it were a living creature.

Here, Ptolemy has lost his grip on the *context* of the subject matter that he is recording.

Now, Aries is a fire sign producing heat. The only reason that it is related to moisture is that it happened, at that time, to be the place of the Vernal Equinox. Therefore, at the historical time of Ptolemy, Aries had become the start of the moisture of spring.

Albiruni affirms (p. 338),

> All that is peculiar to Aries does not move away from the place of Aries, although the constellation of Aries does move away . . . The meteorological influences of this station are peculiar to the first (i.e., original) position of Aries, and in no way depend upon the stars from which the station got its name.

Here, Albiruni confirms the overriding influence of the Universal Seasons. Albiruni also confirms the motion of our solar system through the galaxy which changes our perspective of the constellations; whose stars do seem to move away to form new pictures. Albiruni's statement makes perfect sense in the universal context that we have rediscovered.

Unfortunately, his translator has interjected parentheses further on in the narrative, where he relates Albiruni's statements to the Precession of the Vernal Equinoxes.

Extreme Conditions of the Planets

Ptolemy (i.19) explains,

> The so called exaltations of the planets have the following explanation. Since the sun, when he is in Aries, is making his transition to the northern and higher semicircle, and in Libra is passing into the southern and lower one, they have fittingly assigned Aries to him as his exaltation . . . and Libra as his depression . . . Saturn again, in order to have a position opposite to the sun, as also in the matter of their houses, took contrariwise, Libra as his exaltation and Aries as his depression.

Once again, Ptolemy is trying to say that the sun and planets derive their original power from the present position of the Vernal Equinox. Again he has confuted the theory of the Thema Mundi with *the coincidence* that the Vernal Equinox just happened to be near Aries during his own historical lifetime. These coincidences have not only fooled Ptolemy, but have led to the utter confusion of modern astrology and cosmology.

Boll, in his *Sphera* (p. 235), says that Firmicus's and Ptolemy's term for exaltation is *hypsoma*—that is, when the bodies of the planets stood at their greatest height or altitude in their course through the zodiac, in which position they were considered most powerful.

In our own time, the orbits, axial inclinations, and eccentricities are at a minimum. However, this may not always have been the case in the far reaches of the past. Josephus (i.70) relays the tale of "Adam, having predicted a destruction of the universe, at one time by a violent fire; and at another by a mighty deluge of water." Seneca (iii.29) says,

> Berosos, who translated Belus, says . . . earthly things will burn . . . when all the planets which now maintain different orbits come together in the sign of Cancer, and are so arranged in the same path that a straight line can pass through the sphere of all of them.

The deluge will occur when the same group of planets meets in the sign of Capricorn.

It may be noticed that Cancer, where the fire occurs, is the exaltation of Jupiter whose Greek name according to Aristotle (Cosmos 2–6.) is Phaeton: "Flaming fires from the heavens once burnt up the Eastern parts, they say, in the time of Phaeton, and others gushed and spouted from the earth in the West."

Following the hint contained in the testimony of Seneca, it may be supposed that the meaning of the planets coming together in Cancer, and in Capricorn, was a mistranslation of a cosmological concept. Namely, that our galaxy was in the universal perspective of Cancer during the fire, and of Capricorn during the flood.

The ancients, furthermore, held that the exaltation and depression of Jupiter and Mars were counterpoised in these two regions. It may be that this was their expression of a law generalized by Laplace (1749) and Lagrange (1736): *that the total eccentricity* of the planetary orbits of the solar system had to stay constant. They further said that if the orbit of one planet increases its eccentricity, that of the others must decrease sufficiently in eccentricity to strike a balance. This same sort of constancy holds for the inclination of a planet's orbit to the plane of the ecliptic.

It may be, then, that by hypsoma or exaltation the ancient cosmologers were referring to the greatest eccentricity in the distention of the ellipse of the orbit of a planet. The term depression may have signified the nearest approach of the orbit of a planet to that of a perfect circle. The counterbalance of Jupiter and Mars would take place in the galactic regions of Cancer and Capricorn. This extreme *aphelion* and *perihelion* of these two planets, whose elementary natures were held to be completely opposed, gave sufficient reason for the great cosmic fire and the great deluge experienced on earth.

The entire theory of astrology and cosmology is derived from the genesis of the universal season and galactic revolution. And these theories are embodied in the Thema Mundi.

Ancient history and climate are illuminated by the cosmic order of the universe. The idea of an order of transcending cosmic cycles explains an all encompassing theory of nature based upon the four elementary natures of Moist, Hot, Dry, and Cold. All this can so easily be understood, once one can master the influence of the highest cycle upon its inferior cycle, and so on down to the daily cycle of the rotation of the earth. It is all a matter of astronomy, physics, and the supreme balance of a transcending order of cosmic cycles.

Chapter 5

That Knowledge by Astronomical Means is Attainable

When I sit on a bench in the park, watching all the people passing by, I cannot help but marvel at how completely different they all are from one another. Not just the different races and nationalities; but each and every specimen is totally unique. Our special individuality is the best proof that God loves each of us personally. We are not only different in our superficial appearance, but in our thoughts, feelings, and physiological makeup.

Therefore, it is hard to believe that the incidental aspects of the planets during our creation or birth could have an extraordinary influence upon us.

First of all, in order for astrology to have any input on our lives it would have to deal with the total amalgamation of the imprinted influences of the planets upon all our past ancestors. Our genetic inheritance must be one of the most powerful determinants in our lives. If we were to trace back in anyone's extended gene pool and DNA makeup, the combination of the astrological influences affecting the mixture of their parents, grandparents, and their forefathers, this individual history would be unmanageably complex.

The so-called fate at the time of our coming into being may give a certain direction as we enter into the stream of time and events. But, that influence is so very minuscule in relation to the immense background and heritage of our breeding that it should be admitted that we are essentially free and independent in our thoughts, actions, and in our will. We have been given *freedom of will*, and we are a unique component in nature. This enables nature to draw upon a great pool of humanity whenever it requires change or originality.

So, we should say that genethlialogical (personal) astrology is without merit—because it cannot even begin to fathom the complexity of individuals. The ancient cosmologers never intended their science to suffer the degradation of becoming a fortuneteller's art.

Though we enjoy freedom of the will, this does not mean that we have all been granted a multiplicity of choices. For, there are some of us whose birth or family heritage has slipped into conformity with the cosmic flow of time and events. And some current events do represent the ordained themes of the world.

Some individuals are the actors and understudies on the stage of life. Most of us are the audience who observe them. These great and often horrible personalities, like Alexander, Napoleon, and Hitler, enact the political theme of the world. They are the personified cataclysms and hurricanes of the human drama. And it requires no great wisdom for philosophers to learn to keep their distance from these mighty but devastating forces. Also, we should not be taken in by their wondrous speeches for they have been given the power to sway the masses.

That is why the astrologers of ancient times were only allowed to be the attendants of the kings and great rulers. And, I think, this is the basis of the Doctrine of the Divine Right of Kings. They are not divine; but their genetic history is such that they have slipped into the stream of fate, and the development of national political history. Namely, that fortune, or the divine influence in this world, has chosen certain people to guide the state, and their personal fate has become inextricably co-joined with the fate of the state or nation that they govern. Because the state has become personified in one individual, the astrologers rightly felt that they could prognosticate the fate of the nation through the horoscope of the individual ruler.

The reason why astrology does not work in our present day is the same reason why there are calendar reforms. Astrology was placed out of synchronization because the so-called savants of that art did not know how to deal with the Precession of the Vernal Equinoxes or any of the other cosmic cycles.

We must once again reiterate a misleading instruction from Claudius Ptolemy in his four part *Mathematical Treatise* or *Tetrabiblos* (I.10) *Of the Effects of the Seasons and of the Four Angles,* where he states, "For this reason, although there is no natural beginning of the zodiac, since it is a circle, they assume that the sign which begins with the Vernal Equinox, that of Aries, is the starting point of them all." He goes on to say that the individual power of the signs is derived *only* from the point of the Vernal Equinox, which determines the seasons of the year. Coincidentally, at the time of Ptolemy, the vernal sign had just moved from Aries into Pisces.

But, as the Vernal Equinox moved into Pisces, the astrologers were not sure how to repredicate the powers of the signs of the zodiac. So, they just pretended that there was no such phenomenon as the Precession of the Equinoxes. And they adjusted their *Ephemeredes Catalogues* backward to the sign of Aries. So that if you were to go outside and clearly observe that Saturn was in the sign of Taurus, the astrologer's Ephemeredes would tell you to calculate that Saturn was *astrologically* in the sign of Gemini.

It is no wonder that astrology became totally discredited by acting the buffoon of all the sciences. And rightly so, because its practitioners had trespassed against the possibilities of the art by attempting forecasts for private individuals. The charlatans had failed to understand the real fundamentals of the science, which are cosmological and sacred, steming from long research and divine inspiration.

Napoleon's Waterloo

Just as an interesting diversion, let us examine the case of the Emperor Napoleon at the Battle of Waterloo.

Napoleon Bonaparte had unified Europe for the first time since Charlemagne. He had given it a Civil Code that survives today. Because of his personal ingenuity and bravery on the battlefield, Bonaparte ranks alongside the greatest commanders of history such as Ramses, Alexander, Hannibal, and Frederick of Prussia. How could anyone defeat such a man? Goethe would rightly imply that he defeated himself.

One of the best accounts of the battle of Waterloo can be found in Stephen Zweig's *Sternstunden der Menscheit*. He dwells especially upon the actions of the leaders of the reserve contingents of each of the armies. The French general, Grouchy, was as dull and contrary a man as could ever be found if the reports of that day do him justice. He was educated in the

Napoleonic tradition of fanatic obedience. Another French officer, who had recently disobeyed an order from Napoleon, obliged the great man by fetching down a book from a high shelf which the Emperor could not conveniently reach. Napoleon replied, "General, you are a full head taller than I am. Should you disobey me again on the battlefield, I will see that the difference in our height is instantly remedied."

On the English and German side appeared General Bluecher. He was a product of the philosophy of Frederick the Great of Prussia. The Prussian military manual emphasized personal decisiveness, responsibility, and accountability from generals to officers down to the man in the field. To Frederick, the greatest sin was failure to respond and take incentive! These were the rules and virtues which won the day. The rigid obedience; which made Napoleon's army such a perfect tool of his genius, became the very cause of his defeat.

The astronomical picture of June 18, 1815, is an astrologer's dream. It is perfect, simple, and utterly remorseless in its consequences. The marshals of the engagement, Napoleon and Wellington, are represented by the sun and the moon, who are the marshals of the heavens. On this day, the powers of the sun and moon are checked in total abeyance. The great commanders, just as their heavenly counterparts, are held ineffectual because Mars controls the Sun; while Saturn controls the Moon. What is created is an absolute astrological checkmate.

In this great drama, Napoleon and Wellington had parried, checked, and counter-checked each other's forces as if they were playing a giant chess match.

As Clausewitz says in his astute *Vom Kriege*, when armies of equal strength and determination meet, they can do nothing more than wreck equal destruction upon one another, without a decisive result. Wellington lamented, "I wish it were nightfall, or that the Prussians might come!"

Returning to the astrological positions, Venus is in opposition to Saturn who controls the Moon. The benign Jupiter is in opposition to the warrior Mars who dominates the Sun from the house of Saturn. All this while Saturn is visiting the house of Mars, in Capricorn.

The very heavens are checked and counter-checked, just as the commanders are below. Both stars and people are interlocked and intertwined in total ineffectuality.

But, look, there is something in the skies that is independent and unfettered. It is the planet Mercury, standing alone, without any aspect or relation to any other cosmic body. He alone could permit a decisive movement by someone.

And so it proved. Down below, the Prussian General Bluecher had heard cannon fire. He immediately proceeded in its direction, and the small weight of his advancing forces broke down the French lines. Bluecher alone turned the gigantic, but frozen formations into a battle rout. General Grouchy, had he likewise responded to the cannon's roar, could have matched the advances of the Prussian, in order to promote a further stalemate. But, because he was mindful of Napoleon's instructions to obey his commander, he firmly held the position he had been ordered to maintain.

For private individuals like us, there is a plethora of freedom to be enjoyed. This is because fate develops in many different cycles of time. However, for people like Napoleon, there is little or no freedom. For they have become the tool of fate and the personification of their nation.

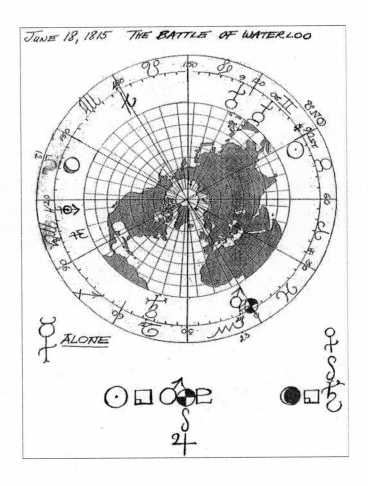

Chapter 6

On the Nature of the Ancient Sites

Standing in front of the entrance to the Palace of Versailles, constructed at the behest of the self-styled "Sun King," Louis the XIV, one cannot help but be impressed by the startling use of perspective, with ascending and diminishing proportions. These special effects were precisely calculated to make the visitor feel small; and to foster an impression of grandeur and power upon foreign dignitaries as well as upon the subjects of the French king. The proof of this determined presentation, a view well calculated to impress, is born out by the reports that King Louis also hired some of his subjects to impersonate ambassadors from Siam at his royal court, to impress the world of his global fame.

When we look at the monolithic works of Stonehenge, the Pyramids of Egypt, the Cyclopean walls, and Lion's Gate of Tiryns and Mycenae, we are immediately impressed that a great people must reside here. And if we were enemies, or ambassadors of other powers, trying to negotiate treaties, our first impressions of these great works would color our attitudes and actions.

Therefore, we might conclude that the architecture of ancient and modern people is created to serve a very political function—to impress outsiders, as well as the very subjects of our own realm. Great buildings also help to reaffirm one's own prestige. And the grandeur of architecture makes a memorable impression of an important heritage—in the minds of subsequent generations of rulers. This wish to make impressions is a common and natural desire shared by the ancient and the modern worlds.

There is, however, an important difference between ancient and modern structures.

Seneca (iii.15–29) considers "whether the world is an animated being or a body governed by nature." He says that the earth is like the system of our bodies, and, "in the same way this whole body of the entire earth is a passageway both for water, which takes the place of blood; and for winds, which you might simply call respiration . . . echoing the belief of those who are fond of the theory that the earth is a living creature."

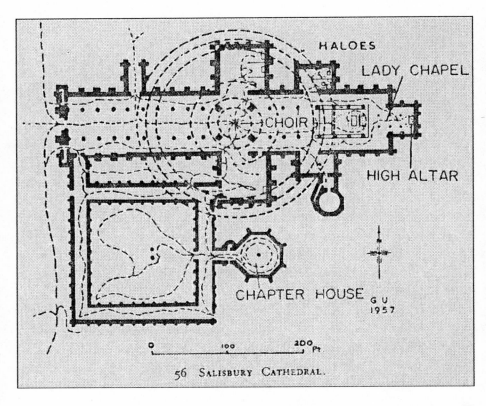

56 SALISBURY CATHEDRAL.

What distinguishes ancient sites from modern constructions is that the ancient structures are founded in specific relation to underground patterns and sources of water. These special patterns determined the function of the structures that were to be placed above them. They also prescribed the very size, proportions, and directions of the walls built above the influence of their waters. The reason for the placement of structures above subterranean aqua-spirals is that these water courses are acted upon by the positions of the heavenly bodies; especially the moon. The moon draws these underground waters as it does the tides of the ocean. And, in conjunction with the sun during its annul course, and in aspect and conjunctions with the planets, the moon's power upon these underground water spirals is further amplified in respect to the specific characteristics which those water spirals produce.

The reason that the ancients adorned these special underground water sites with megalithic stones and temples is as follows: *These places produce a powerful field of electromagnetism under certain astronomical conditions.* These strongly felt currents of energy would stimulate prophetic trances, or inspire congregations in the midst of their worship. They might also help to sooth and calm assemblies of people at times of decision and judgment. A powerful and seemingly magical influence was produced, when it was successfully anticipated and coordinated by priests and rulers, who had correctly interpreted the astronomical phenomena acting upon these water streams—for a special ceremony, at a specific time.

We might be tempted to call these ancient people, "water worshipers." The ancients obviously appreciated the beauty of streams and waterfalls in nature, but they had a most especial veneration for the subterranean streams which serve as the circulatory system of our planet. It is important to understand that this is not "water worship"; nor did the ancients ever adore fire or any of the other elements of nature. They only revered water because it served as an intermediary and a vehicle which demonstrates the unity between earth, man, and the heavenly cosmos. So, if we read of any ancient people who profess to have a special regard for any of the elements of nature, we should, right away, understand that whatever element they have chosen is their intermediary between earth and the cosmos.

My conclusions were formulated after reading Underwood's masterful account of these phenomena in his *Patterns of the Past.* This unfortunately disregarded work gives the most simple and explicit description of the variety and strengths of the emanations of these water forces. It is also written in such knowledgeable simplicity, that one cannot help but embrace his conclusions.

Colin Wilson, in his *Atlas of Holy Places*, writes that,

> All good dowsers will verify that the stones of Carnac are charged with some magnetic force . . . The people who built Carnac were obsessed by the moon because it affected them, as it affects tides and "lunatics" during a full moon. Experiments today prove that the area in which the stones of Carnac stand has a magnetic or electrical force . . . at the center of a rich source of earth energy.

At the other side of the world we have the famous Nasca lines depicted upon the desert of Peru. These may not be just works of art or astronomical signs. Hydrogeologist, Stephen B. Mabee and archeologist, Donald Proulx, from the University of Massachusetts suggest that some of the mysterious lines demarcate streams of underground water.

This dependence upon a subterranean water pattern seems to explain why ancient sites have such a very long and peculiar history of their own. In most cases they were reused and reconsecrated, even by conquering people from different civilizations.

These seemingly magical sites were resanctified and accepted by subsequent invasions of new colonists. This is why Ireland serves as such an excellent and isolated microcosm of the long-term preservation of an ancient cultural order and context. For, on the place where a medieval church stands today, there once stood a carved stone cross from early Christian times, erected upon the coronation stone of ancient kings, where before had been a druid's altar, and before that a place of oracular inspiration. Around the medieval churchyard is a Christian graveyard, where formerly the dead of another revelation of God were resting. Thus, the saints and sinners of one order of people are sleeping in the Lord with those of other generations.

Water force is not that difficult to perceive and understand. Underwood has experimented with young school children and found that almost all of them were able to use a water-divining apparatus, and perceive the subterranean flows of water. I have found an easy simile. Namely, the veins and arteries of the human body are analogous to the network of underground water streams that nourish and vivify the earth, in the same way that our veins carry blood throughout our bodies. Personally, I have used a variety of supple divining sticks from hazel to willow, held in tension, to read the water forces below. But the most precise and effective instrument has proved to be a very light copper wire held with forefinger and thumb, utilizing one loop held in light tension by the other thumb and finger. Anyone should be able to use this instrument to convince themselves of the existence of underground water forces, for this simple apparatus even detects the minute hair lines that surround these subterranean streams.

Underwood states that ancient people observed how wild and domestic animals would invariably return to a specific spot in the land to give birth to their young, because that place seemed to facilitate ease of delivery. The story of Cadmus, who was enjoined to follow the cow until she came to rest, seems to relate to this phenomenon; that is, the cow will find the most salubrious site. Underwood, in *The Pattern of the Past* (p. 60), states that horses, cattle, pigs, sheep, dogs, badgers, moles, hares, rabbits, tortoises, lizards, geese, owls, rooks, wild bees, ants, and gnats all respond to geodetic lines, water spirals, and underground water forces.

Willows, apple, yew, cedar, elm, hawthorn, mistletoe, crow garlic, and hazel, in their natural state, seem to be attracted to these special places. Insects, gnats, and ants are drawn to them, and the track-lines of domestic and wild animals trace these underground waterways exactly. Early roads and pathways were founded upon these animal track-lines, which explains the seemingly irrational twisting and convolutions of many of the ancient roads. The specific size or the unusual bending of walls of ancient structures often follow the underground pattern of the water courses.

The ancient natural philosophers and priests made a study and a science of these patterns, which they regarded as the blood of the earth. They laid out the boundaries of the farmers' fields, their towns and temple precincts upon this unalterable and easily traceable grid. This became a natural plot map, obviating all disputes over boundaries and land use. Also, every country is like a distinct individual whose body is serviced by its major organs. In this simile, the land is united through networks and major confluences of underground streams to produce the most important organs, which are designated by knots and spirals of tremendous force and perceptible activity. Underwood declares Stonehenge in England to be sited upon one of the most important heartlands of water activity within the entire country.

According to Giraldus Combrensis, these stones were stolen by Merlin, the magician, from Ireland where they stood at the true umbilicus of that island. Pausanius reports (x.16.), "What is called the Omphalus [navel] by the Delphians is made of white marble, and is said by the Delphians to be the center of all the earth." Omphaloi, like that at Delphi, have been found by Reisner in the temple of Amon in Egypt. They occur as well in Ireland, where at present several of them occur as the capstones of the most ancient stone crosses of Ossory.

Underwood contends that different patterns and arrangements of the subterranean water spirals produce different effects above the ground. Some of these sites induced a penitent or purgatory effect, and these were maintained in Medieval times as stations for pillory boxes, prisons, and cells. There is a site in Ireland bearing an ancient name of the moon that is said to induce madness in anyone sleeping there. The local lore of Killamery says that those depressed by headaches should visit their ancient stone cross, where they will be cured of their malady.

Masimo Pitau, in his excellent work on the stone fortress-like astronomical observatories in his native Sardinia, called Nuraghi, has noticed that these are often called after a special thermal or mineral spring, over which they were founded. Many churches have been built on the ruins of these Nuraghi, and employ their ancient well as a source of holy water. There is a certain tradition that in one of these churches, this water compels its drinkers to tell the truth; and many a suspected person has been taken there, and unwittingly confessed to his crime. The ancients were fascinated with the different efficacy of local waters which seemed to vary as much as the different tastes of the same grape-stock when it is transplanted in various climates or environments. There is no doubt that the different mineral formations that water flows through will taint and formulate the water in a very special way. But for the purposes of this inquiry, we would like to consider only the force and effect of underground water *upon the life above.* The different influences are due to the particular arrangement, number, size, and twisting of the individual water spirals, and these are depicted at Gavrinis and Newgrange as guide maps to the subterranean forces.

Underwood mentions that in the course of his investigations of water-divining that the force seemed to oscillate in accordance with the phases and rising of the moon, and positions of the sun. It is our contention that the ancients founded their sites in accordance with these underground water patterns, whose distinctive convolutions they were able to characterize for a special use, and, whose force and influence, in close attendance with astronomical forces they used to heighten their experience of religious ceremonies. Also, they employed these water forces to magnify their judgments during public assemblies, and to increase their sensory perceptions in scientific observations, or philosophical contemplations.

It is also easy to imagine that music and dancing helped to heighten and express the mystic interplay of earth, water, mankind, and the heavens above. I would guess that the so-called Irish fairy music and the chants of the Native Americans were the accompaniment of such mystic cosmic ceremonies.

For these reasons, the detection and use of these underground water emanations became a very important part of the ancient worldview. In their philosophy they considered themselves to be naturalists, who closely inspected everything around them upon land, upon the oceans, and in the heavens. Therefore, it would seem to be an abomination to destroy, tamper with, or change the courses of these ancient walls or holy sites given the painstaking efforts of the ancient natural scientists, who so carefully surveyed the countryside and fashioned a stone-built grid upon its features. They did this in the name of a natural science to aid in the celebration of the land, the stars, and their lives. We can only wonder if this careful systemization led to an ordered and tranquil appreciation of all things, which resulted in a society at peace with itself, its neighbors, and its environment. One wonders if such a purposeful and perceptible ordering of nature could have created a semi-paradise here on earth, reminiscent of the Golden Age?

As with all things of great beauty; there is always the chance of misuse and violation. The special captivation of the balance of heavenly, human, and underground water forces may have prompted some individuals to hedonistically play at the control of these mystic forces. There is always a very fine line of intention between a cosmic religious ceremony and blatant wizardry.

We have spoken of the worldwide practice of the reuse of ancient sites: pyramids built over and upon older megalithic temples, new facings placed upon older structures, churches placed in ancient holy precincts. This was all done in appreciation of the special water influences present at these sites. Could the combination of astrological and water forces have served to facilitate moving heavy stones? Could water forces also assist in the stability of these stones, by helping to keep them in place over a great duration of time and seismic disturbances?

Archaeologists and engineers have had difficulties explaining how some of the more ancient core structures could have been built of megalithic stone blocks weighing more than 600 tons. There is even more difficulty in explaining how monoliths of such weight could be carefully fitted together with such remarkable precision. In our modern world, there are few cranes that could even lift such stones. None of these cranes could align such massive stones.

I believe that the ancients utilized the special power of these water spirals to raise and align these great stones. And naturally, they utilized the powers of the sun, moon, and planets acting in unison with the water forces, to compound the levitation forces. In addition, it seems that they used music and special chants, producing specific harmonious sound wavelengths *to activate* the stones, or the water molecules within them. And this could only be done while the stones were on site, and placed in between the field of influence of the springs and that of the sun, moon, and stars.

Finally, we need to consider that nature is the ultimate teacher of mankind. Certain groupings of water spirals actually demarcate sacred propositions of geometry. I believe that Newgrange in Ireland is conformed upon water spirals that depict the Golden Mean Proportion of *Phi* in geometry. It was for this reason that Newgrange was honored as a holy place for such a long period of time, and by such diverse groups of invaders.

I also feel that the Great Pyramids of Giza somehow have something to do with the direction of Jerusalem. I imagine that the plateau of Giza contains some particularly rare water spirals in geometric arrangements exhibiting sacred mathematical proportions. And, these geographic-aquatic configurations were demarcated by very ancient stone buildings which existed long before the constructions of the Pyramids were superimposed upon this most ancient holy site. There are also some interesting findings about the geometric form of the Giza plateau available from Morphvs of the AIWAZ Institute of Slovenia.

Also, for those who doubt the special power of water forces, I would like to remind them of the words of Patrick Abbott in his *Natural Disasters*, when he remarks that just because water is so common on our planet that does not mean that it is not an unusual element, which acts quite differently than most substances. To cite just one example, water expands when it freezes—while most other things shrink.

Finally, we must understand the motivation of the ancient people to honor these special water-navels on a worldwide basis. These special water-knots are created by star groupings within our galaxy branding their influence upon the receptive clay. Our earth is therefore a complete model microcosm of our galaxy. Hence, these places are holy places where there is a great possibility of establishing communication with the Divine.

The motivation behind all this extreme reverence of natural places and natural science is the overwhelming desire to stay in touch with the Almighty. It is all about communication with God. Therefore, the measurement and correct estimation of cosmic cycles, astronomical positions of the sun, moon, and planets are the keys to establishing the precise avenues of Divine communication.

Throughout the world, researchers continually express surprise at the elaborate and precise observatories and stone formations used by ancient people to mark the Vernal Equinox and the other cardinal points. It is remarkable how accurate a simple scratched line on a stone can serve this purpose. But, what we do not realize is that the ancients did not just wish to recognize the cardinal points for agricultural purposes. They wanted to know the exact astronomical position of the cycles within the zodiac, so that they could perform the correct and perfect ceremony in accordance with the revelation that took place during that cosmic era.

Therefore, an ancient place is not just about underground water and astronomy; it is also about history, time, and revelation.

PART VII:

REVELATION: THE MOST IMPORTANT SCIENTIFIC FACT

Introduction

In the cosmological philosophy of the ancients, *religion will determine the key piece of scientific information.* Our most careful observation cannot determine the specifics of time and its correspondence to global geography as well as the actual act of divine revelation. God sends messengers to us at the end of cosmic cycles to tell us about his wishes for the future cycle. The place and time of the appearance of these messengers are the most important scientific facts.

It is for the above reason that technologically advanced communities have successfully and continually adopted the principle of the priest/ scientist. Life is dualistic, a combination of material and spirit. Ultimate wisdom can only be achieved through the study of the laws of nature and the laws of the divine.

We have gone to great lengths to establish an ancient historical and cultural context. History and culture is really the story of the divine interaction with the world. Natural science uses theories based upon long-term observation. History is the foundation and edifice upon which long-term observation and its subsequent theories are arranged.

The priests of religion use their art to certify the authenticity of the divine messengers. This is not something that they can achieve independently without close cooperation with astronomers and historians who establish that the time and context are near to the end of a cosmic cycle, and that it is appropriate for a divine messenger to appear.

We can estimate the Precession of the Vernal Equinoxes by the use of sighting stones and a few generations of observation. But we cannot measure and precisely observe the millions of years of Galactic Progression. The Revelation of these messengers defines a specific geography upon our globe which is congruent with Time and the heavens.

For example: the birth of the Messiah in Bethlehem, and His trial and agony in Jerusalem, is the most important fact in all of science. The reason for this is because these events define Time and Place upon our earth relative to our position within our galaxy. In other words, they define the correct time of the Galactic Cycle.

And to review again, these events mark a specific geography on our globe, which is the Place in which that specific Time is physically embodied. Revelation reminds us of God's continuing love and care for each of us and His creation.

The correct information of Place and Time are the ultimate scientific coordinates necessary to all studies of climate and the physical development of the planet—now, in the past, and in the future. These coordinates are the key to investigating the slow dissemination of culture, and the more pressing advance of civilization. These coordinates will serve as the outline for the studies of anthropology, archaeology, and geology. *This is, indeed, the information that the world and science has been waiting for!*

It is the same type of information that the minds of the ancients gleaned from their lesser revelations. This information, derived from religion, became the basis of ancient science and cosmology. The thoughts of the ancient priest/scientist cannot be understood without an appreciation of this system of cosmic time and global geography.

The Magi, or astrologers, as they are sometimes called, followed a wandering star to the place where the Messiah was to be born. There is no doubt that there was a significant planetary configuration, or wandering star, associated with this holy visitation. What that configuration was is not important to our discussion here. What is vital to the comprehension of this event—is that the Vernal Equinox in its Precessional Cycle demarcated the first point of the zodiac sign Aries, the sign of the Ram. This point is to be understood as the part of Aries that is next to the sign of Pisces.

The mythology surrounding the Messiah is repeatedly associated with the Lamb, the Wrath of the Lamb, and the Fish of Pisces.

It must be understood that the demarcation of the sign of Aries as the point of the Vernal Equinox is a very important fact in the cosmic determination of the Revelation—but it is by no means the ultimate factor. Let us say that the Vernal Equinox is the minute hand of the cosmic clock. But, since it spins around every 25,920 years, it is not enough of a determinant to produce such a great cosmic event as the appearance of the Messiah.

There is a much greater cycle which revolves counterclockwise to the Precessional Cycle. It is like the hour hand of the cosmic clock, which comprehends the many millions of years that our planet has been in existence, as a member of our solar system as it journeys around the center of our Milky Way Galaxy.

From our perspective of the earth, the advance of this Galactic Cycle would show that it had just finished that portion of the galaxy which we see as Pisces. And it had just entered into the first degrees of Aries *at the very time* of Revelation. The two cycles, which travel in counter directions, intersected and crossed each other at the precise moment of the Crucifixion.

This supreme coincidence of intersection produced a window of Divine Communication with the world. If we can appreciate the uniqueness of this event, in respect to the devolution of all time, the majesty of these events must impress us with awe. The form of the ancient Irish Crosses, with their circling ring of cosmic time, prominently crossed by stone, shows their anticipation of this most sublime universal event.

Such is our explanation of Time, as it was understood by the ancient mind.

Let us review again. The birth and death of Jesus not only took place in Time, but was realized in a specific geography on earth. And the ancients would have concluded that if this event was the ultimate realization of Time, expressed as the celestial geography of the first point of Aries, then, the earthly geography of the Revelation, which is Jerusalem, *must* also be the global and geographical expression of Aries. That is, Time is expressed as global geography.

The ability to divide the globe into twelve fields, corresponding to the celestial zodiac, with Jerusalem as the first point of Aries, opens the door to a wide range of scientific speculation. First, let us look at the correspondences:

Europe and Africa .... Pisces
West Africa, Spain, Ireland, and England .... Aquarius
Brazil and Greenland .... Capricorn
South America, Eastern United States .... Sagittarius
Mexico, Canada, Middle United States .... Scorpio
Northern California and Alaska .... Libra
Pacific Ocean.. Virgo
Eastern Siberia .... Leo
Australia, China and Japan .... Cancer
Southeast Asia, Mid-China .... Gemini
India and the Indian Ocean .... Taurus
Jerusalem, Saudi Arabia and Russia........................... Aries

We notice that what the astrologers call the dry and arid triangle of Taurus, Virgo, and Capricorn dominates the great oceans of the world: the Indian, the Pacific, and the Atlantic.

We notice the moist triangle of Cancer, Pisces, and Scorpio rules over the great deserts like Australia, the Sahara, and the deserts of the southwestern United States.

We also notice that if we are to look at a globe with Jerusalem in the center (that is, an Azimuth projection), that this perspective comprehends Africa, all of Asia, and all of Europe, while, diametrically opposite there is almost no land at all, but mostly ocean.

The central position of Jerusalem is a unique expression of all the astronomical cycles and forces. Jerusalem is also the ultimate expression of culture, science, and religion. The ancients would have recognized that *the earthly city of Jerusalem has become the heavenly city of Jerusalem!* It behooves us to recognize the three major religions which have historically chosen this locality. Let this be a place of peace, and forever dedicated to research into true knowledge and science.

Finally, the crossing-over and intersection of the Vernal and Galactic Cycles always produces momentous changes in human society. This is because the Cycle of Civilization is crossing the Cycle of Culture. As there is a war and a confrontation in heaven there is, likewise, a great upheaval here on earth. All the old beliefs and sacred images are shattered and thrown from their pedestals. A New Age is born and change is the theme of the new cosmic day.

Chapter 1

The Expectation of the Coming of the Messiah

Theodor Hopfner in his excellent work *Uber Isis und Osiris* tells us that the Mediterranean and the Near East was alive with prophecy and the expectation of the Coming of the Messiah. There was a deep conviction of belief in this great forthcoming cosmic event that cannot be understated. The wars and the historical events of that epoch have disturbed the wealth of worldwide prophecies which predicted the Advent of the New Savior.

The reasons for this overwhelming expectation were based on astronomy and cosmology. These sciences observed that the Precessional Cycle of Aries was coming to an end, and would move on into Pisces. This phenomenon alone would produce absolute changes in the significance of religious cults, and promote the need for new heroes, demi-gods, and rituals more appropriate to a new cosmic time. Also, the cosmological shift in Precession would give priority to a new city and nation which would assume the mantle of the power of civilization within the world.

Schwaller de Lubicz (*Sacred Science*, p. 117) confirms this in saying,

> An epoch of such destruction, between the ending and the beginning of a time, can only be explained in the light of similar

crises. The existence of precisely such a period is observed at the end of the Precessional epoch of Taurus [the Eighth to the Tenth Dynasties], as well as at the end of the epoch of Aries, at the moment of passage into the Christian era; and again we see the beginning of an identical crisis during the present epoch of passage from Pisces to Aquarius.

Schwaller de Lubicz continues with this same discussion in the next sentence to say, "The same symptoms characterize them: a democratization that casts into oblivion the achievements from the time of the kings and repudiates a religious metaphysics; the social disorder, moreover, is accompanied by climatological and telluric disturbances."

Schwaller de Lubicz intelligently appreciates the crisis of change—due to this one astronomical cycle quitting one zodiac sign and entering into another. However, he does not exhibit an awareness of any other or greater cosmic cycle. For, this Precessional changeover was not the only thing happening astronomically. At the precise moment of the Precessional change from Aries to Pisces, a momentous changeover of the Galactic Cycle was occurring simultaneously as our solar system was crossing over from Pisces into Aries—an event of the highest and most sacred order!

What had occurred was an event—millions of years in the making—namely, the Cycle of Culture, in direct confrontation to Cycle of Civilization, all happening exactly upon the boundary of Pisces and Aries.

It is because of the clash of these two astronomical cycles that everything changed in the world. All the ancient idols fell from their pedestals; the Great Pan was dead; the gods fell to earth from their thrones in Olympus; the mysteries and incantations no longer held their charms; the stones would not move to the sounds of music and dancing.

Most people and nations were disappointed in the fulfillment of their expectations. They thought a great king of immense power and authority would come to unite and rule the earth in peace and prosperity. This did not happen. On the contrary, there came wars and dispersion; and an end to traditions and homeland!

But, what we must realize is that the cosmologers were correct. The great astronomical crossing had produced a new world order.

Jerusalem became the Holy Place of three of the world's great religions: Hebrew, Christian, and Islam. Curiously, these share many of the same traditions, prophets, and holy sites. These three religions are partners in the development of the New World Theme. This theme will develop over long periods of time. We see the worldwide evangelization of the globe. We also see the worldwide dispersion of the Jews to many countries where they have prospered and enjoy immense influence, political power, and control of information and media. We see the spread of Islam worldwide to the Far East and the West.

The conquest of Spain by the Moors serves as a special preview of the interaction of these faiths. Here in Spain; Christianity, Judaism, and Islam co-existed for a time of mutual respect and appreciation. It should be noticed that this union promoted a spectacular advancement in philosophy, art, classical literature, and science, which was only possible because of this unique cultural exchange.

There is good and evil in the world. Everything under the sun has a pure and cultural side. On the other hand, everything also has a pragmatic, self-fulfilling, monetary, and power-driven visage. This duality is a consequence of the two astronomical cycles: the Galactic Cycle of Culture, and the Precessional Cycle of Civilization. Heraclitus has taught us that *War is the mother and father of all things.* This so-called war is just how nature works. If the world was run on cultural principles—it would be too staid and complacent. If the world was run purely on civil and political principles—it would be too selfish and domineering.

All religions agree about God. What they disagree about is the priority of their national prophets. Religion is the vehicle of our manifest connection with the Eternal God. But, religion also operates in the context of temporal and historical development. Therefore, we cannot ever discount the revelation and religious experience of other nations. If we deny aspects of other religions, we take away from the completeness of our own religious perception. Every religion will fulfill its place in the course of history and time.

The Carpenter's Son

Schwaller de Lubicz in his *Sacred Science* (p. 240) covers a very unusual subject called qualitative exultation, which "refers to a kind of spiritualization of the thing's characteristic quality." Figure 49, a botanical bas-relief in the so-called Garden of Thothmes III, shows a new plant with its flower emerging from the main flower of the parent plant.

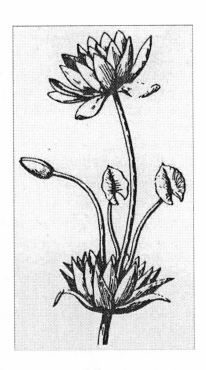

The Egyptians always investigated any anomalies in nature and humankind, thinking they might lead them to some higher truth. I do not know if this has anything to do with our investigation, other than to convince us that under certain conditions all things are possible in nature and the cosmos. These are not super-natural events. They are natural events, which only occur after very long intervals of time, and under specific cosmic relationships of different astronomical cycles. Like the one-time blossoming of certain plants and cacti, these events are rare in time, but quite natural.

We would like to consider some special matters that are connected with the person of Christ.

1. It is said that Christ was born of a *virgin* birth by his mother, Mary. According to ancient Atlantic traditions, her own mother, Anna, had likewise conceived her daughter in a virgin state, through the power of the Holy Spirit. The Egyptians, who were supreme naturalists, firmly believed in the

possibility of insemination by light and spirit. Their proof was the creation of the Apis bull by the means of a cosmic beam of light (though some have interpreted this as a flash of lightening). According to St. Matthew (ch. 1):

> *". . . behold, the angel of the Lord appeared unto him*
> *in a dream, saying, Joseph, thou son of David, fear not*
> *to take unto thee Mary thy wife: for that which is*
> *conceived in her is of the Holy Ghost.*
> *. . . that it might be fulfilled which was spoken of the Lord*
> *by the prophet, saying,*
> *Behold, a virgin shall be with child,*
> *And shall bring forth a son, and they shall call his name*
> *Emmanuel, . . . God is with us."*

I truly love the simple beauty of this passage of St. Matthew. I do, in a fashion, distrust the Britannic tradition of a generation to generation virgin birth. One might imagine that the laws of nature, being forever balanced, would prescribe that the special circumstances of one birth might bring about sterile consequences of the next. Therefore, dual virginity or the fatherhood of Christ would be negated in the natural order of things.

There is a German Chant of the 15th century:

> *Lo, how a rose e'er blooming, from tender stem has sprung;*
> *Of Jessie's linage coming, as those of old have sung!*

How can a rose be forever blooming, and then spring from a branch? This is mixing the supernatural and the natural. The Rose Cross is the Rosicrucian symbol, because the rose is Mary, the Mother of God. But the rose is also the symbol of geometry, the heavens and God. The meaning of the ever-blooming rose is God continually reestablishing His connection with man. We have been taught to believe that because God is all powerful, that this connection is one sided. You must learn to believe that our love, patience, and prayers drive the motion of the universe. Our part in the higher development of God's plan is crucial. Our successful partnership with Him illuminates the radiance of His creation

2. Jesus was able to restore sight to the blind, raise the dead, cure innumerable ailments and disease, drive out evil spirits, walk on water, multiply loaves and fishes, change water into wine, and perform numerous other miracles. He was in essence All Powerful, *Pantocrator*, and could do all things. These are attributes of God. Yet, he purposefully chose never to use his power against the religious or civil authority. This would have been unfair and opposed to his purpose, which was to convert the hearts and minds of his adversaries. He wished to show humanity how to love his Father and their fellow man. In this he proves himself to be the true god-man, and the incarnation of the Holy Logos, the word of reason. He must allow himself to be humiliated and spat upon; to prove his human nature. He *never* uses his power in any act which would lead to his self-fulfillment or aggrandizement. He never abuses his power. Indeed, we rarely hear of Christ commanding some one to do a thing. He is not a ruler or a commander of the political world of civilizations and nations. He is truly God, whose spirit resides upon the higher plane of culture and sanctity.

Many refused to believe in him because of this unimaginable humility. Because they expected a demi-god or a powerful king, they never realized the rare and extraordinary cosmic forces in play which produced this special commingling of human and divine nature.

3. Everyone knows of the symbolism surrounding the Christ. The Gospel of St. John reports that when John the Baptist sees him he hails, "Behold the Lamb of God, which taketh away the sins of the world!" The Book of Revelation likewise proclaims, "Worthy is the Lamb that was slain" Christ is a lamb in the context of his revelation. Consider, however, his position as judge of this world; and *beware of the Wrath of the Lamb!*

Some of his miracles are in the context of fishes, which he catches and multiplies at his will. Many inquirers have seen the astronomical symbolism of reference to Aries, the ram; and Pisces, the fishes. And this naturally relates to the dual crossing from one house of the zodiac to another. Yet, we should realize that the Cultural and Galactic crossing into Aries is of principal interest. For the Book of Revelation refers to Christ primarily under the name of the Lamb. For those who understand, it says in the same work, "I am Alpha and Omega, the First and the Last." In astrology, Aries is the head, while Pisces is the feet—the beginning and the end of the zodiac. Two of the major events of his story are the baptism of his head, and the anointing of his feet by Mary Magdalene. Jesus also washes the feet of the disciples.

4. There is no doubt that Christ has a sophisticated organization of disciples, propagandists, and evangelists. Yet, how did these simple and common people manage to bring a new religion to life in the world? The rapid introduction of a new religion is one of the greatest of all the miracles. Jesus never discloses his own name or who he is. Rather, he asks others, "Who do they, or you, say I am?" In St. Mark, He has purged a man of an unclean spirit, which cries out, "I know thee, who thou art, the Holy One of God!"

5. One of the esoteric symbols of Christ is that he is the carpenter's son. In religious art, Joseph, his stepfather, carries the hammer and the carpenter's square. This shows that his stepfather represents the true father, the Holy Spirit, who makes and designs all things. In making the sign of the Cross, Christians first touch their head (Aries, the exaltation of the Sun) and say, "In the name of the Father." Then they touch below their belly by the intestines (Virgo, the sign of the Virgin and the exaltation of Mercury) saying, "and of the Son." Then they touch both shoulders (Gemini, the house of Mercury) saying, "and of the Holy Spirit, Amen."

Christ says that if you destroy this temple, in three days he will raise it up again. Our Lord refers to his own body, while his listeners think he is speaking of the Temple in Jerusalem. Schwaller de Lubicz in his *The Temple in Man* shows how the Temple of Luxor is designed in the proportions of the human body. No doubt he got this idea from the above saying of Christ. The point is that the temple, the human body, and the universe, are one unity.

Schwaller de Lubicz speaks (p. 143) of the unusual symbolism of the carpenter's ax in Egyptian hieroglyphic titles. One of the many distinguishing titles of the great sage, Hesy, of the Third Dynasty is Carpenter of the Royal Science. Another high personage of the court of Horus Den, fifth king of the First Dynasty, bears the title, "Carpenter and Mason of the Golden Palace." These are personages of high learning and wisdom. Yet, they are distinguished as carpenter. In the Catholic Religion, the Pope is called the Chief bridge-builder, the Pontifex Maximus.

6. Christ is crucified, and dies in the spring—during the Vernal Equinox—at the precise moment of the dual crossing. In addition, He was conceived during the Vernal Equinox. In some countries in South America, the cross is a holy sign of the wind, and perhaps; this is representative of the Holy Spirit. The cross is the symbol of the exact cosmic point in time, of the astronomical dual crossing. The famous and unique Irish crosses, with their cosmic circle around the cross arms, seem best to represent this symbolism and prophecy of the coming of the Messiah.

7. Christ is born during the winter solstice. This is the rebirth of the sun. His crucifixion sign of Aries is the exaltation of the sun. It is also the house of Mars, the angel or messenger of war. While Christ is the spirit of personal and inner peace, some of his statements are quite martial. He speaks of the contentions within families, and that He has not come to bring peace to the world, but rather fire, wars, destruction, and poverty.

Because part of the character of Christ comes from the Precessional Cycle crossing over from Aries to Pisces, we must realize that the Precessional Cycle controls the advance of civilization, which necessitates empires and wars. Christ will not bring us this peace, because it is contrary to the natural order of the rise and fall of civilizations. Christ will bring us His Peace, which is part of the Galactic Cycle of Culture and Science. This Peace is everlasting and pure—and even war, pestilence, and disaster cannot disturb its heavenly form.

8. In Luke 21, it says that some spoke of the temple, how it was adorned with goodly stones and gifts. Here, Christ speaks as a prophet, because he knows that a new cosmic age is about to come forward. Interestingly, Christ also speaks as a natural philosopher and scientist when he recounts the probability of natural disasters, "The days will come, in which there shall not be left one stone upon another that shall not be thrown down . . . Nation shall rise against nation, and kingdom against kingdom. And great earthquakes shall be in divers places, and famines, and pestilences."

9. Jesus is the judge of the living and the dead. He fulfills the prophetic example of Dionysus, as Lord of the Underworld. Also, He is Osiris, as *Chenti-Amentiu,* the first of the Westerners (those who have gone to the Underworld and have risen again). He is like Harpocrates, the son of Isis and the murdered Osiris. He has come forth again, as the Holy Word, to honor all the true prophets who spoke the Word of God but who were slain by the hand of man.

10. The Persian Magi, the so-called Three Kings, traveled with their gifts of gold, frankincense, and myrrh to worship the newborn cosmic king. They were prompted by a revelation of the ancient astrologer, Zarathustra, who had foreseen the coming of the Messiah and the fulfillment of the cosmic cycles.

11. The majority of ancient religions feature an omnipotent deity. Even in the Eastern Orthodox Faith we meet the all-powerful, *Christ Pantocrator.* Yet, Christ is not a Precessional demi-god of minor cycles. He is the Son of the Universe. His dual-nature is as diverse as culture and civilization. He is a God whose ways we do not understand. He is so grand that His strength is in His weakness. His grandness is in his humility. Egyptian lore prophesizes of the future triumph of Horus over Seth. Christ's triumphant entrance into Jerusalem is upon the humble back of the donkey. There is a multiplicity of meaning contained in this procession. One aspect is that the donkey is the totem animal of Seth.

12. Most important of all is the mystical formula adopted by the early church fathers who specified that the person of Christ was "Begotten, not made." That is to say, that Christ was a totally natural event of creation. He was not an artificial thought or action of God, outside of the development of nature within the course of time. Christ was with God in the beginning, now, and at the end of time

The outrageous and horrendous flagellation of Christ is beyond our comprehension. It is chilling to understand that everything that Christ suffered, from the Crown of Thorns to the Nails through His Hands, were the very most excruciating forms of human punishment and based upon the most sensitive areas of the body. God has given us the blood-offering to which we stand indebted for all our generations. He cares for us, feeds us, and is even beaten and dies for our sins.

This bruised, beaten, and bloodied image shows the character of the material form of the New Savior. Everything about Him is full of contradiction in our human eyes and limited understanding. He is weak and ineffectual in His lifetime—yet His effect is cosmic. He is the God of Love whom the world Hated. He is truly a god of contradictions,

> I am not come to bring peace into the world, but to throw fire upon it—Let the dead bury the dead [for this is not the land of the living, but of those who die]—you are the salt of the earth, but if the salt has lost its flavor, where with shall it be salted?—Those are they who have washed their garments *white* in the blood of the Lamb.

How can blood make a garment clean and white? How can God be beaten by lesser creatures? The contradiction becomes the truth—the truth of a new age.

As the true God, we can only know Him sometimes in these contradictions. Many of the great programs to convert native people to Christianity resulted in the most brutal, heinous, and self-serving examples of barbarity, cruelty, and disrespect that the world has ever seen. Yet God appears in the eyes of the lost child who for the first time sees their mother and father again.

H. G. Wells, who by his own admission was not a Christian, called Christ the Greatest of all Men. His criterion was: that person, that by his words and example had prompted humanity to think the most profoundly—and thereby changed the world forever.

Lastly, the Hebrew Scriptures are vital to the prophecy of the Coming of The Christ. Abraham takes his only son, Isaac, to be sacrificed. This Isaac, like Christ, carries the wood upon which the sacrifice is to be performed. Abraham represents humanity. God asks him if he, on behalf of humanity, will perform the ultimate sacrifice of his only son. This is the covenant with Abraham: if he will do this, God will do the same. Namely, in the future, God will also sacrifice his only son. Therefore, there will be a union between the divine and the human flesh in the person of Christ.

Christ also says that God can raise up these stones to become the children of Abraham. I would assume that God can also raise-up stones to be the children of Christ. Let no human sanctify himself because he belongs to the Jews, the Christians, the Moslems, the Buddhists, or any other religion or sect. All are important in the development of the history of the cosmos, and in the eyes of the Creator.

Also, there are records in different nations of Christ living and appearing among them. The message of Christ is presented to all the nations of the earth. For cosmological reasons, the gospels are first preached in Jerusalem, and from there, outward to all the nations of the world.

Because the cosmic cycles touch every corner of the globe; we must conclude that all nations participate in the formation of Culture. And, therefore, we all share a common religion through the messages of all the prophets, who are the speakers for the Holy Spirit of God. This ought to be our highest thinking about these matters of God.

But, we must caution against those who would try to unify all religions under one person or sect, for such a goal would necessarily be subject to politics and corruption. The fervent belief in one's own family, national, or ethnic prophets is the most wholesome, natural, and secure vehicle of preserving the message of God over vast periods of time.

It is righteous for us to appreciate the greatest gift of God's love by sacrificing His only Son to redeem his creation. In recognition, all the nations of the world should revere and honor Jerusalem as the Seat of Revelation, Culture, and Science.

Chapter 2

The Circular Stone Zodiac of Dendera

Sir Norman Lockyer in his *The Dawn of Astronomy*, written at the turn of the century, was one of the great pioneers who carefully demonstrated that Stonehenge and the temples of Egypt had been aligned to the sun and particular stars. He also concluded that the ancients were capable of calculating the length of the year and the Precession of the Equinoxes to the greatest degree of accuracy.

So, we must understand that the study of the astronomical knowledge of ancient people is only about 100 years old. This basically means that we really know almost nothing at all about this subject!

Schwaller de Lubicz's final statement on Precession is (*Sacred Science*, p. 179),

> It has now been fully documented that the basis of the religious cult changed coincidentally with the astronomical phases of the precession of the equinoxes. The possibility that the ancient Egyptians might have possessed knowledge concerning precessional cycles had been hitherto excluded. Herewith the reasons for the

change of the cult of Hap the Bull into that of Amon the Ram stands clarified.

Sicilus (I.12) reports, "For the Egyptians consider Ocean to be their river Nile, on which also their gods were born." The first Atlantic colonists who came to Egypt naturally called the great river after the name of their homeland, just as the Greeks had brought the name Triton to their new homeland. I believe that these Oceanic Egyptians went a step higher than just recognizing the phenomena of Precession. I believe that the Circular Zodiac of Dendera was their show-piece, created to demonstrate that the Galactic Progression of our solar system was well-known to the ancients.

The Circular Zodiac of Dendera is so particularly fetching in its proportional design that one must believe that it represents the ultimate *piece de resistance* of the ancient cosmologers. In this creation of graceful workmanship, they were undoubtedly trying to disclose the entire treasure of their astronomical science.

Below, I would like to list some of my observations on this zodiac:

1. The circle is supported by twelve Heaven-Holders. Four of the supporters are female goddesses. And, four are pairs of falcon or hawk-headed gods whose forearms and hands overlap to demarcate different segments of the circle. This is a very clever way of combining the number eight of the geographic-cartographic system with the number twelve of the astronomical system. Brown, in his *The Story of Maps,* reports that there are some rare examples of compass roses which are divided into twelve parts of a circle, instead of the usual eight.

Moustafa Gadalla in his *Egyptian Divinities* (p. 38) says that,

> Egyptian texts state that Nun—the precreation Chaos—possessed characteristics that were identified with four pairs of primordial powers. Each pair represents the primeval dual-gender twins—the masculine and feminine aspects. The four pairs are equivalent to the four forces of the universe . . . The manifestation of creation in eight terms [Ogdad] is expressed in all four Ancient Egyptian cosmological centers.

He also says that Nun is the cosmic ocean. One should notice that the symbol for water appears on the top and bottom borders of the Dendera zodiac.

2. Herodotus has commented that the Egyptians seem to do things contrary to the way of other nations. The viewpoint of the actual heavens is as if you were an observer looking up at the sky. We, however, usually like to draw things so that we can look down on them in order to study them more closely. It is of the utmost importance to notice that the direction in which the vast majority of the figures of the disc of the zodiac are walking, or facing, is counterclockwise. This counterclockwise direction is the direction of the Cycle of the Precession of the Vernal Equinoxes. One would think that these figures should be facing in the direction of the annular course of the sun and the seasons of the year (clockwise direction). Because

the special festivals that mankind celebrates are during the course of the year.

3. It is extremely important to recognize that if we draw a line between Aries and Pisces from the center of the circle and then construct a right-angle cross through the center of the circle, that this cross line through the latter portion of Gemini and Sagittarius divides the 36 decan figures on the rim of the circle; so that 71.4% of them are on the Aries/Pisces side. That is, 21 of the 36 total figures are in the hemisphere around Aries/Pisces. I must think that the cosmologers are telling us that the Aries/Pisces hemisphere reflects the *current* Galactic Time.

4. The symbolic decan figures which appear under Aries/Pisces are significant. The headless and armless man sitting upon a golden mean throne could be prophetic of John the Baptist, who was beheaded. John was also a messenger, like Hermes (patron of the arms). A headless man also appears on the ancient Irish crosses. Other decan figures in this region are a hawk-headed god, and the youth, Harpocrates, sitting upon a lotus flower. The lotus has immense cultural significance (see Schwaller de Lubicz). To the right of the headless man is a Janus-like figure of rams' heads facing in both directions, which is a certain sign of a vital demarcation (connects to the navel of the giant outstretched Hathor). The Linear Zodiac at Dendera also shows Harpocrates under Aries, and the Ibis-headed god, Thoth, under Pisces.

5. Outside of the circle of the constellations and decan figures; and below Aries/Pisces are two falcon-headed Heaven-Holders, below whom there is a broad band of hieroglyphs. Below all this appears the gigantic image of the outstretched Heaven Goddess, Hathor. Her generative organs, from which the Egyptians say that the sun is born, are directly below Aries/Pisces. The position of the birth canal for the emergence of the sun in the region of Pisces/Aries is the cosmologer's special design in order to show the precise time of the Galactic Cycle. Furthermore, it will be noticed that at right angles to Pisces/Aries are Gemini/Cancer in one hemisphere, and Sagitarius/Capricorn in the other, exactly where they appear in the night sky in the foreground of the ocean/river stream of the Milky Way which is denoted outside the squared circle by the chevron zigzag symbols for water, in this case, heavenly water.

I think that the sign of the birth canal, the giant Hathor, and the great band of hieroglyphys present a guidepost from the cosmologers who originated this piece indicating that *this is the Cosmic Time and Position*, read and focus from here.

Looking at the entire presentation as a whole; it appears that the zodiac was created entirely to demonstrate this major theme of cosmology, namely that the Precessional and the Galactic Cycles were about to cross each other in Aries/Pisces. It was done to show that Galactic Time and Place were on the borders of Aries/Pisces, and that if we were to imagine the great recumbent heaven-goddess standing up, she would face in the direction of Galactic Progression!

Let us now see what others have said about the amazingly articulate Dendera Stone. Franz Boll deals with the subject of the Dendera Stone, now in the Louvre, in his work *Sphaera* (Ch. 14). Concerning the origin of some of the figures on the monument, Boll shows that Sagittarius and Capricorn are fashioned after old Babylonian models, and that there are also Egyptianized renderings of Greek figures. He therefore concludes that the work is the "product of mixed cultures."

Boll explains that many have tried to find the principle on which the projection is based, and cites Karl Riel who affirms that it was made after the rules of Alexandrine science. It should be viewed from the meridian of Sirius. Standing underneath the center of the stone and looking up at it— is the same as if one was observing the night sky outside the temple. Riel says it was intended to be a star and feast calendar. However, Latronne, one of the pioneers in examining the work, had already remarked upon the extreme stylization of the upright standing figures which appear like a religious procession. Boll says that this artistic arrangement forces the displacement of some of the constellation figures, notably in the region of Virgo, which harms the exactness of the projection.

Also, Brugsh has demonstrated that the author of the Dendera Stone has included figures of the planets among the constellation figures, and located in the vicinity of the zodiac houses of their exaltations. That is, the planet Mercury as a man-headed deity by Virgo; Saturn as an ox-headed man by Libra; Mars as falcon-headed over Capricorn; Venus with Janus-like double-faces by Pisces; with Jupiter as falcon-headed behind Cancer (these are the so-called houses of the exaltations, or highest power of the planets). Boll's conclusion is that "the circular zodiac of Dendera is a representation of the Sphaera under an astrological viewpoint." I wish Boll had said, "under a cosmological viewpoint." But, in this context, *astrological* and *cosmological* should mean nearly the same thing.

Boll gives a translation of the Arabian text of Abu Masar (848 AD) by Karl Dyroff. Abu Masar reveals the astrological significance of the entire regions of the heavens which rise along with the twelve zodiac signs. He says that the old sages recorded that certain figures (one for every ten degrees or decan of a sign; 3 decans x 12 signs = 36 figures) were thought to be the embodiment of the entire sphaera. Some resemble human and earthly forms, while some are amalgamations of many different things. The sages of the various nations differ concerning the form of these figures, and again some record very ancient figures which for the most part are now forgotten. Abu Masar is concerned that the phenomenon of the Precession of the Vernal Equinoxes requires a timely review of its significance and influence upon these decan figures. Yet, he reports that the Indians, Persians, and Egyptians are adamant that *these figures proclaim the inherent reality* pronounced and transmitted upon the earth by those regions of the heavens near which they appear.

Astrology is based upon the experience of events which repeat themselves, time and again, under the same region of the heavens. Namely, certain regions produce specific themes and individuals when they are indicated by any of the cycles of time. This experience is derived from noticing gifted, prominent, or troublesome individuals in the history of the world whose birth or actions are associated with specific regions of the heavens. It may therefore be supposed that the Dendera Stone is also a historical document, an icon which presents a calendar of time in terms of pictures. Riel has already said that it was a star and feast calendar; and feasts are based upon the commemoration of venerable individuals that have appeared in history.

Schwaller de Lubicz in his *Sacred Science* (p. 103) says that all temples were built according to *"The Book of Foundation composed by Imhotep, son of Ptah* [Third Dynasty], a book descended from heaven to the north of Memphis. The Temple of Dendera, however, followed an even earlier plan namely *a plan recorded in ancient writings dating from the Companions of Horus* [an allusion to prehistory]" (italics mine). Therefore the Temple of Dendera is among the most ancient of all temples. It was restored during the time of the Ptolemys. Some authorities suggest that the round zodiac was carved at that time, though they admit that it is probably a copy of very ancient Egyptian astronomical thought.

Peter Tompkins in his excellent work, *Secrets of the Great Pyramid* (pp. 165–175), says that Maspero pointed out that, "All the Ptolemaic temples and most of the Pharaonic temples have been reconstructed" during the many periods that they were in use. He also writes that it was clear to Lockyer that there had been two temples of Dendera, one dedicated to Hathor, and the other to Isis. Both these deities were heaven goddesses. Again, according to Lockyer, the present temples of Dendera were renovated in Ptolemaic times, but were built upon much older sites.

Tompkins continues to say that Jean Baptiste Biot staked his academic reputation on his analysis of the circular zodiac. He said it represented the skies in Egypt in 700 BC, and that it had probably been copied from older drawings made on papyrus or stone. Lockyer confirmed that the Isis temple had been directed at Sirius in 700 BC, when Sirius rose "cosmically," or in unison with the sun, at the Egyptian New Year. But Lockyer quoted an old inscription which described a temple of Hathor in the time of Khufu (Cheops) in the Fourth Dynasty (which he dated to 3733 BC), "when the star shone into the temple and mingled with the light of her father Ra." In Lockyer's opinion the temple of Dendera may have been rebuilt at least three times. He further hypothesizes that the temple could have been in use as early as 5000 BC.

Tompkins then reports on Schwaller de Lubicz's analysis of the circular zodiac. He says (following Lockyer) that it was indeed carved in Ptolemaic times, but incorporates a palpable demonstration of the Precession of the Equinoxes, as well as three important historical dates.

Schwaller de Lubicz proclaims that the zodiac is in a circle at the center of which is our north pole. This circle is in a square oriented with the walls of the temple, or about 17 degrees east of north. Our north pole is correctly located in the constellation of the Jackal, or Little Bear, as it was at the time when the zodiac was carved, sometime about the 1st century BC. But the zodiac also shows the pole of the ecliptic located in the breast of the Hippopotamus, or the constellation of Draco. He says that the zodiac thus becomes *a calendar going back to remote antiquity.* Later, Stecchini concluded that the ancient Egyptians not only understood the precession of the axis of the earth, but considered the true meridian to be the one passing through the pole of the ecliptic of the solar system. If the Egyptians could determine the pole of the solar system as Stecchini says, that means that they ascribed a definite movement to the entire system. That movement would be Galactic Revolution.

Conclusion

Many of the experts admit that the Circular Stone Zodiac of Dendera may be from extreme antiquity. The temple itself is extremely old and has been remodeled several times.

One avenue of investigation would be to discover important astronomical features which the Egyptians failed to portray. Perhaps in this way we might find out where the inventor of this zodiac is trying to lead future generations who are contemplating his work? Therefore we should try to stay with what the Egyptians have actually portrayed, and also, what they have not portrayed.

First of all; there is no directional indicator pointing directly to the pole of the ecliptic (the pole of the zodiac, which is in the breast of the Hippopotamus).

Therefore, we must ask, why is there no such line? And our answer must be: that the very reason that they do not show this important point is the key to understanding the true theme of their representation. Sometimes the solution to a problem is not to be found in the evidence at hand, but rather, in what should be there, but is missing.

It is apparent that the Egyptians celebrated the movement of the Precession of the Equinoxes. During the course of their history, it is evident that they had changed their predominant cults from the Gemini, to Taurus, to the Ram, because of Precession. While the Egyptians were celebrating the sequence from Gemini, Taurus, to Aries, they did not dismiss the other zodiac signs and their accompanying decan figures from their pantheon of gods and influences. This was because these cults and deities will cyclically reappear into prominence again, in the course of time.

So, in attempting to find the pole of the ecliptic, around which the sun moves through the twelve signs of the zodiac during the year, we could not find any major bisecting lines or other outside indicators. This is very unusual, considering how important the year, its festivals, and its seasons are. Rather, we found this pole by experimentation; namely by asking, "What center of a circle would produce an equitable 30-degree division of the 360 degrees into twelve signs, that each sign would most comfortably fit into each division without too much trespass, or overlap into another zodiac sign?" Thereby, the pole of the ecliptic was found to be in the breast of the Hippopotamus, as Schwaller de Lubicz has suggested. He knew that it was there from other Egyptian texts and expected to find it there. But, he made the mistake of assuming and expecting to find this pole marked in this particular stone zodiac. The only trouble is that this pole is not so marked.

But, again, if we need to find this point by experimentation, it is obvious that the Egyptians did not indicate it. I believe that this very remission is an assertion on their part. They are trying to tell us that it does not really matter where the pole of the ecliptic is stationed, because it moves around considerably during the course of time. Viewed in this light, the Dendera picture represents a more inclusive overview, and a representation of the totality of Egyptian cosmological science. The Egyptian cosmologists wish to show that there are many cosmic cycles represented at one time, here on this stone tablet. And they were not going to show you the pole of any of these cycles—because those poles all move.

In evidence of this, we should look at the supporting members of the entire circle. In the picture, six of the Heaven-Holders are facing clockwise and six of the Heaven-Holders are facing counterclockwise. This seems definitely to show that there are many cycles involved in their cosmology. The daily cycle of the sun and the Precessional Cycle both move counterclockwise. The yearly cycle, and the Cycle of Galactic Progression both move clockwise.

The Egyptians are showing us that Precession is only one of the cycles of the cosmic scheme. They show that the pole of the ecliptic circles around in the semi-permanent vault of the heavens. So, they purposely showed it *without any indications* as to how to find it within the picture!

Again, the giant recumbent Hathor figure, whose generative parts are directly below Aries/Pisces, is indicating the major cosmic theme of the entire representation. Namely, it represents the Expectation of the Coming of the Messiah. As the words of the prophet have sung to us; "Out of Egypt have I called My Son."

Boll had concluded that this stone was in part an astrological representation. He thought this because the planets were shown in the houses of their exaltation, which is the highest position of their powers. Again, this seems to prove that the Egyptians were attempting to show the entire heavens, planets, and cosmic cycles. The only fixed position that they were indicating is that of the most majestic of cycles, the Galactic Position of our solar system directly opposite the genitalia of Hathor, upon the borders of Pisces/Aries.

Finally, we should appreciate The Egyptian's interesting display of cosmic geometry within the bounds of the Zodiac of Dendera. First, we need to quarter the entire square of the circle and Heaven-Holders, and then bisect each one of these quarters in half. And then from that bisection point on the baseline, take a compass whose other point touches the center of the circle. If we then drop a diagonal down again to the baseline, it produces the Golden Mean Proportion. That is where A is to B, as B is to $A + B$. This divine formula is the basis of Egyptian art and architecture. We have already met this divine rule as shown by Leonardo da Vinci in his famous representation of the Vitruvian Man in the circle. We have also shown that it is found as far afield as in the proportions of the Killamery Cross in Ireland.

Therefore, it is not surprising that the span from fingertip to fingertip of each of the Heaven-Holders is exactly equal to A of the Golden Mean Proportion. The height of the line between the knees of the hawk-headed supporters from the baseline of the great square to the rim of the circle of the heavens is also equal to A.

A note of caution must be exercised here, and everywhere, regarding the possibility of distention of photographic images. It would be wise for the scientific community to directly examine this piece in the Louvre in Paris, where it now resides—in order to recheck if all the spans of the arms of the Heaven-Holders are equal. And, if these spans were not equal, it would give us important scientific information regarding the precise Egyptian measurements of our galaxy.

The height, from feet to top of head, of the female Heaven-Supporters is approximately B of the golden section. The radius of the great circle is also close to B, but not quite. We do not wish to be carried away in our zeal for discovery by committing the error of Schwaller de Lubicz, who erroneously connected two particular markers outside of the circle by a straight line.

The circle inscribed upon the apparent path of the sun through the figures of the zodiac appears to be ½ of B. There are many such relationships to be found in the lines and the figures on this piece.

Of all this cosmic geometry, what struck me as the most revealing is the line which passes through the knees of the Heaven-Holders under Sagittarius. The point where the line intersects the circle of the zodiac appears to be exactly the length of A of the Golden Mean. Did the ancients mean to show that our galaxy, and the cycles within it conform to relationships expressed by the Golden Mean?

It is likely that they did. Because in the philosophy of the ancients, the Creative Spirit imposes form upon inert matter of any size by dividing it into the proportions of the Divine Golden Mean.

We must marvel at the artistic ingenuity of these cosmologers in creating a such a beautiful scientific picture of so many dynamic astronomical cycles. The Circular Zodiac of Dendera is the final testament to the beauty and simplicity of Egyptian art and thought.

Chapter 3

The Twelve Regions of Geography and Earthquakes

In another part of this work we suggested that the oceans and the deserts of the globe were an expression of certain regions of the zodiac. These zodiac regions are all different in their character and influence. Our modern age is like a mirror-image of the Tower of Babylon. All the languages of the world are not confused, but rather, destroyed through unification into one major language group. English has nearly become the universal language and Western fashion and trends overwhelm the planet. But less than 200 years ago, every region of the planet had a distinct local, regional, and national style of dress, language, family, tribal, racial, and human anthropological type. Everything was so unique, while now, everything is all the same.

Two hundred years ago, the twelve unique geographies of our globe could express themselves with a unique production of their own soil. We have read in Theophrastus, the eminent Roman horticulturalist, that wine is a product of its region of geography. "Time," says Theophrastus, "has proved this over and over again." You may take a parent vine stock and divide it several times. Then you may plant these offspring in different places of the world. Each new planting will exhibit a special taste, aroma, and color, completely different from its root stock. Wine is the expression of its home soil. Wine is the proof of the diverse character of the twelve geographic zones of the globe.

We have continually said that the first part of Aries is joined with the city of Jerusalem and the region of Palestine. Because the Messiah was born in the Galactic Period of Aries—His birthplace must also be related to Aries.

We have tried to use ancient literature, mythology, astrology, maps, art, and science to demonstrate this point. We will now examine the geographic position of major earthquakes in order to illustrate the coincidence between *heavenly position* and *earthly geography*. We hope to illuminate the proverb, "On earth, as it is in heaven"—verbatim.

It is now 2,005 years after the appearance of the Messiah. The Precession of the Vernal Equinoxes is *now* moving away from Aries and Pisces in the direction toward Aquarius. We have ventured to define the Precessional Cycle and the Galactic Cycle as the minute hand and the hour hand of the Cosmic Clock.

As well, we defined Jerusalem as the true geographic coordinate to the astronomical position of Galactic Time. We intend to use this data in scientific investigation. That is, Galactic Time is on the border of Aries/Pisces which defines Jerusalem as the global geography of Aries/Pisces. The rest of the globe will be laid out in zodiac fields starting from Aries/Pisces being centered upon Jerusalem. For I believe that the astrological forecast of great quakes is possible if you can coordinate earthly geography with heavenly geography (which is another way of saying cosmic time or astronomical position).

The ancients appreciated the correspondence between heaven and earth. L. A. Brown in his *Story of Maps* (p. 34) tells us that the famous Archimedes had a celestial globe of glass with a small terrestrial globe suspended inside it. Hero of Alexandria, the geometer, had a similar glass orb which also surrounded a terrestrial globe.

Diodorus Siculus (I.81) writes,

> For the positions and arrangements of the stars as well as their motions have always been the subject of careful observation among the Egyptians, if anywhere in the world; they have preserved to this day the records concerning each of these stars over an incredible number of years, this subject of study having been zealously

preserved among them from ancient times . . . not infrequently they foretell destructions of the crops . . . and as a result of their long observations they have prior knowledge of *earthquakes* and floods (italics mine).

The reason that no one has been able to duplicate Egyptian prognostication of earthquakes is because—until now—no one had rediscovered their Galactic Cycle and cosmological system. That is, no one had been able to redefine cosmic time and its relation to geography. Let us take a hindsight look at earthquakes, and see if this Egyptian cosmic system can help us.

Earthquakes

Earthquakes are strangely defined. Seismologists measure them in terms of magnitude. Other organizations and individuals tend to qualify them by the amount of damage to human life and architecture that they cause. This tends to cloud the issue and disturb the scientific appreciation of genuine Great Earthquakes, namely those which cause the largest amount of geophysical displacement and upheaval.

Generally speaking, thousands of minor earth tremors occur daily, as part of the natural constitution of our planet. And indeed, some of the historically destructive earthquakes have not been "Great" at all. The calamatous destruction of San Francisco during the 1906 earthquake was more the consequence of the disruption of the water pipes which allowed the city to be engulfed by fire. The fire was the primary cause of the destruction, not the earthquake itself. Indeed, it was reported that when the citizens realized that the ruination of their homes was not covered in their insurance policies, they set fire to their damaged property to reclaim their investment by causes that were covered!

Again, The Loma Prieta, or "World Series" quake of October 17, 1989, exposed flaws in human engineering and building practices, but, this catastrophic occurrence was by no means a "Great Quake." At first, it was reported that the Golden Gate Bridge was down. But actually, a timeworn and distressed metal section of the Bay Bridge had given way. Some un-reinforced brick buildings came crashing down, and an architecturally unstable building collapsed at its ill-supported garage level. Because of the important World Series many people had left their workplace early to watch the game at their home. Thereby, they luckily avoided the collapse of the badly engineered Cypress Freeway, which did indeed claim many lives.

Another tragic example is the December 28, 1908, quake in Messina, Sicily, where 100,000 people died due to the poorly constructed buildings of that time. The point that we are trying to establish is that the investigation of Great Earthquakes must be differentiated from minor earthquakes, even though minor ones may have produced major calamities in terms of human life. We all sympathize with the loss of life in Sicily, which could have been averted by better construction methods, while in the Bay Area of San Francisco the bridge has been mended, the freeway and buildings torn down and replaced, and thousands of potentially weak structures have been retrofitted.

Our concern is to attempt to identify Great Earthquakes in the past which have had a monumental geographical and geophysical impact. Furthermore, had these occurred in populated centers, they would have wrecked devastation, not only upon the weak points of civil infrastructure, but upon the entire surrounding geography. A Great Earthquake would be one that had completely and utterly destroyed a great city or a legendary island like that of Atlantis, or the 100 miles of westward California coastland that anciently plummeted into the ocean in one instance of time.

In the catalogues of historical earthquakes that we have available for review, there are, unfortunately, no true Great Earthquakes, but there appear to be some instances of nearly great earth tremors.

It is our contention that the primary factor in the production of an earthquake is the specific conformation of the planets of our solar system, acting in aspect with the sun and the moon. The total massed relationship of these heavenly bodies to a specific plate, or fault line, of our global geography becomes the final trigger and cause of these events.

Therefore, the proper investigative method is as follows: Construct a simple circular zodiac divided into twelve equal houses. Then, by means of an astronomical ephemeris, plot in the correct positions of the sun, moon, and planets for that particular day and hour. Next, using an atlas, and using Jerusalem as the prime meridian located on the border of Pisces/Aries, locate the geography of the place of the earthquake. Plot the position of the place of the earthquake in relation to the zodiac, which starts with Pisces/Aries directly upon Jerusalem.

Our best candidate for a *near*-Great Quake is the first earthquake of the New Madrid, Missouri, series of quakes that started on December 16, 1811. This quake measured an estimated magnitude of 8.2 on the Richter scale (according to the *U.S. Geological Survey Circular #1083, Responses to Iben Browning's Prediction of a 1990 New Madrid, Missouri, Earthquake; USGPO, 1993*).

The 1811–1812 earthquakes were felt as far away as the Gulf Coast, the Atlantic shore, and the Canadian province of Quebec. The February 1812 event leveled the town of New Madrid and, apparently for a time, reversed the flow of a section of the Mississippi River. It caused widespread surface deformation, including the formation of Reelfoot Lake. It toppled chimneys in Louisville, 250 miles away.

New Madrid, Missouri, is located about 89.5 degrees west longitude, which corresponds to about the first degree of Sagittarius, according to our theory of geographical and celestial coincidence. On that date of December 16, 1811, the sun, moon, and planets constituted a near-direct hit upon that geography:

Astronomical degrees of separation from geography

Sun .... 23 degrees .... Scorpio
Saturn .... 28.5 degrees .... Scorpio
New Madrid .... 1 degree .... Sagittarius
Mercury .... 7 degrees .... Sagittarius
Venus .... 10.5 degrees .... Sagittarius
Moon .... 17 degrees .... Sagittarius
Jupiter .... 2 degrees .... Gemini
(*Jupiter is in opposition to 2 degrees of Sagittarius*)
Mars .... 28.5 degrees .... Capricorn
(*Mars is sextile to the geography and disjunct to the Moon*)
Uranus .... 21 degrees .... Libra
(*disjunct*)
Pluto .... 7 degrees .... Aquarius
(*sextile to the Moon*)

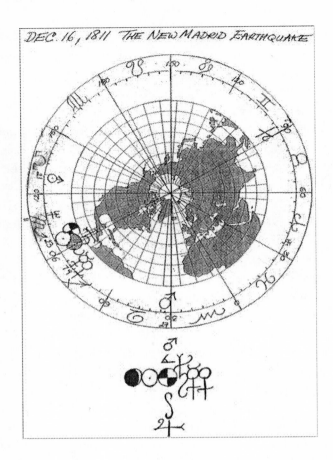

This *coincidence* of celestial conjunctions, alignments, and relationships—*all of which are positioned relative to the geography*—has without a doubt triggered the earthquake. We must notice how the celestial spheres surround the geography in a nearly equidistant pattern, and how they are relatively positioned in respect to one another to execute this kind of leverage. Had they been more precisely related, the extent of the quake would have been more devastating!

There are numerous undeveloped theories about the cause of earthquakes. For the reader's interest one of these is reported by *The U.S. Geological Survey Circular #1083* (p. 4) comments upon the failed 1990 prediction of Iben Browning's suggested earthquake. His hypothesis was that peaks of tidal loading in the solid earth could trigger earthquakes in regions of high tectonic stress. The *U.S.G.S.* (p. 12) replied, "Because high tides occur with each new and full moon, and because about 110 earthquakes greater than magnitude 6 occur each year, there is a significant random chance of occasional major earthquakes roughly coinciding with a high tide."

Our Conclusion

The above demonstration *does not mean* that we can now predict earthquakes. We have demonstrated in another article that astrological prognosis for private individuals is absurd and meaningless, because of the incomprehensible amount of factors which produce a unique individual. In the same way, most earthquakes are individuals, quite unique, and difficult to analyze.

However, from reviewing so many large and near-Great Earthquakes, we feel that we have made some useful general discoveries. These are listed below:

Saturn and Jupiter, when they are related to each other, as well as to the specific geography, seem to play a major role in causing quakes. Mars is also decisive. In truth, though, any planet properly positioned can cause a tremor.

1812. New Madrid: Saturn in conjunction with geography, and in opposition to Jupiter. Mars is quartile to geography.

1886. Charleston: Saturn in opposition to geography to which Jupiter, Moon, and Uranus are quartile.

1906. San Francisco: Jupiter quartile to Saturn quartile to geography. Moon quartile to Mars, and in opposition to geography.

1908. Messina, Italy: Jupiter triangular to Mars who both hold Saturn who is in conjunction with the geography.

1923. Tokyo: Sun, Mars, and Venus apply to Saturn and Mercury which apply (30 degrees) to Jupiter, which is quartile to geography.

1934. Nepal: Jupiter triangular to Saturn, Mars, and Venus which are triangular to geography.

1960. Chile: Saturn and Jupiter are in conjunction with geography to which Mars is quartile with the Moon.

1994. Northridge, CA: Moon is quartile to Sun, Mars, and Venus which apply to Saturn which is quartile to geography.

1989. San Francisco: Saturn applies to the geography while in opposition to Jupiter.

Again, these are only minor individual quakes even though we call them major episodes. They are minor because the *degrees of separation* between the celestial spheres and the geography are too far apart. They are not direct conjunctions, oppositions, or triangularities perfectly related to the geography. Only absolute direct-hits can result in the Great Quakes of supreme devastation which change the face of the regional landscape forever.

Therefore, it will require a genuine Great Quake, where the celestial bodies are nearly congruent with the geographical fault line, to finally prove the scientific validity of astrological cause. Again, we prefer to use the detective's theorem of *what is missing?* Therefore, what did not happen in most earthquakes was—a direct congruency between global geography and celestial phenomena.

Frederic Golden in *The Trembling Earth* reports that migratory birds and animals sense the changes in the earth's magnetic field prior to earthquakes. The Chinese scientist, Chang Heng (78–139 AD) constructed an 8-foot diameter bronze vessel seismograph, which operated with a heavy pendulum and eight dragon heads and eight frog figures. The Portugese, Miguel Tibero Pedegache Brandao Ivo stated emphatically in 1756 that earthquakes were caused by the sun and the moon. Newton, himself, propounded upon the interrelation of the gravitational force of the planets, saying that celestial bodies are bound to each other by their mutual gravity. Their attraction is directly proportional to the masses of their bodies, and inversely proportional to the square of the distance between them. By examining the disturbed layers of the soil of the San Andreas Fault line, Kerry Sieh of Stanford surmised that big quakes would hit San Francisco about every 160 years.

It is of further interest that Peter Tompkins in his *Mysteries of the Mexican Pyramids* (p. 271) reports on Alfred Schlemmer, who had been analyzing the recurrence of large-scale earthquakes around the globe. He theorized repetitive cycles of earthquakes based upon torsional pull on the earth's crust by the sun, moon, and planets. He further postulated that there had been a series of harmoniously designed reflecting pools at the pyramids of Mexico City which had allowed the ancient *Teotihuacanos* to investigate the occurrence of earthquakes around the globe. That is, they had constructed a precision seismograph which would allow them to predict the occurrence of earthquakes on a worldwide basis as well as in their own area.

Chapter 4

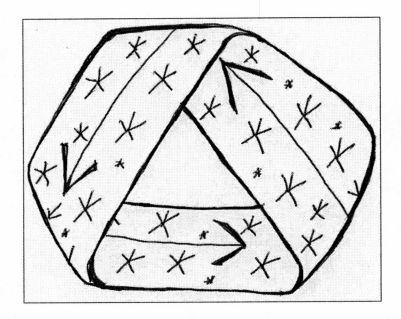

Paleo-Climatology and the Mobius Universe

It would be wonderful if we could predict climate changes in the future, or investigate climate changes in the past. Is this possible? We have gone to great lengths to discuss ancient cosmological cycles. This has given us an insight into the ancient scientists' concept of Time and Place.

What if we were to apply this ancient thinking to the task of unraveling the mysteries of the cycles of climate?

We have spoken at length about the cycles of Precession and Galactic Progression. But what we have not mentioned is that our entire Milky Way Galaxy is on the move within the universe.

We shall not call this movement a cycle because it is incomprehensible. Yet believe it or not, the cosmologers of the Dendera Stone have shown evidence of this phenomena, which we will now only call an indication of the Universal Season, which is now winter.

The cosmologers theorized that the seasons of the universe were as follows: Springtime begins in Taurus until the end of Cancer. Summer begins in Leo until the end of Libra. Autumn begins in Scorpio until the end of Capricorn. Winter begins in Aquarius and ends in the last part of Aries. The effects are typical of any season and develop from Moist to Hot to Dry to Cold.

The ancients have constantly told us that the life giving cycles proceed from Moist to Hot to Dry to Cold, and that once the cycles are put into motion, they generate and regenerate this life-like sequence over and over again. Perhaps, if there is enough space and time; a Mobius-Strip like chain of galaxies can achieve perpetual motion. In this form, energy is recycled through the strip where all galaxies travel in the same direction—but on opposite sides of the strip! Therefore, there is no defeating influence of gravitational friction, because everything is moving the same way, even though each galaxy is on the other side of the universe!

In reference to global climate, the influence of the Universal Season must predominate over the Galactic Cycle. If the Galactic Cycle now stands at Aries, and the Universal Season is at winter, then we would expect the temperature to be excessively cold. This is *not* how harmonious cycles operate. They promote and sustain life by opposing extreme effects. The region of Aries is of itself conducive of the element of heat. And therefore this opposition of extreme heat against the universal season of cold produces clear, mild, static, and temperate conditions. However, harsh extremes are generated when we introduce the effects of the Precessional Cycle added to Universal Season and Galactic Progression.

After the time of Christ, Precession moved into Pisces, which produces moisture. So that we experienced Universal Seasonal cold, mixed with Galactic Progression in Aries, which renders heat. These three influences when mixed together produce a balanced temperate mix. In fact, the mixture of Moist–Cold–Hot is so generative and productive of food supplies that we have experienced the most unprecedented population growth ever to appear on our planet.

After the year 2,160, the Precessional Cycle moves into Aquarius, when the mixture will be a combination of Cold–Hot–Cold.

The combination of Cold–Hot–Cold is not fruitful. It may be assumed that population figures will decline with the less productive food supply induced by moving from a temperate climate to one of predominant cold. No doubt, world temperatures may be more extreme and forces of the atmosphere may become stronger and more violent. In truth, one would hope the difference in general temperature would be minimal, though the general character of the forces of nature will become more extreme and violent.

Therefore, it is my opinion that Global Warming itself is not a firm climate change but an *intermediary event* preparing us for a forthcoming change. A temporary surge of heat will introduce us to a harsher and colder global climate. The discoverer of Global Warming never meant to describe his research by the term, warming. His studies indicated the emergence of a greater range of extreme weather conditions.

We are aware that there was an ancient deforestation of Greece and many other parts of the world in order to provide fuel for the smelting pots of the Iron Age. We also decry the ruination and despoiling of the magnificent rain forests of Brazil and Mexico—only to provide sub-standard farm land.

Recently, in the Sonoma-Napa Wine Country of California, scientists warned that impending climatic changes would alter the profitability and, possibly, bring about the destruction of the vineyards. The immediate and ensuing screams and cries of the local landowners of that blessed region quickly silenced the scientists, whose ill-considered remarks might possibly have influenced future land values in that golden region. The results of all this was that everyone agreed that one must take into consideration different weather cycles at different time periods. Just as the nearby Russian River had recently fulfilled her 500-year-highest flood level, so too, the vineyards were experiencing a small adverse blip in the weather cycles.

The reason for the above paragraph is to show how easily the conclusions of science may be altered when they get mixed up in commercial matters of high importance, where the consequences are judged in terms of millions of dollars. Therefore, I would think that in the interests of truth that it would be well to study these ancient systems of assessing climate where the results are not measured in terms of millions of dollars, but rather, in terms of millions of years of accurate knowledge.

Those of our heirs that have prepared wisely enough to endure 2,160 years of Aquarian climate may look forward to the following Precessional Era of Capricorn, which will be a mixture of Cold–Hot–Dry. This combination is well balanced and temperate, but tending toward drought-like conditions in places not naturally favored by protected coastal regions; or in the presence of abundant streams and rivers.

None of this futuristic thinking means anything, unless we can backtrack into the past to show that this climatological system effected past ages. Perhaps we could shed light on some of those periods of astonishing technological accomplishments of the ancient's. Archaeologists have seen certain ups and downs in science, human progress, art, and architecture. Those who study antiquity are at a loss to explain the occurrence of these cycles of creativity and sloth. I believe that much of our human endeavors are dependent and conditioned by the weather.

Therefore, let us look at the past by going back to the Precessional Epoch of Taurus. The Universal Season would still be winter, and therefore Cold. But the Galactic Position of our solar system was in Pisces which is Moist. The Precessional Position was in Taurus which is Dry. The resultant mixture is Cold–Moist–Dry, which is temperate and relatively productive, except that it lacks heat for a great abundance of food supply. And when food is lacking; human population is scarce. Yet, we can probably date many important renovations, constructions, and discoveries to the epoch of Taurus. Bouche-Leclercq (p. 54) notes that the majority of the equinoctial position points of Egyptian manuscripts and zodiacs fall into the Precessional time of Taurus! This must be evidence of an extremely fruitful scientific time.

Moving further back in time to Precessional Gemini, we find that the mixture combination results in Cold–Moist–Cold. This could definitely have resulted in the last minor Ice Age, because of the admixture of the dual Cold with Moisture. These circumstances would have created an atmosphere producing frost, snow, and ice.

Going back in time another 2,160 years, Precessional Cancer would have been Cold–Moist–Moist, resulting in extremely swampy conditions, fostered by continual rainy downpours. In Ireland and Britain archaeologists

	4320AD	2160AD	+0-	2160BC	4320BC	6480BC	8640BC	10800BC
Galactic Season *is Winter for all dates*								
	Cold	Cold	Cold	Cold	Cold	Cold	Cold	Cold
Galactic Progress by Zodiac Sign								
	Aries	Aries	Aries/Pisces	Pisces	Pisces	Pisces	Pisces	Pisces
	Hot	Hot	Hot/Wet	Wet	Wet	Wet	Wet	Wet
Precession of the Vernal Equinoxes								
	Capricorn	*Aquarius*	*Pisces/Aries*	*Aries*	*Taurus*	*Gemini*	*Cancer*	*Leo*
	Dry	Cold	Wet/Hot	Hot	Dry	Cold	Wet	Hot

The results of the combination of the *above* three influences upon climate periods of 2160 years

4320AD	2160AD	+0-	2160BC	4320BC	6480BC	8640BC	10800BC
Balanced	Cold	Balanced	Balanced	Balanced	Cold	Wet	Balanced
Favorable	*cold*	*Favorable period of human developments*			*cold*	*wet*	*Favorable*

have noticed extremely moist climate conditions which resulted in unusually raised and protected forts and habitations. David Banks Rogers in his *Prehistoric Man of the Santa Barbara Coast* speaks of the earliest inhabitants called the Oak Grove People. These people had to endure a constant wet period of storms and inundations during their long occupation of those regions in California. As well the latest excavations of early man in Brazil have shown that a similar wet climate existed here during the Precessional period of Cancer.

The epoch of Precessional Leo would have been a *hall-mark* of beneficent climate which would have exalted human ingenuity, progress, and productivity. This assertion has also been confirmed by archaeologists and researchers of the ancient past. The cosmic mixture of forces at this time would have generated a general climate of Cold–Moist–Hot. This combination elicits the most balanced of conditions and is, therefore, one of the most extremely fruitful of all the combinations favoring human activites. Some inquirers believe that it was during the Leo period that the Sphinx and the original temples nearby the Egyptian Pyramids had been built.

Inquirers into the past have found strange evidence of human habitations which curiously suggest the possibility of the many climatological conditions that we have discussed above. We could now imagine the Wet influence of Precessional Cancer revitalizing the Sahara Desert for a short period of time into the oasis of lakes and water-ways that appear to have existed there in the far distant past. Of course, there is traditional, cartographic, and geological evidence for these assertions. The appearance of water-erosion marks upon the body of the Sphinx also seems to fit in with these conclusions.

This cosmological system could be compared with geological and other scientific data in order to better illuminate a climatological picture of our planet. Below we compare the major cycles in terms of precessional periods of 2,160 years.

It should be noticed in the above chart that only those eras were designated as *balanced* which had three different cosmic elements at play. It seems most likely that these temperate periods facilitated invention, technology, and construction. Any astronomical and climatic condition that prevails over 2,016 years will, undoubtedly, have a profound influence on human productivity.

Many Egyptologists, down from even the earliest investigators, have noticed distinct periods of extraordinary excellence in culture, science, and building. Curiously, these productive periods were abruptly terminated and transgressed into eras lacking in all those former achievements. In later periods Egypt seems to have blossomed again and experienced a Renaissance. These types of scientific, sociological, and cultural fluctuations certainly seem to indicate cycles of climatic change.

We notice that there was a great age of primeval building during the Leo period when the global climate was favorable and temperate. This subject has been well covered in *Fingerprints of the Gods* and *The Message of the Sphinx* by Graham Hancock and Robert Bauval. This standard of excellence in building technology lapsed during Cancer and Gemini, but was rekindled in the time period of the Taurus Age when, once again, the global climate was more temperate and agreeable to human art and building activities.

The world climate that we have experienced since the time of Christ has been *especially* fruitful. This must account for the diversity of human inventions and enterprise. However, all this fruitfulness does have its dark-side, namely, the outrageous growth of world population, spurred on by the simple expedient of exceptional agricultural production, sophisticated methods of transportation, refrigeration, and dried and canned food preservation.

As we said above; the Precessional Age of Aquarius should bring about a predominance of colder climate accentuated by stronger storms and harsher, more dramatic weather. One immediate consequence of this type of climate change will be that the electric based economies of many nations will be put to the test. Survival is going to be a major issue for those nations which have not made adjustments to account for the possibility of dramatic climate change.

Triangles of Empire, Culture, and Global Politics

Within the discussion of the climatic effects of Precession, we would like to have a brief discussion on the subject of empire and politics. This is not so odd, because politics nearly obey the same rules that determine climate.

We said how beautifully cosmic cycles complimented, compensated, and balanced each other. Yet, when I hear that there is only one Cultural

Seat and only one Political Imperial Seat on the entire planet, I cannot believe that this is a very fair and balanced system. This is all too true. In astrology we learn of geometric relationships such as triangularity, sextile, quartile, conjunction, opposition, and other configurations.

Therefore, any position on our globe that is in a direct geometric relationship with the Seat of Culture or the Seat of Empire, derives *some* portion of that power. In astrology, quartile (90 degree) and opposition (180 degree) are bad, contrary, and disjunctive relationships. The other relationships are good and in unison; such as triangular (60 degree), sextile (20 degree) and conjunction.

On the map we notice that the eastern seaboard of the United States and its capital are in triangular relationship with the Holy Land, the Seat of Culture. Ties of this nature are incredibly deep and lasting. During the Second World War, Germany, which lies within the Seat of Empire, made its strongest compact with Japan which lies in a triangular relationship with Europe.

PART VIII:

THE REMAINING JEWEL OF ATLANTIC CULTURE

Chapter 1

Ogygia

Ireland might well be called a Galapagos Islands of ancient traditions and folk-ways. Not only was classical Mediterranean culture preserved on this isolated island, but also, in the very earliest of times, it became a vehicle of transmission of the New Revelation to Europe. Even into our modern era, Ireland served as the homeland of devout and dedicated nuns, priests, missionaries, and teachers to the entire world.

Ireland has always been a retreat and a bastion of safety to those who were fleeing from the ills of the world. From my own personal experience of the Irish people, and also by the admission of their own histories, the Irish are a blend of almost every representative culture and tribe of the ancient world. This is the reason for the great charm of the Irish, and above all, their humanity. The people of "The Island of Saints and Scholars" have also been forced by cruel necessity to travel to the ends of the earth.

They are known for their ability to mix easily with other people because of their keen interest in customs and history. This has been a trait of their own historical experience. It is little wonder, then, that it is in Ireland that we may find such a paradigm of the preservation of examples of ancient Atlantic culture.

Our authority for this study will be the *General History of Ireland*, composed in 1625 by the Rev. Doctor Jeoffry Keating. He was educated at the College of Salamanca in Spain. His work is much disparaged, though widely used, by modern scholars, who have as yet not undertaken to offer a replacement for this excellent work. His compilations included readings from manuscripts which are *no longer in existence*.

Keating says that the first name of Ireland was the Wooded Isle, so-called by a messenger sent there by Ninus, the son of Belus. It is said that during all history, "Three times Eire put three coverings and three bareness off her," alluding to her woodlands. Keating says that Plutarch called Ireland Ogygia, which means "the most ancient Isle." We have already mentioned that Homer in the *Odyssey* tells how his hero is detained on Ogygia, *the navel of the sea;* "Tis a wooded isle, and therein dwells a goddess, daughter of Atlas of baneful mind, who knows the depths of every sea."

The third name of the island was Inis Alga, "the noble island," which name it held in the time of the Fir-Bolg, an ancient colony of people who settled here before the Scythians or Gadelians came to Ireland.

The next name of Ireland was Eire, called after Aeria, an ancient name of Egypt and Crete, for the Gadelians were banished out of Egypt to Crete. Most of the old authors however claim that Eire was the queen of the Tuatha de Danaan, who came after the Fir-Bolg. Ireland also held numerous other names, such as Fodhla, Banba, Fail, Hog's Isle, Scotia, Hibernia, Juernia or Verna, Irin, and Ir.

Keating excuses himself for relating some fabulous antediluvian accounts of Ireland, but since the poets have thought worthy to pass on these stories, he declares that, "I shall offer them faithfully, as they are recorded in the most ancient manuscripts." These preflood inhabitants include a daughter of Cain, called Banba; three fishermen from Spain who were contemporaries of Noah; and Fors, Fearon, Andord, and Fiontan, who survived the Deluge; and divided the world between them.

After the Flood, came Adhna, a messenger of Ninus, who was followed by Partholanus from Macedonia in Greece. This Partholanus brought learned men, druids, artisans, and merchants to Ireland. He caused many new lakes and rivers to be created. Some say that he fought a great battle with a descendent of one of the prior inhabitants of the island, Uadhmoir.

The next colonization of Ireland came from the Euxine Sea, led by Nemedius who was said to be a full brother to Partholanus. Nemedius felled several woods opening up the countryside, and created several new lakes. He was met in several battles by a people called Fomorians, who were master builders and seamen. These Fomorians came from Africa and were said to be descendants of Sem, trying to separate themselves from the posterity of Ham, who was cursed by Noah. The Fomorians vanquished the Nemedians and took possession of the country, and established a great fortress and tower, called Conuing's Tower, on Tory island off the coast of Ireland.

The next invasion of Ireland was by the Fir-Bolg, descendants of a grandson of Nemedius, who had escaped to Greece. Another grandson of Nemedius, named Briotan Maol, fled from the Fomorians to inhabit Scotland, where his posterity long endured. The Fir-Bolg divided Ireland into five equal provinces and ruled for eight successive kingships. The last of their monarchs married a daughter of Maghmore, King of Spain.

The next invasion of Ireland was by the Tuatha de Danaan, descendants of another grandson of Nemedius, who had escaped from the Fomorians to Boeotia and Achaia in Greece. There they learned the magical arts. In the course of their return to Ireland they wandered in Denmark, Norway, and Scotland. The Tuatha de Danaan defeated the African Fomorian pirates and later routed the Fir-Bolg in another battle. These they expelled to the coastal islands, such as the Aran Islands. The leader of the de Danaan was Nuadha Airgiodlamh, so-called because of his artificial silver limb, which he had fitted to him, after he lost his hand in the battle with the Fir-Bolg. The Tuatha de Danaan brought four treasures to Ireland: a magic sword, a spear, a cauldron, and the *Lia Fail*, or the Stone of Destiny, which is now, or for a time was, under the coronation chair in Westminster Abbey.

The Lady Danaan and Beochuill who were of great beauty, charm, and quality, were nonetheless feared commanders of their armies. Lady Danaan's sons were experts in the black arts and the mysteries of charms and enchantments—which their enemies were not able to withstand. Their female deities were Banba, Macha, and Moriogan. Their heroes were Breas and Lug, "the long handed," master of all arts, who instituted the Irish

Olympic games called *Tailtean*. Other heroes were the Daghdah and his grandsons: Macuill, who worshipped the hazel tree; Maceacht, who worshipped the ploughshare; and Mac Greine, who worshipped the sun. In short, a great majority of Ireland's druidical learning, institutions, music, and dancing, fairy folklore, and superstitions come from the age of the Tuatha de Danaan. This great tribe was likewise instrumental in preserving histories and traditions of the former conquerors of the island, in great part by intermarriage and assimilation. Again and again in human history, we should be grateful to those who steal and borrow culture, and then make it their own, for they are the agency of preservation.

The next invaders of Ireland were the Gadelians, or Gaels, in about 1300 BC. These were the sons of Gallamb, also called Milesius, or Miles, who was the king of Spain. Their descendants ruled Ireland for over 2,000 years until the coming of the Norman-English under Strongbow. Forty brave commanders and Scota, the wife of Miles, set sail for Ireland from Brigantium on the northwest coast of Spain. Among them were the issue of Breogan, grandfather of Miles, the founder of the Brigantes of Spain, Ireland, and England. Scota engaged Queen Eire, the wife of Mac Greine, in battle. Scota was killed in this fight, but her army was successful. In the battle of Tailton, the Milesian commanders, Amergin, Heremon, and Heber Fionn slew the three kings of the Tuatha de Danaan.

In the course of time jealousy between these brothers grew to civil war, and Heremon proved victorious. He divided the island into five provinces among the generals who had helped him. The province of Leinster he gave to a gentleman of great worth, a descendent of the Fir-Bolg. The two Munsters he gave to Er, Orbha, Fearon, and Feargna, whose names were identical to the four sons of the original Partholanus. Connacht he gave to two noted generals of Spain, while Ulster was conferred upon Heber, son of Ir, son of Miles. At this time the Picts came to Leinster from Thrace, but were thwarted in their attempt to gain the kingdom, and removed to Scotland. A few of their nobles and an eminent druid remained in Ireland.

Thus stands the report compiled by the Reverend Keating of his vast readings into ancient Irish manuscripts. I think the reader may appreciate his unbiased and faithful compilations, and gain a small understanding of just how varied Irish history is, and how many and varied races and tribes have contributed to the multicultural formation of that which we now simply call *Irish*. And this does not even include the later Viking, Norman, and

English influences. To my mind, Ireland serves as a select microcosm of the adventurous intermixture of different people. And we should use this Irish model when considering Mediterranean history, in order that we may not mask the divergent forces at work in those vast regions by over simplification and the wish to create simple, teachable, and historical abstracts.

In this vein we would like to continue on and give a more extended review of the more important groups that invaded Ireland. Especially, we would like to focus upon that group called the Fomorians of Morocco.

First of all, the Fomorians seem to validate the Greek mythographer's assertions that their gods, heroes, and cultural usages originated in the West, on the bounds of the ocean. For we will see that the Fomorians were a very knowledgeable and talented people, who like the Veneti of Brittany, were accustomed to deep-ocean travel, guided by astronomical sciences, and naval technology. Second, we will see that the Fomorians, even after defeat, were allowed to intermarry with the new conquerors, as we see from studying the subsequent genealogies. The inference also arises that the culture and sciences of the Fomorians were absorbed in every new formation of Ireland. And this again gives us a comparative model to consider how Atlantic culture and technology might have been transmitted to the Mediterranean lands.

Our main theme here is to show the diversity of Ireland, which had so very many names, and so many different people coming to its shores. These were people who intermarried, shared, and assimilated each other's culture. And all this upon the foundation of an older Atlantic culture, brought into Ireland by the first Fomorians.

Chapter 2

The Prophetic Stones

Could anyone imagine that the ancient Cross of Killamery in County Kilkenny, Ireland, is based upon Egyptian geometry? Peter Tompkins in his *Secrets of the Great Pyramid* says that,

> In the Great Pyramid the rectangular floor of the King's Chamber [which consists of two equal squares, or a 1 x 2 rectangle] also serves to illustrate; and to obtain the Golden Section. If you split one of two squares in half, and swing *the diagonal* down to the base, the point where the diagonal touches the base will be 1.618 in relation to the side of the square, which is 1.

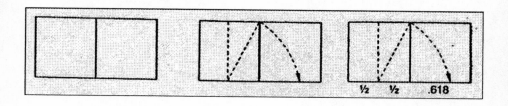

½   ½   .618

The Golden Section or Golden Mean is the division of a line in such a way that A is related to B precisely the same as B is related to the entire line, that is, $A + B$. The reason why this proposition is so important is that nature uses this principle as one of its *formulas of creation*. Many plants and animals are designed according to the Golden Mean. Johannes Kepler regarded it as the symbol of creation or generation. It is something Divine and may extend to the creation and form of the universe.

Leonardo da Vinci's famous sketch of the human figure encompassed by a circle demonstrates his interest in the Golden Section. What I find remarkable is that an analysis of his construction is based upon the same geometry that Tompkins has shown us to be a factor in the King's Chamber of the Great Pyramid. Indeed, starting with Napoleon's expedition to Egypt from the time of Jomard, researchers have shown that Egyptian art and architecture is based upon the Golden Section. The Greeks adopted Egyptian geometry, and the artists and architects of the Renaissance inherited the same fascination with this special creative formula.

When we look at da Vinci's sketch it is not hard to see why humans are delighted with fabrications based upon this principle. What is pleasing to our eye is the elements of our own shape embodied in art. We most easily recognize and appreciate material things which are in likeness and proportion to our own shape. But more important than this; is that *God created man in His own image,* and therefore, the Golden Section is a Divine geometrical form of God, the Creator. When the ancients wished to represent the Holy and the Divine, they used the Golden Proportion.

The alluring question for me is: "Why is the Killamery Cross based upon these Renaissance proportions, and geometrically laid out according to the same rules that constructed Egyptian art?"

Let us look at the genius involved in designing this work of primeval Irish art. And let us imagine that we are the artist laying out the important lines of the cross. In front of us we have a large rectangular block of stone. And just like the Egyptian example, the height of this block is twice its width. Where do we begin?

First: A line is drawn which divides the length in half, creating two perfect squares. The three flowers, each with four leaves, begin below this line. Above this line begins the interlacing which becomes two of the serpent's heads. The circle of the cross also rests upon this line.

Second: These two great squares are each bisected. The horizontal bisection of the lower square of the eventual cross divides the base spud and the first flower from the two flowers above it.

Third: The horizontal bisection of the uppermost square becomes the top of the cross arm.

Fourth: A compass or string is placed upon the left side of the bisector of the lower square. The other end of the compass, or string, is placed upon the right side of the block at the point of the division of the two great squares. When the radius is drawn from this point on the right side toward the left side of the upper square: It divides that left side of the upper square into the Golden Section whereby A is to B as B is to $A + B$. Please note, that on the finished cross that, this Golden Section line goes right through the center of the mysterious spiral, below the crocodile's mouth, from which the upper serpents spring.

Fifth: Take the length of B from the top of the proposed cross and it becomes the center of the cross arm defining the central boss of the circle. Take the same length of B from the bottom of the cross and you have the exact center of the middle flower.

Sixth: A further division of one half of the bisected squares into the Golden Section produces the means X and Y. Thereafter A and B, and X and Y, make up all the subsequent details of the cross. The width of the shaft above the base spud is A. The radius of the petals of the lowest flower is Y. The length of the lowest base is apparently the length of the diagonal which produces the first Golden Mean.

It can only be concluded that this elaborate and rigorous display of geometry is beyond the realm of coincidence. The geometry involved is so definitive and absolute in the final creation of this masterpiece; that it seems to serve a higher purpose. That purpose was to celebrate an earthly revelation of the Divine.

The proposition that the Killamery Cross is based upon pure Egyptian Divine Geometry poses a number of intriguing and difficult questions. Do I think that there were Egyptians in Killamery? Do I think that this cross is of ancient Atlantic origin? The answer may be that both Ireland and Egypt share a scientific tradition that stems from a more ancient past related to events that happened upon the greater Atlantic coastlands and those regions which communicate with this ocean.

It may be appropriate to review the history of the origin of the Golden Mean in Western thinking. I would also like to speculate upon the local history of this most enchanting geography of Ireland. Hopefully, these two matters will help us to gain additional information about this interesting cross whose stone work seems to speak to us.

Egyptian Theory of Numbers

Diodorus Sicilus (i.98) records that the Greek Pythagoras (582–500 BC) had three silver flagons made to give as presents to the priests of Egypt. The talented Pythagoras learned their language and was admitted to their temples. There, he learned the Egyptian teachings about the gods, geometrical propositions, and their theory of numbers. He was also the first to use the term "philosopher." Pythagoras was one of the earliest of the Greeks to study in Egypt. The philosopher, Plato, paid a huge sum of money to obtain books of his lectures, which were attended by thousands. Pythagoras also spoke about the science of music, and that geometric and harmonic means are indeed fundamental ratios in nature: "There is geometry in the humming of the strings. There is music in the spacing of the Spheres." This saying was used by Bode in his harmonic ratio to compute the distances of the planets from the sun.

Pythagoras was a real poster-child for the advertisement that travel broadens the mind. He is said to have visited Delos, Sparta, Lesbos, Egypt, Persia, Babylon, Chaldea, and Croton in Italy. Plutarch says that Pythagoras studied under Oenuphis, priest of Heliopolis. He remained in Thebes and Memphis for over 22 years according to Iamblichos, who also says that he had to submit to long periods of examination before he was permitted to advance with his studies.

Pythagoras lived to be over 100 years old. Schwaller de Lubicz in his *Sacred Science* (p. 259) says that Pythagoras learned geometry and astronomy in Egypt; astrology, astronomy, and the science of numbers from the Phoenicians and Chaldeans; and the magistery of the cult and its observances from the Magi of Babylon, where he lived for 12 years.

Pythagoras said that the source of all numbers is the Monad, which is divine. It is also the origin of both odd and even numbers. Like our present day understanding of cell division, the Holy Monad splits into two units in order to produce the undefined Dyad. The Dyad, according to one ancient reporter, then splits itself into something where one part is longer than the other.

I cannot help guessing that the Killamery Cross represents the Divine Monad and the undefined Dyad. The idea behind the description "undefined" is that it has no specific length. The Holy Spirit, the Divine Artificer, or Plato's Demiurge finds matter which is of no exact length; and then he imposes Form upon it, by means of geometric division. The geometric divisions produce numbers, life, and formality in the universe, and ultimately create our world and the life within it. It would seem, then, that the very specific geometric form of the Killamery Cross makes it a holy object in the eyes of the ancient people.

We are ever indebted to Pythagoras for his communications regarding the Golden Mean. This, however, does not prove that the idea originated with the Egyptians. Interestingly, the ancients were very serious about the sanctity of their theories of number. Schwaller de Lubicz in *Sacred Science* (p. 261) reports that Hippasos of Metapontion was deemed to have perished in a shipwreck because he had divulged the doctrine of the irrational numbers, namely that some geometrical quantities cannot be expressed in terms of whole numbers (like the Golden Mean Proportion).

The Time Period and Meaning of the Crosses

The Ossory Group of Stone Crosses is unique and puzzling in that the iconographic ornamentation *never* portrays Christ. There is one image that shows Adam under the Tree of Life, but this is common to several cultures, and also related to the constellation of Gemini. The Killamery Cross has a creature with a mouth like a crocodile as its topmost feature. This creature's skin is also portrayed in a scaly pattern, although it lacks the typical crocodile's tail.

There is a crocodile which appears on the ancient Dodekaros Zodiac in the place of the present day sign of Pisces. Plutarch says (*Isis and Osiris*, 381),

> The Egyptians declare that the crocodile is the living representation of god, since he is the only creature without a tongue. This creature usually lives 60 years and lays 60 eggs, which are

hatched in 60 days. The number 60 is the first measure for such persons as concern themselves with the heavenly bodies.

Isha Schwaller de Lubicz in her *Her-Bak* (p. 287) says that although the crocodile is classified as a reptile, it also shares some common features with fish and birds. It has a dualistic character, in that it spends the night in the water and is on land during the day. She says that Plutarch and Elien established a relation between the crocodile, Seb-Sobek, and Cronus, the god of time. The crocodile is reputed to be unable to look backward. Since the crocodile can only look forward, I would think that it is also a symbol of prophecy. Definitely, it is related to Cronus and Time. I would think that it represents one of the most majestic of the cosmic cycles, namely, the Galactic Cycle. Therefore, in all its simplicity, this crocodile-like form represents one of the most powerful, prophetic representations of holy art.

Most of the fragments and crosses that I have examined bear figures that are related to star groups and the science of cosmology. I was able to make these identifications by using the text of Franz Boll's *Sphaera*. But, it is not this involved and specialized subject matter that we wish to discuss here. We only wish to remind ourselves that these crosses do possess cosmological symbolism.

If there are no images of Our Savior, does that mean that these crosses are of a pre-Christian date? I do have some experience with the weather resistant qualities of some types of stone, including the type of sandstone used for these crosses. I do know that wood will sometimes petrify like a stone, and I have seen that marble can warp just like a piece of wood. Also, there are some stones that are soft when quarried, but then get harder and harder with age.

Mary Miller in the *Courtly Art of the Ancient Maya* writes (p. 74), "The volcanic tuff used in Copan construction was ideal for such three-dimensional architectural sculpture: soft when first quarried, the stone later hardened to a surface that defied wind and rain." In the experience of my work, I have discovered that there are several types of stone that when they are quarried fresh, they are soft and easy to work. If they are placed outside they will weather for several hundred years; until they become hard and petrified in themselves. The weathering process then stops, because the stone is now hardened. It is impossible to determine the true age of certain stones. Perhaps these stones have become super-petrified; and are much more than 2,000 years old.

Another interpretation could be that these crosses date from a time of 300–400 AD, just at the beginning of the evangelization of Ireland. In either case, they could be a product of a pre-Christian mentality. They may represent the efforts of a very ancient and extremely conservative and enlightened scientific community, who wished, as a last chapter of the old world order, to express their science before the actual and complete revelation of Our Lord transformed the island to Christianity. Perhaps this interpretation may be true, in one way or another, because these designs were so readily and completely adopted by the religious monasteries that followed. And, these institutions absolutely approved and copied this art form because, as Dr. Healy informs us, the majority of Druids became priests of Christ.

It is well-known to biblical and historical scholars that the Orient was alive with the expectations and the many prophecies of the Coming of the Messiah. We read in the New Testament that the Magi, or astrologers, came to search for the new-born Son of God. In Irish history it is recorded that the Druid Bacrach of Leinster had foretold the coming of Christ to King Connor Mac Nessa of Ulster some hundred years before the time of the Crucifixion.

Christians have become accustomed to the image of Christ crucified. It is a vital symbol of their religion. But, let us transport ourselves back to that epoch. The cross was a symbol of utter humiliation. The very idea of associating this sign with the Most Holy Messiah would have been repugnant to the early church. The cross, as a shameful way of death, was not immediately elevated by philosophical appreciation and dogma to that most revered state. This did not happen until the mystical humility of Jesus was associated with the humility of the instrument of the cross within the entire mind of the new Christian community.

What, therefore, would possess the Irish to make such a leap into the dogmatic mind of the future church as to erect crosses, without the image of Christ? For the pure and simple cross was not accepted as a Christian sign until later periods of history. I believe that the cross, and the combination of the circle and the cross, were accepted as cosmological signs of a New Cosmic Age and the hoped-for appearance of the Messiah.

It is my contention, therefore, that the Ossory Crosses were erected as a prophecy of the expected appearance of the Son of God, an event which cosmological science and the prophets had already predicted. The circle of these crosses represented the cycles of the sun, moon, and stars, and the Galactic Progression of our solar system. The cross is an ancient symbol of the wind and the Spirit of God. It overlaps the circle of the universe to show that a Great New Epoch of time was soon about to take place. Also, nearby Killamery is a place called Windgap. Perhaps, this locality was sacred to the wind?

Ireland and the Locality Around the Ossory Group

The localities where these several crosses and fragments are found are ancient holy places of the Druids. They are marked by underground springs, water spirals, and aquifers; whose power is heightened and amplified during the solstices, full moon, and the conjunctions of the planets. Assemblies gathered by the Druids during these astronomical occasions would have felt a transcendental sensation when brought within this field between these springs and the stars. I believe that some of the bases of the crosses were original Druid stones, upon which rested the famous capstones, like the one at Killamery that cured headaches. The proof of these assertions are several capstones that rest upon the crosses at Ahenny. They are, without a doubt, the exact image of the famous Omphalos at the Oracle at Delphi. These types of beehive-shaped stones are also found in the temple precincts of Egypt.

When the Druids wanted to celebrate the New Epoch of the Messiah, they caused these crosses to be carved, and they placed them between the old base-stones and the Omphali. Some of the bases were replaced, as were the omphali, which were now carved into the shape of medieval church-roof capstones.

This is where the tradition of the Irish capstones originates. Obviously, the actual Omphali at Ahenny were never replaced, and appear in their original state. This may also serve as evidence for the possibility that the crosses were carved during the transition from the Druidic to the Priestly period. This is because most of the Ossory Crosses do not have the church-roof style capstones. They are, therefore, the oldest and most original of the Irish Crosses because they still have their original omphali caps.

My assertion regarding the original Druid base-stones comes from the presence of powerful underground water spirals at these sites, which these great stones were originally set to demarcate. But, even more importantly, the assertion is based upon the story of *The Seven Holy Bishops,* of which there are many local versions.

The Seven Holy Bishops at Ahenny

The remarkable thing about these local stories is that they are classical fables. In the stages of the degeneration of the historical fact, the last stage, after myth, is fable. And the fable is the oldest form of human recall—where the time period or the succession of the ruling kings has become oblivious, where the true names of the protagonists have even been forgotten. The only thing that is remembered in a true fable is the *place* where these events occurred. And since fable has been erased from the realm of history, only a very few of the local people cherished and preserved the memory of these events. Therefore, I would say that this region is historically very, very old, indeed.

The Story of the Seven Holy Bishops

On the west side of the base of the Ahenny North Cross is a picture of seven holy men dressed in long robes and holding crosiers, which are staffs similar to shepherd's hooks, often used by bishops. Crosiers are very ancient religious symbols which appear as early as the cave paintings of Alta Mira.

According to Catherine Norris of Tibberaghny, this version of the story was told by the schoolmistress of Owning:

> There was once a woman of the village of Owning who gave birth to seven boys at a single birth. She and her husband were astounded at the miracle; and because they were in poor circumstances, and indeed, somewhat afraid, they resolved to drown the infants, and be done with this unnatural prodigy altogether. The next morning, the husband set out with the babes, parceled in a bag. But, on the road, he was accosted by a holy man who asked him the nature of his burden. "Puppies, sir," answered the husband, "to be drowned." The holy man was not to be deceived by this falsehood; and taking charge of the bag, he told the husband that he himself would perform the office. But, rather, the holy man baptized the youngsters, and had them brought up and educated to be great religious men like himself.

The version by Rose Springfield in *Romantic Slievenamon* relates that the seven boys were educated in France, but returned again to Ireland. Once here, however, they were taken for spies from France and were pursued and killed by knights from Granny Castle: "And the people of the country set up crosses where the bishops *were killed, of carved stone of the pattern as they have in France, with a line that has no beginning and no end,* to show that the power of God goes on forever."

In the Armorican region of France this legend is recorded almost word for word in accordance with the Irish tale. *The Guide de la Bretagne Mysterieuse* reports that the cult of the Seven is venerated throughout Brittany under a Christian mask, to conceal a more ancient cult. There are numerous fountains with seven separate basins dedicated in their honor. In Plestin-Les-Greves, they even report that The Seven came from a place in the British Isles to evangelize Armorica. It seems most probable that the story of *The Seven Holy Bishops* is related to an ancient astronomical religion, for nearby the astronomical stone alignments of Carnac, is the Chapel of the Seven Saints. Close to this chapel are the ancient megalithic Dolmens of the Seven Saints. There is a circular souterrain by Josselin with seven great stones disposed about its interior. At Vieux-Marche there is an ancient chapel of the Seven Saints founded upon a dolmen, which forms a megalithic cavern in which the cult of the ancient Seven is still apparently celebrated. By the chapel is a sacred fountain whose waters are led out through seven troughs set out in the form of a triangle.

Back in Ireland, on the Island of Aran of the Seven Churches, is the burial place of seven holy persons under an ancient flagstone, whose inscription has been interpreted as the Seven Romani. Healy (pp. 169–184) reports, "Who they were, or whence they came, they have no notion whatsoever." On Tory Island, ancient base of the Moroccan navigators, the Fir-Moricchi, is the Church of the Seven, whose foundations are still traceable.

The Fomorians, or *Fir-Moricchi*, the men from Morocco, were the first conquerors of Ireland. Keating reports (p. 124) of,

> Africans who often landed upon the island; and there we have an account of certain stars, and the names of them, that were worshipped by the mariners, and were supposed to derive a power from the god of the sea, either to misguide the ship, or to conduct her safe into the port.

They were experienced deep-ocean navigators, well versed in the astronomical sciences. They must have been related to the Veneti, of the astronomical alignments of Carnac. This must be so because of the concurrent tradition of the Seven Holy Ones, which prevails in Brittany and Ireland in localities associated with sea peoples. As well as being the first tax-collectors, the Fir-Moricchi were also the premier builders of fortresses, towers, and castles in Ireland. The Fomorians came from the homeland of that most famous astronomer, Atlas, the Heaven-Holder. And, it will be remembered, that the seven daughters of Atlas were revered throughout the ancient world.

The Killamery Cross and the other Crosses of the Ossery Group are all found near by, or upon, the mountain named Slievenamon. Curiously, the Fomorians are connected with the Slievenamon in the literary accounts of Ireland. James Maher, in his *Romantic Slievenamon,* reports that the actual name of the mountain is *the mountain of the women of the Plain of Femin,* named after the Danaan princesses, Fea and Mean. On the mountain is the Sidh, or fairy palace, of Donn Mac Midir, the great-grandson of the Fomorian, Ealathan. The *Book of Lismore* connects the mountain with the ancient stronghold of the Fomorians on Tory Island. It begins a legend of the Fianna by speaking of "a beautiful and timorous fawn that was roused by us at Tory Island, in the North of Ireland." This young deer, or stag, then led the warriors directly from Tory to the Slievenamon. It will be remembered that in many Irish tales that Druids assume the form of a deer. A stag is represented on the north side of the Tibberaghny stone. The Stag is also an ancient constellation of the heavens.

Keating tells us stories of the rebellious Deise tribe, and the curious tales of the Deise Druids. These stories show that the people of this area were possessed of a great single-minded, conservative, and traditional temperament. They were noted for their strict adherence to druidism, and an aversion to outside influence. Healy (p. 62) notes that the Gospel of St. Patrick was said to have been drowned in the nearby River Suir.

The 18th-century poet James Lalor called the mountain "Erin's Parnassus." But, because of this area's wealth of megalithic monuments, and truly original form of Irish art, these environs of the Slievenamon may more rightly be called "Ireland's Arcadia." The Reverend Carrigan in his *History and Antiquities of the Diocese of Ossory* describes the multitude of giant's graves, cromlechs, and underground chambers of the area, where every township possesses its own Druid's altar.

One of the versions of the legend of the Seven Bishops tells us that the babes were said to be puppy dogs. Getty, in *The Island of Tory* (iii., p. 149), says that when St. Columkill came to consecrate the island, he was attacked by a dog whose paw print is still to be seen imbedded on a stone on Tory Island. The imprint of a dog's paw is also to be found on one of the promontories of the Slievenamon at a place called Carrignagun, the rock of the dog. Here was said to be the resting place of Bran, the famous hound of Finn. This place marked a megalithic burial chamber of the category called *leaba na g-cuin*, a grave of the hounds. Sadly, around 1850, this monument was destroyed by English rent collectors. On a high hill above Owning village, there still exists a magnificent, but much mutilated, *Leaba* or "dog's grave." This suffered the same ignoble fate of the Slievnamon monument. Carrigan in his *History of Ossory* says that the local pronunciation is *Leobba na Gueeng,* and that tradition variously calls it the grave of hounds or heroes, or longmen or giants. There is a concurrent tradition in Sardinia, whose ancient builders of their unique astronomical observatories, were, like the Irish Fir-Moricchi, originally from Africa. Masimo Pittau in *La Sardigna Nuragica* explains that Sardinia was first colonized by African giants. The most ancient cemeteries there are styled *Domos de Jana*, the homes of Jana, or Diana, the moon. Dogs are always the companions of Diana and Artemis, the great huntress.

The dog is a symbol of the moon. It is also a symbol for death, in his character of Cerberus, who is the hound and guardian of the underworld. Boll (*Sphaera, pl. 5, 6*) shows that on the very ancient Dodekaros Zodiac that the constellation of the Dog appears in the place of the zodiac sign of Taurus. In astrology, Taurus is the exaltation of the moon. This sign is also the home of the Seven Atlantic Pleiades, the daughters of Atlas.

Plutarch in *The Face that Appears in the Orb of the Moon* tells of the ancient Atlantic religion on the island of Ogygia in the Western Ocean, identified with Ireland. The ancient philosophers of the West conceived that the oceans of the world were a physical manifestation of the Heavenly Ocean, the Milky Way Galaxy. These philosophers also recognized that a great bond existed between the moon and the natural oceans. They identified the moon's attraction of the underground and ocean waters with Fate, which directs the spirits who vivify the realm of plants, animals, and humans. These Spirits bring earthly bodies to fruition, and finally to destruction. The death of these bodies is only a natural event in the cycle of material birth and death. The spirit does not participate in death. Plutarch relates that upon parting from the body, the soul wanders between heaven and earth, in the regions of purgatory, and these spirits manifest themselves on earth in many forms. But, according to Fate, the soul is finally attracted to the orb of the moon. There are certain damned and unwholesome regions on the dark side of the moon. On the other hand, there is the Elysium, or Abodes of the Blest, which are on the moon's illuminated side. The Abodes of the Blest are in a place called The Meads of the Moon.

In connection with this religious philosophy, it is noteworthy that the cross, which depicts the Seven Holy Bishops, is found in a place called Ahenny. There are several derivations of this particular place name, one of which is Ath, meaning a ford. Another variation is Achad, meaning a field or a meadow. The latter root of the name Ahenny is based upon Aine, the Irish Goddess of the Moon. Therefore, Ahenny could actually mean The Meadows, or Meads of the Moon, just as in Plutarch's account. Considering the special originality of this unique area, I will boldly surmise that the basis of Plutarch's account came from here!

Lady Gregory, in her *Gods and Fighting Men* (p. 86), records that Aine, a goddess of the Danaan was the daughter of Manannan, the God of the Sea. But, some say, that she is the Morrigu herself, the Divine Crow, who presides over the fate of battles (note: a crow picking a headless body, draped over a horse, is depicted on the south side of the Ahenny Cross). O'Kearney (*Folk Lore.1 Kilkenny Arch. Soc.*) proclaims that Aine, or Ana, is none other than Diana, the Goddess of the Moon. He mentions the Chair of Aine near Dunany, called "the chair of the lunatics," because demented people from all over Ireland flocked to this place, driven by some insuperable impulse. Rabid dogs often flocked around this stone as well, and threatened neighbors and cattle of the district before they killed themselves by plunging into the sea.

O'Kearney also associates Aine with the Greek Athena, goddess of wisdom and inspiration; frequently invoked by the bards as Leanan-sighe. Athena is also the patron of crafts and weaving. And, on the Slievenamon, there is a rock called Carraig an Turna, the rock of the spinning wheel. According to Maher, this was the home of the Fairy Women of Peafield. O'Brennan (*Ancient Ireland ii.*, p. 139) associates Aine with wisdom. He tells of Ane, who was an actual Sybil prophetess of Cork and Kerry.

Finally, I would like to mention a report contained in *Atlantis in Spain* (p. 95) saying that the Andalusian mariners preserved the tradition of Atlantis, the fabulous Island of St. Brandan; and the legend of the Seven Cities. The Seven Cities were founded by seven bishops who fled to the west from Spain at the time when the Visigoths were conquered by Musa, and when Roderick disappeared in 714 AD. The author says that it is a historical fact that the Finians took their name from an early Irish race associated with the region about the Straits of Gibraltar. I myself have always sensed a relationship between the Gadelians and the name Gades, now called Cadiz.

I hope that we have put forward enough information to establish that a very ancient Atlantic-based culture existed around the immediate area of the Ossory Group of Stone Crosses. I especially think that the verbatim concurrence of the tradition of the Seven Holy Bishops, both in Ireland and in Brittany, is of vital importance in establishing a link between the Veneti and the Fomorian navigators who originated in Africa.

Engineering

The Killamery Cross appears humbled by the wayside in a disheveled locale, an ill-kept cemetery graveyard. Yet, to the learned eye, it is an absolute gem. It is an extravagant piece of artisanship. Like its fellow crosses, it required the will of the local rulers and their people to endorse its creation, which was time-consuming and extremely costly. I work for the oldest monument maker in California, Donohoe & Carroll, in the largest cemetery complex in the world, and though we have made crosses of this size, we have never been asked to execute a cross of such delicate and refined interlacing as is exhibited by any one of the Ossory Crosses. In today's money, the Killamery Cross could not be made for under 200,000 American dollars. Some of the other crosses would cost considerably more. Therefore, we must realize that the creation of these crosses was of supreme cultural importance for the community to expend such energy and cost in their creation.

In a different context, Dr. Healy, in his *Ireland's Ancient Schools and Scholars*, reports on the Celtic art at Clonmacnoise, saying that the architect, or *ollamh-builder*, had his remuneration fixed by law. Besides a kind of fixed percentage on the work which he superintended, he had a fixed annual salary, rated at twenty-one cows, from the king-in-chief, in whose service he was engaged. He mentions the medieval artists like the O'Duffys. But, it cannot be denied that Ireland possesses an architectural tradition that may be older than that of Egypt. Among the gods of the Tuatha de Danaan were Credenus, the craftsman, and Goibniu, the smith. There is also the famous builder, the renowned Gobban Saer, whose memory is still traditionally preserved in various parts of the country. Dun Angus of the Aran Islands and the fabled Tower of Glass of Tory Island, all speak of a heritage that goes back to the first conquerors of Ireland, the Atlantic navigators from Morocco.

Within the last two decades, a very important discovery was made in the locality of the Slate Quarries nearby the Ahenny Crosses: a miniature "Newgrange" type of stone alignment. This one works accurately for the determination of the winter solstice. This megalithic construction is called the Knockroe passage tomb. It is even decorated with a frieze of quartz, just as in Newgrange. The view from this site is dominated by the outline of the Slievenamon, with its great cairn on the summit.

We are but in the early stages of a determined and scientific investigation of this very significant area. This discovery would seem, without a doubt, to demonstrate that a culture possessing astronomical science and engineering wisdom flourished in this area. And if, as they say, Newgrange is older than megalithic Egypt, then a real case could be made for the supreme antiquity of Irish and Atlantic sciences, because the Golden Mean proportion signifies the birth of the advanced sciences and engineering. I am certain that researchers in the future will confirm that both Ireland and Egypt have inherited Atlantic culture, science, and religion.

In conclusion, when we join the Killamery Cross to one of its later descendents—we notice that the crocodile-jawed creature has been replaced by a four-armed solar spiral. But, considering the totality of the cosmological evidence that we have advanced throughout this book, we might perhaps look at these symbols as representing images of swirling galaxies?

The mystical knot of Killamery has now been superceded by the ram within a circle, which we assume to be a reference to the zodiac sign of Aries.

We previously showed that the big boss in the middle of the Killamery Cross corresponded to the stomach of the Vitruvian figure. This same spot is now adorned by the stomach of the Ancient of Days (Cronus or Time) holding the Aries symbol.

Our prototype portrayed an interlacing which was over the bowels of the Vitruvian Man. This knot-work is now only suggested at the feet of the small figure of the Ancient of Days.

The Killamery Cross begins with three flowers of four petals. This represents nature as a product of the twelve regions of the cosmos. The interlacing above these flowers shows the weaving of the astronomical cycles. These cycles fulfill themselves as shown by the intertwined serpents of time. The crocodile-jawed Cronus who controls Universal and Galactic Eras, now dictates from above that monumental events and terminations of the higher majestic cycles are about to take place. Thus, from this now desolate place, a report of great wisdom and expectation comes to us once again!

The Ahenny Cross shows that the artists were experimenting with the problem of representing the Divine Golden Mean in terms of cosmological art. Here they include the base and omphalus as part of the equation. While on the Killamery Cross, a more pleasing proportion was achieved by eliminating the base and the capstone in the equation.

Chapter 3

The Final Equation of the Golden Mean

We have already spoken about a mysterious subculture in Ireland. This stemmed from the earliest Sea People who inhabited the island and brought with them building technology, science, and astronomy from their own ancient traditions in Morocco. These navigators were generally categorized under the term Fomorian. But their achievements were belittled and denigrated in subsequent generations; because they were disenfranchised by the Act of 79 AD whereby all non-Milesian and non-Gadelian pedigrees were made illegal in the records of the Kingdom of Ireland.

This conveniently brings us to a definition of mystery. A mystery is a situation where important elements of fact are missing, or where specific elements of fact appear out of their usual context.

Therefore, by denigrating and disenfranchising the Fomorians from their rightful place in the record of Irish history, the Irish themselves, *created a confusing mystery about the roots of their own culture.*

Ancient Irish Crosses Founded Upon Megalithic Sites

Wherever you encounter numbers and geometry associated with art, you may rightly conclude that science and religion are also part of this equation.

Let us resume our investigation of the Killamery Cross and other crosses of that generation. The Killamery Cross, with its three quadra-petaled flowers on its shaft, cries out to the observer to fathom its geometric construction. It seems to suggest, "Here is a secret, and I will also direct you how to solve it."

As we have already discussed, the Killamery Cross is constructed upon the principle of two squares, which are then subdivided into eight equal segments which divide the height of the cross from above the base to below the capstone. The top square is then divided by the Golden Mean into one segment of .618 and another segment of .382. Traveling upward from the middle line which separates the two original squares, .382 (of the top square) defines the horizontal line of the center of the cross arm and its central boss. Again, .618 (of the top square) defines a line which goes through the center of the mystical knot underneath the alligator jaws.

KILLAMERY

We have assumed that this mystical knot represents *a mystery about to be revealed* concerning the fulfillment of several of the great cosmic cycles. We imagined that it concerned the much anticipated coming of the Messiah of God. In the following photo-diagram, we have joined the Killamery Cross with the later Cross of Durrow. At the position where the mystical knot of Killamery appears, the Cross of Durrow shows a circle surrounding a lamb, or a ram. The importance of Aries, the Ram, has already been discussed in our section regarding the circular zodiac of Dendera. It should not be surprising that here, as in Egypt, the importance of the Divine Golden Mean and Aries come into play as the prime message which the stones relate. Also, just below this encircled ram stands a figure holding a cross and a staff with the astrological symbol of Aries.

Another important member of the Ossory Group, the Ahenny Cross, is nearby the Slate Quarries. This cross has always struck me as somewhat disproportionate because of its low cross arm. But, when you divide the entire monument, including base, cross, and capstone, into eight segments, then five segments from the base becomes the center line of the cross arm. Each segment is based upon the height of the capstone.

Looking at the Ahenny Cross, the ring of the stone circle always appeared much too large to the artistic eye. Yet, the diameter of the circle (when measured from within its outer rope work) multiplied by *Pi*, 3.14, equals the height of the entire monument. In fact, multiplying the diameter just inside the rope molding of the circle of any true ancient Irish cross by 3.14 will yield the height upon which the geometry of the two squares is based.

The Ahenny Cross with its apparently low cross arm, its huge circle, and its obvious omphalus capstone which is = 1/8 of the entire height. When we place the Durrow Cross alongside the Ahenny Cross, we notice that the cross arm of the Durrow Cross is slightly higher than that of the Ahenny Cross. This is easily explained when we discover that the sacred geometry of the Durrow Cross is based upon where the ornamental panels begin and end. Its geometry begins at the baseline of its bottom ornamented panel, and ends at the top line of its uppermost ornamented panel.

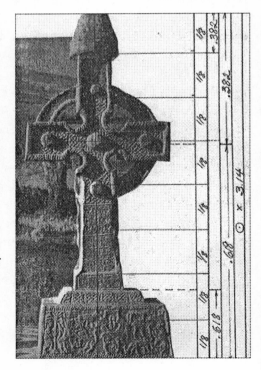

The Killamery and Durrow Cross placed side by side.

Why are crosses of different proportions chosen to display the mystical geometry? I believe it is a question of the progressive development of this art form to select the most beautiful way to combine the cross and circle, and the more ancient base-stone and omphalos.

I believe that the Ahenny Cross was the first monument where the Druids attempted to place the cross upon the primeval base-stone and underneath the omphalos cap. Measurement of these two pieces of the monument reveals that the base is .618, while the omphalos is .382 of their combined height. This proves that knowledge of the Golden Mean predated the addition of the crosses. As we said, the entire monument is based upon two squares divided into eight portions. Therefore, we believe that the Ahenny Cross was the first design to attempt to combine all these elements under the geometry of the Golden Mean.

The Killamery Cross represents the next stage in the evolution of the Druids' attempt to incorporate the mystical Golden Mean directly within the body of the cross itself. Again, the circle is not in 3.14 relation to the total height of the monument; but it is in 3.14 relation only to the height of the cross itself. The Killamery Cross becomes the archetype of all future Irish Crosses. We must remember that these crosses have nothing to do with the crucifixion of Christ. They represent a cosmological prophecy that a great new time period will soon come upon the world, because all of the ancient cycles are about to complete themselves on the borders of Aries/Pisces.

Next in development after Killamery comes the Cross of Durrow. As we said, the Golden Mean Proportion is no longer incorporated into the total height of this cross. It is only related to the artistic panels which ornament the cross. Even the division of the cross into two squares of eight sections is no longer represented. Even still, there is no image of Christ crucified. There is only an image of, what we might call the Ancient of Days and Time, holding a cross and the sign of Aries. Therefore, we cannot absolutely determine if the Durrow Cross falls within the Christian era, because its symbolism and proportions still relate it to the cosmology of the ancients. But, let us also remember that the majority of Druids were immediate and avid converts to Christianity, because they expected and longed for the promised appearance of the Messiah.

The Golden Mean and Newgrange

According to the publication of *Newgrange* by the Midlands East Tourism Board, Newgrange was anciently called *Bru na Boinne,* the Palace on the Boyne:

> The passage graves of Newgrange, Knowth and Dowth . . . are older than Stonehenge, Mycenae or even the pyramids of Egypt . . . Their survival through more than five thousand years reflects the sophistication of their design, and the ingenuity of the Stone-Age culture which constructed them . . . Of all the megalithic tombs discovered, only Gavrinis in south-east Brittany can in any way compare with Newgrange for richness of ornamentation and variety of motif as well as in the technical excellence of its execution.

These great wonders of the ancient world are acknowledged to have been built between 3500 and 2700 BC.

We know that every ancient site on the planet from Baalbek to the Great Pyramids to Stonehenge was at one time discovered, and then reused and reused again, and later added to by subsequent cultures. The reason for this continuity was out of respect for antiquity. But, just as important, these sites had scientifically demonstrable energy properties emanating from specialized formations of underground water spirals. As we saw at Killamery, the conformation of the water spirals produced mental equilibrium and effectively cured headaches.

These special places were marked by their discoverers by means of upright stones and omphalai. Later cultures expanded upon the demarcations of these sites to better represent their total functions. Sometimes these sites, or navels, represented greater conjunctions of larger water patterns over a greater area of the landscape, and focusing upon a central navel, which was like the eye of a spider web. I would think Stonehenge, the Pyramids, Carnac, and Newgrange each represent one of these greater focal navels. Those who wish to gain a better understanding of these matters should consult Underwood's *Pattern of the Past*.

My interpretation of Bru na Boinne, Newgrange, is that the ancient water diviners discovered a very potent *triple spiral* within this especially rich underground-water region of the Boyne Valley. A triple water spiral is indicative of a holy site. Its properties heighten adoration and communion with the divine. The rock art of Bru na Boinne represents these triple spirals.

Furthermore, the diviners discovered that the major track-lines formed a huge circle (the present boundary walls of the tumulus) around the triple spiral and communicated directly with the center of the triple spiral along the passageway. This direction of the passageway coincided with the direction of the setting of the winter sun at solstice. In addition, the freestanding stones outside the tumulus demarcate the halo or *cliphus* of the outermost track-line spiral. Upon drawing a diameter of the halo circle along the passageway finds that the southwest basin on the left is located at .382, or the Golden Mean Proportion of the entire diameter of the exterior halo.

Such wondrous and striking coincidences found in nature indicate that Bru na Boinne was not only a divine holy site of great significance, but that it possessed astronomical and cosmological significance as well. It is therefore no wonder that the site was maintained and held in high regard over such an immense period of time and by very divergent cultures.

In review, Leonardo da Vinci has reminded us that the human proportion is based upon the Golden Mean. "Man is the Measure of all Things," he is the expression of all creation, and his form represents the cosmos of the universe. As man is the Golden Mean, so the cosmos is the Golden Mean. The ancient Irish Crosses and Bru na Boinne combine art, astronomy, and geometry to express their appreciation of science and religion in one cosmological context.

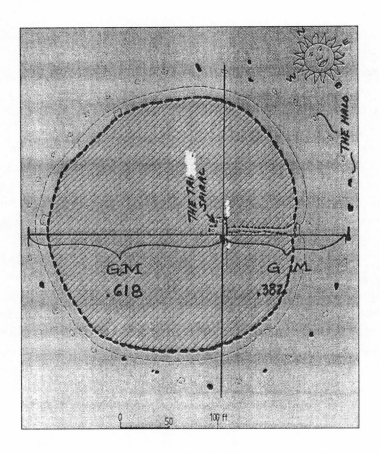

APPENDIX I

Review of the Time Periods of the Zodiac and the Cosmic Body

Christ said, "If you destroy this temple, in three days, I will build it up again." He was referring to the temple of his body, while his listeners thought that he meant the Temple in Jerusalem. Schwaller de Lubicz was inspired by this saying. In his book, *The Temple in Man,* he shows that the design of the Temple of Luxor was based upon the human body and its proportions. This is all *pure cosmology.* Namely, the human form, the temple, and the cosmic universe are all one. Each is an expression of the other.

The microcosm of the human body is a representation of the body of the galaxy and, in turn, of the universe. The cosmologers related these parts to the houses of the zodiac. These houses of the zodiac serve to define specific regions of the heavens as a backdrop to determine the annual progress of the sun around the heavens, the position of the Cycle of the Precession of the Vernal Equinoxes, the position of the progress of our solar system around the galaxy, and any other heavenly cycle that we wish to study. The specific regions of the heavens refer to parts of the universe which transmit certain characteristics and themes down through the lower cycles. The macrocosm of the universe relates to the human body as follows:

The head = Aries; *the neck* = Taurus; *the arms* = Gemini; *the breast* = Cancer; *the heart* = Leo; *the bowels and womb* = Virgo; *the forearms* = Libra; *the genitals and parts of procreation* = Scorpio; *the thighs* = Sagittarius; *the knees* = Capricorn; *the lower legs* = Aquarius; *the feet* = Pisces.

When we see Egyptian gods without arms, we should see a relation to Gemini (shoulders) which is a house of Hermes/Mercury/Thoth, the god of intellect and science. Indeed, the Egyptians regarded people who were born without arms, as sacred persons. Often the ancients used the opposite symbol to what they wanted to show, because nature herself presented these opposite influences. Therefore, sometimes the symbols showed the exact opposite of what they wanted to show. Without arms means the sign of Gemini, patron of the arms. The symbol of a body without a head, most probably refers to the sign of Aries, patron of the head.

A figure that is ithyphallic is related to Scorpio (genitals and private parts). We hear of the bloodletting ritual from the penis of Mesoamerican kings. This seems very peculiar to us until we see that the global geography of Mesoamerica corresponds to the heavenly regions of Scorpio.

The images of the great Buddha with a magnificent belly naturally seem to portray fruitfulness and abundance. But cosmologically, this physical appearance relates to the cosmic region of Virgo (stomach and womb), which is the house of the exaltation of Mercury, god of wisdom. So, if we read that Zeus sewed up Dionysius in his thigh (to later give birth to him) we should understand that the chronological shorthand of this system refers to a period of the time related to Sagittarius.

Let us compare the unique genealogy of Skytobrachion, as recorded in the works of Diodorus Sicilus, to the classical Greek account of Apollodorus as well as to the Egyptian version recorded by Manetho.

Skytobrachion	Apollodorus	Manetho

The Galactic Age of Scorpio:

Skytobrachion	Apollodorus	Manetho
Uranus & Cretan Zeus	Uranus & Ge	Hephaestus

The Galactic Age of Sagittarius

The Great Titans Titea & Idaea	The Hundred Handed	Helios

The Galactic Age of Capricorn

Basilea, Hyperion, Helius & Selene	Cyclopes	Agathodaemon Thoth

The Galactic Age of Aquarius

Cronus & Rhea Atlas & Pleione Hesperus & Pleiades	Cronus & Rhea Iapetus & Asia	Cronus

The Galactic Age of Pisces

Olympian Zeus Poseidon, Pluto	Zeus & Hera	Osiris & Isis

Amazingly, the different genealogists seem to agree to a remarkable extent. It must appear astonishing at first to realize that mythology follows the Galactic Cycle which revolves over a period of millions of years! This Galactic Cycle follows a counter-clockwise order from Aquarius to Pisces to Aries—therefore, coming from the west and traveling to the east. The Galactic Cycle is the *Cycle of Culture* which we have been continually demonstrating as having its origin in the West. Therefore, the development of culture and its historical myth comes from the West, where the first images of the waxing moon appear.

Again, this cycle involves millions of years while the Precessional Cycle moves from one house to another in only 2,160 years. This cycle promotes the rise of civilizations from east to west. Precession also expresses universal forces, themes, and characters as it more rapidly travels through the various houses of the zodiac. But, Precession is under the overriding influence of the Galactic Cycle. Let us review this mythological-cultural sequence of the Galactic Cycle in more detail:

1. Zeus/Jupiter is the lord of the Galactic Age of Pisces. Osiris and Isis are the Egyptian versions of Jupiter and Hera. In astrology, Pisces is the lunar house of Jupiter. This house is also the exaltation of Venus, wherefore we have Hera, Isis, and Aphrodite. Heracles, whose name means the fame of Hera, is the Heaven-Holder.

2. Cronus/Saturn is Earth-Holder of the Galactic Age of Aquarius, which is the lunar house of the planet Saturn. Mercury is a governor of the triangle of Aquarius, Libra, and Gemini. Atlas is the Heaven-Holder, and his son, Hermes, is the prophet of the sciences. Because of the dark influence of Cronus, The Heaven-Holder is called *olofronous*, or dark-minded.

3. Capricorn is the solar house of Saturn/Cronus. It is the exaltation of Mars. The triangle of Capricorn is governed by Venus and the moon. The Agathodaemon and the wise Cyclopes are associated with this time.

4. Sagittarius is the solar house of Jupiter. The governors of the triangle of Sagittarius, Leo, and Aries are the planet Jupiter and the sun. According to Manetho, Helios, the sun, rules this galactic cultural age. The Greater Titans and the Hundred-Handed make this an age of giants, great building, and scientific accomplishments.

5. Scorpio is the solar house of Mars. The governors of the triangle of Scorpio, Pisces, and Cancer are Mars, Venus, and the moon. The ithyphallic Hephaestus, the god of artisans using fire, and his mythology (including adventures with Mars) fits well into

the setting of Scorpio. The fact that Uranus is castrated of his genitals exactly fits into the lore of Scorpio.

6. Libra is the exaltation of Saturn. It is the solar house of Venus. It is part of the triangle belonging to Mercury and Saturn. It is the depression of the sun. I would say that this cultural period reflects the Golden Age when animals could speak, and everyone lived in accord and tranquility. During this age, the regions now occupied by California enjoyed the climate of an earthly paradise.

This record of the history of *world culture* is preserved in these ancient myths with their allusion to the members of the cosmic body. They also refer to the planets, whose natures are akin to the elementary forces that dominate these vast cosmic periods.

In terms of our present global geography, this obviously does not represent the shapes of the land masses of many millions of years ago. The cultural age of Libra was located in California. The age of Scorpio is Central America and the mid United States. The age of Sagittarius corresponds to South America and the very easternmost parts of the United States. Capricorn comprehends the mid Atlantic Ocean. Aquarius is Western Africa, Spain, France, Great Britain, and Ireland. Pisces is the region of Libya, Egypt, Europe, and Greece.

This scheme is predicated entirely upon the fact that Jesus Christ is the true Messiah who was born in Bethlehem and crucified in Jerusalem, the new Heavenly City, in Palestine. This sole scientific fact establishes a new Prime Meridian for cultural geography upon the new Heavenly City. This Prime Meridian of Culture is located precisely on the astronomical borders of Pisces and Aries. All of this heralds the dawn of a new Cultural Age of Aries. *On earth, as it is in heaven.*

APPENDIX 2

The astrological Decan Figures on the rim of the heavens, especially those of the circular Dendera Zodiac.

We notice that on the Circular Zodiac of Dendera and many other ancient zodiacs that smaller figures are depicted below the circle of the zodiac. What are these, and what do they mean?

Usually 36 images are used to represent every ten degrees of the twelve divisions of the sphaera.

Sicilus *(ii.30.6)* says that the Chaldeans had a system of 30 stars called "counseling gods," twelve of which were the gods of the months, and beyond the circle of the zodiac, they had 24 stars called the "Judges of the Universe." Bouche-Leclercq in his note to Sicilus responds that the author has confused the 36 stars known as the decans with the 30 stars of the month of the Egyptians.

Abu Masar mentions that the Persians, Indians and the Egyptians all use the idea of a **cosmic personification of the heavens**, which the 36 decans may represent. Abu Masar also says that these figures may represent stations of the moon, national heroes and feasts, as well as markers of chronological cycles.

Franz Boll, in a note on a tract of Hermes Trismegistus, tells of amulets of 36 decans in which 36 lords of the zodiac are mentioned by name and form. Also, Boll records 36 gem stones engraved with names and also the existence of 36 magic herbs. The Papyrus Oxyranchus mentions 72 lords of the zodiac.

The ancient writers say that there is much disagreement among nations and different astrological schools about the character and meaning of the Decan Figures.

This disagreement is only natural because the influence of the regions of the heavens is modified according to the positions of the many cosmic cycles. Also, the same heavenly regions have different influences on the twelve regions of the globe. Therefore, the Decan Figures must change according to time and region.

We do not agree with the vagaries of these types of astrological influences. We prefer only the pure cosmic consequences. Yet, we will discuss them here as information for the reader.

The idea of *earthly personification of the heavens* is quite simple. The astrologers, through long observation, have noted that when the sun, moon and planets are strongly related to a 10 degree portion of a certain zodiac sign that special apparitions and manifestations take place. These become the subject of legend and lore. In Ireland we find the story of *the headless coachman and his team of headless horses.* There is also the story of *Jackie the Lantern,* which is a supernatural light hanging as a lantern from the sky. These ghostly forms frequently appeared in November and have become a part of American Halloween lore.

For the sake of information, we will cover some of the Decan lore for a few of the zodiac signs.

Aries

Abu Masar says that in the first decan of Aries rises Athena. In the second decan rises a cultivated field. Boll, in the appendix to the *Sphaera,* says that according to various feast calendars, the time of the sun in the Ram is devoted to the child-bed days of Isis after the birth of Horus, the feast of Hathor and the eye of the sun, the birth of Hor, the birth of the sun. The name of Seth is not to be spoken. Some of the calendars report the birth date of Hor going into the beginning of Taurus. In mid-Taurus, there is a feast when an antelope and pig *(Seth animals)* are savagely cut apart. On Dendera there is a figure sitting on a lotus beneath Aries. Plutarch

(Isis and Osiris 355) says that, "They believe that the sun rises as a new-born (child) from the lotus…allegorically…the enkindling of the sun from the waters."

Pisces

According to Hopfner *(Isis and Osiris)* at this time occurs the entrance of Osiris into the moon and also his burial in Busiris. Later there occurs the spring festival of Isis. Abu Masar tells of a bull deer called Jamar, in whose nostrils appear two snakes. Teukros says that there is a scorpion in whose mouth are a pair of snakes. In the mid-portion rises a mysterious identity called "the middle of the heavens." In the last part of Pisces rises the head of the crocodile whose head is averted like Aries and Taurus. The Indians say that here appears a naked man with feet outstretched with a lance in his stomach. On the rim of the Dendera zodiac is a seated naked figure that is armless and headless.

Scorpio-Sagittarius

There are some very curious Decan and rim figures in this region. Above Scorpio is a seated figure riding on a barque. Sagittarius' front hoofs are riding on a barque. The rim figure of a seated ape rides on a barque, and next to him is a ram's head with a solar disc on a plinth. Below all this and outside the circle is the blunt marker which seems to point near to the pole of the ecliptic. Boll says that the Sphaera Barbarica shows the outrageous long sting of Scorpio touching a circle at the feet of Sagittarius. There is also a circle or *clyphus* over Scorpio and also surrounding Aries.

Appendix 3

Cosmological Synopsis of *Origin of Culture and Civilization*

1. The Middle East, Greece, and Rome transmitted Western Culture but none of them are the original homelands of Western Culture.

2. The rise of Nations, Civilizations, and Empire directly follow the Cycle of the Precession of the Equinoxes from East to West traveling 30 geographic degrees in about 2,160 years.

3. The much slower Cycle of Culture is from the opposite direction from West to East responding to the progress of our solar system around the center of our Milky Way Galaxy. This cycle completes itself in many millions of years.

4. By necessity, because they travel in opposite directions, these cycles cross one another and must clash about every 25,290 years. When this happens there are horrendous scientific, religious, and cultural consequences. If this confrontation should occur upon the boundaries of the zodiac signs so that the Galactic Cycle enters into a new sign, the upheaval is magnified and a new cultural theme is born. This is what happened at the crucifixion

of the Messiah. It is upon these principles that the ancients founded their scientific cosmology. These became the foundation of an all encompassing worldview comprising astrology, revelation, and a sequential genealogical mythology of gods and heroes.

5. For the ancient mind, science and religion were intertwined and mutually dependent upon each other. Religion defines the magnitude and importance of human genius, true revelation, prophecy, and incarnation. Religion asks the question, "Is this done by the agency and will of *the Holy Spirit of God* or is this the work of man alone?" Then, science determines the astronomical position and the time of this inspiration or revelation. The geographical place on the globe where the appearance of genius occurred establishes a congruency between the astronomy of the heavens and the geography of the earth. Time becomes the equation between these two points—one in space, one on earth.

6. Therefore, according to ancient thinking, the Revelation and Appearance of Christ is undeniably the most important of all scientific facts. The majesty of this event is singular and unique, as it occurred not only during a clash of the great Cycles of Culture and Civilization, but the astronomical position was such that it occurred directly upon the borders of Pisces and Aries as the cycles transgressed into opposite signs and regions of the heavens. The results are apparent to us now, for they heralded the utter demise of the ancient worldview, and the inception of the new and modern cosmic age.

7. The ancient worldview employed many ingenious arts and modes of communication. Among these were astrology and myth, as well as anthropomorphism and zoomorphism. These were designedly composed to be understood on three levels: the Hieroglyphic, or sacred and divine; the Philosophical, or symbolic and ideal; and finally, the Demotic, or common, sensual, and material. These triple meanings were always considered vital to safeguard and insure the cultural transmission of these sciences over vast periods of political and natural upheavals.

8. Culture and Civilization are diametrically opposed principles; they are like cold and hot. Yet, they check each other's influence to promote

harmony. All balanced and harmonic cycles appear to be similar to a marriage of mutual convenience—love and respect are not always apparent, but most things work out in the end.

9. Culture and Science are the products of the patient accumulation, preservation, and transmission of occasional sparks of genius and divine inspiration over an immense period of time. The faint sparks of inspired genius which are accumulated become like the fire of Prometheus. We are in a remote corner of the universe, and our drama is our long and hard struggle to emulate and communicate with the Divine intelligence, patience, and love. The amazing quest of our ancient forefathers has produced a concord of history, science, and religion.

APPENDIX 4

The Mystery of Chaco Canyon

During the winter solstice of 1977, high upon the remote Fajada Butte in New Mexico, Anna Sofaer discovered an ancient stone alignment apparatus to mark the appearance of the shortest day of the year.

This mechanism consisted of three thin stone slabs, closely arranged, so that sun and moon light could barely fall through this tight spacing and project upon a larger and a smaller spiral incised upon the stone on the cliff below. This seemingly primitive tool turned out to be a precise chronometer of the seasons of the sun and the passages of the declinations of the moon during its nineteen year Metonic cycle. What was created was an instrument for choreographing the dancing movements of the sun and the moon.

What was so amazing about this discovery was that Fajada Butte was part of a holy complex involving an enormous ceremonial centerpiece which attained a height of five stories, which was in turn, interrelated with other temples and stone works over 25 miles away in the distance. All these interrelated buildings, meeting rooms, dance floors, and other places demonstrated different declinations of solar and lunar phenomena. Astonishingly, this purely religious center known as Chaco Canyon is bisected by an artificially marked North to South road which extends perfectly straight over mountains and cliffs an incredible 450 miles into the distance, like some giant longitudinal marker at 107 degrees West. It might be of interest to investigate if the star Antares of the constellation Scorpio bears any relation to the arrangement of this extraordinary site?

Anna Sofaer's findings were produced as videos by the Solstice Project and narrated by Robert Redford: *The Sun Dagger*, 1982, and *The Mystery of Chaco Canyon*, 1999. Anna Sofaer and researchers of the Solstice Project write that spiral patterns engraved upon rocks also appear in Brittany, Ireland, Italy, Malta, Nicaragua, Peru, and Indonesia.

The Anasazi people occupied the Great Sage Plain which experiences some extra weeks of growing season because it totally tilts toward the south and the light of the sun. Below this special *oasis of the sun* lies the sacred center of the Chaco Canyon.

John N. Harris writes in *Spirasolaris* (Internet),

> It is usually accepted that agrarian societies necessarily require a good working knowledge of the seasons, but hardly to this degree of accuracy, surely. Moreover, what can be made of the technical competence and sustained intellectual effort involved in the construction of such a site? And why in such a remote and relatively difficult location? Even though the Anasazi have other impressive credentials, there still remains the major question of why the "Sun Dagger" project was implemented in the first place . . . this still does not account for the skill and competence inherent in the Site itself.

The two statements above are exactly the most important questions that one could ask about this site: *Why* is there such an extreme scientific level of accuracy required over such a large site extending to great distances? And why has it been constructed upon such difficult terrain?

Sofaer has already shown us that there was no evidence of camp refuse or signs of habitation at Chaco Canyon. Therefore, it must be recognized as a religious center of a pure and sacred magnitude.

There is something that I would like to say regarding the accurate readings of these stone astronomical mechanisms. Back in Ireland I recall making a simple equinoctial/solstical marker *in one year* by marking the most southerly and the most northerly sunsets upon a very flat fixed limestone slab. The division between these demarcations would be the equinoxes. There is nothing highly scientific about this, yet the accuracy is, beyond question, acceptable.

The reason that ancient scientist/priests wanted to achieve absolute accuracy of the four seasons was to determine the exact part of the zodiac sign in which the Vernal Equinox occurred. Finding this special place was necessary to interpret the unique theme of this part of the zodiac sign in order to celebrate the correct and proper ceremonies.

Having said this we should also review what we have said about the nature of the ancient sites. What makes an ancient site sacred? Underwood has told us that it is the presence of underground water spirals, arranged in specific geometric patterns which exhibit sacred proportions or astronomical constellations, directions and patterns.

We have amplified upon the investigations of Hapgood by saying that the priests and druids used the astronomical relations and conjunctions of the heavenly bodies to act upon *the tides of water and blood* of their audience's own bodies. By carefully and scientifically coordinating of the astrological phenomena with their rituals and incantations, their followers were naturally stimulated by their own physical reaction to the heavenly bodies of the cosmos in unison with the melody, song and prayers of their scientific priest leaders. These druids themselves were naturally inspired by being placed between such a powerful interaction of heaven and earth.

The sun at its cardinal stations of Summer and Winter solstice, Spring and Fall equinox, heightens the strength and gravity of all other astronomical phenomena occurring at these periods. Frank Joseph, *Sacred Sites of the West (p.117)*, relates that each autumn, a few days after the Fall equinox, there occurs an extraordinary *gathering of eagles* over the town of Squamish on the river of that same name, in British Columbia. Though food is to be found more abundantly elsewhere, nearly 4000 of the majestic birds gather at this special holy place, at this special time of year.

In my mind, music and poetry are our attempt to delineate and imitate the movements of the Divine Spirit through our song and our word. Therefore, music has always been an integral part of holy celebrations. However, Frank Joseph does notice several so called "Zones of Silence" among Native American peoples. He describes earth energies focused in a vortex at the south end of Vancouver Island, Ohio's Great Serpent Mound, and the Marching Bear Mounds of Iowa.

The awkwardness and inaccessibility of Fajada Butte testifies to the specific appearance of powerful subterranean water spirals at this place. And these spirals are working in unison with other underground water forces of this mighty and magnificent complex and the entirety of Chaco Canyon. The major spirals just happen to be focused underneath this jagged and hard to reach butte.

Harris cites Edwin C. Krupp's *Echoes of the Ancient Skies (1983)* which recount some of the cosmological concepts of the present-day Desana Indians of northwest Colombia. The center of their homeland was determined, they say, by Sun Father, who, when time began, picked a place where his upright staff could cast no shadow. There, at a whirlpool entrance to the womb of the earth, Sun Father impregnated the earth, and from that spot the Desana and their neighbors emerged…Figuratively, the shaft of light from the zenith sun fertilized the earth with the procreative energy…the shaman…acts as an environmental protection agent for the Desana to make sure that they don't consume themselves out of their habitat…A giant hexagon of stars, centered on the belt of Orion, is equated with a hexagon of landmarks on the earth that establishes the limits of tribal territory…The center of the celestial hexagon corresponds to the intersection between the Pira-Paranfi River and the earth's equator. Here, where the sky is said to cohabit with the earth…The Desaria associate a pair of intertwined copulating anacondas with the celestial equator's intersections on the ecliptic…the places occupied by the sun at the equinoxes…the Rock of Nyl…exactly on the equator.

The above language of the Columbian Indians is exactly what we have been discussing throughout this book. Namely, the correspondence between celestial places and earthly geography, and also the underground water spirals which are acted upon by the heavenly bodies (*the sky co-habits with the earth at the whirlpool entrance to the earth's womb*).

We have already said that the Anasazi wished to determine the most exact position of the precession of the vernal equinoxes, because, the correct observation of their religious practices depended upon the Anasazi's correct determination of the appropriate heavenly time. To dishonor the gods through the wrong usages would have placed the entire community in peril.

John N. Harris confirms, "They wanted to be able to predict future astronomical events to coincide with their rituals and prophecy." Therefore, ceremonies for a precessional *vernal point* in the first 1/3rd of **Aries** would not be appropriate when the precessional cycle had advanced to last portions of **Pisces.** These parts of the heavens indicate different spirits and different gods.

The second remarkable mystery of Chaco Canyon is that this holy site was closed up and terminated in a very patient and calculated manner. The film presentations by Anna Sofaer relates that it took an enormous amount of time and effort to dismantle the roofs and seal up the entrances, and consign the remainder to the flames.

It is my guess that Chaco Canyon is of pre-Christian origin. It is a holy place that celebrates the worship of water as an intermediary between earth, humans and the heavens. After Christ, a new Age was initiated. The Anasazi needed revelation concerning what they should do now?

Anna Sofaer has remarked upon the universal usage of spirals cut into rocks at religious sites of great antiquity. Among the oldest megalithic sites are those of Malta. Here, too, are many spiral forms decorating the temples and their altars. Scholars are only beginning to realize the connection between water spirals and astronomical phenomena. The orientation of the Mnajdra Temple is toward the time of the seasons of the year, particularly the equinoxes. Sunrise on the first day of the seasons enters the southern temple and lights up the interior. On the equinox days sunlight not only enters the southern temple, but its beams also light up the temple's main axis, according to *www. Heritagemalta.org.* This ceremony is now celebrated once again for the benefit of visitors to these hallowed monuments.

One of the prime mysteries of Chaco Canyon is the 650 roomed and 5 storied Great House at Pueblo Bonito. The roofs alone required 215,000 mature trees. This amazing structure is an obvious indication of great numbers of people who visited there, yet there is no evidence of camp-rubbish and animal bones signifying long periods of habitation anywhere around this site.

The solution to this enigma will substantiate our basic theory about this place, and the nature of all ancient holy sites of this character. The question to ask is, "When do you need to accommodate large numbers of people congregating at one place? The answer is, *during a special day,* during festivals and religious occasions. Religious festivals are based upon the astronomical relations of cycles, the sun, moon and planets. In other words, the holy day is exactly at a certain hour on a specific day, and only on that day and no other. This is absolutely determined and predisposed by astronomy.

A question arises concerning communication. How do you inform a large number of people, at far distances away, about an important festival? The answer could be that three days after each new moon observers could check for any important smoke signals from the main religious center regarding events to come in the next month. These facts seem to support our thesis about the importance of astrology acting upon the divine waterspirals.

Religious celebration based upon astrology also brings up another important consideration. Events scheduled by astronomical positions permit the possibility of the world community celebrating together with one voice raised to God, at the same time. If this were achieved, it would truly be reminiscent of the Golden Age when men, animals and God lived in harmony.

APPENDIX 5

The Golden Proportion of the Labyrinth

Images of labyrinths and mazes appear throughout the world in connection with ancient sites. Perhaps no one will ever completely solve the meaning of these signs, but we would like to attempt to view them from a cosmological perspective.

Jeff Saward in his *Labyrinths and Mazes* reminds us that the labyrinth has one way in and the same path out. Mazes, however, present optional paths within and sometimes different entrances and exits.

We have explored several reasons for our appreciation of holy sites. The main reason was always the appearance of natural, underground water-spirals which were often in patterns which produced special physiological and psychological effects in humans and animals, birds and even insects. At other times the direction of the water lines followed astronomical phenomena such as the direction of the winter solstice.

One of the prime physiological effects of certain spirals is the special fecundity during insemination and a special ease during the delivery at birth. In respect to the above, we think that a labyrinth symbol is evocative of copulation and the fertilization of the seed within the womb. In rather plain spoken language, there is one way in and one way out.

Later we will see that sacred geometry validates this assumption of symbolizing a fecund and blessed act of union of male and female.

The maze, however, has separate entrance and exit and therefore may symbolize the courses and windings of the human intestinal tract. Aristotle humorously suggested that the food we eat is definitely not inside the stomach, because we would not be able to eat, digest and pass the remainder if it were in a container. He said that food is always *outside* the mouth, throat, stomach and intestines. In the same way it could be said that we are not ever inside the maze, but rather, we are outside the maze!

We have commented many times upon the fact that the natural philosophers thought that the bowels were sacred to the zodiac sign of Virgo, which is the house and exaltation of Hermes/Mercury, god of intelligence. The intestines are not a part of our rational intelligence, but rather, they are our feeling or intuitive intelligence. It is from this tradition that we get our expression, "gut feeling". The moon, also, is the heavenly body that is most related to decisions which the body makes itself, without recourse to rationale, social responsibility or appropriate context. That is why so many of our young people get into difficulties, because they think with their body. They have not as yet learned that the harmonious control unit of our brain can, through long periods of practice, be trained as an intellection processing center.

Perhaps the most famous labyrinth is on the island of Crete, having been constructed by Daedalus for King Minos. The story goes that Pasaphae, the wife of Minos, conceived a desire for the Cretan Bull. To satisfy this unnatural lust, Daedalus constructed a model of a cow, and —well, so on and so forth. This union was cursed by the production of a monster which had a human body and a bull's head. Indeed, most of the Egyptian Pantheon of deities are represented in this fashion. But, we know that this is not a token of monsters, but direct astrological-cosmological symbolism.

The story of King Minos and the Labyrinth is all about the zodiac house and epoch of **Taurus,** the sign of Venus and exaltation of the moon. It is a history all about *bulls.* According to Apollodorus *(II.5-III-i)* in one story, the Cretan Bull is said to have been the one Zeus turned himself into when he abducted Europa on his bull's back. Zeus took her to Crete, and of this union Europa gave birth to Minos.

Minos wished to reign over Crete after Asterius died childless, even though he had taken Europa as his queen. Minos then alleged that he had received the kingdom from the gods. In proof of this, he said that whatever he prayed for would be done. He, therefore, sacrificed to Poseidon, and prayed that a bull might appear from the sea. Minos further promised to sacrifice whatever Poseidon should send forth out of the waters. Poseidon sent him the most beautiful of bulls, *perhaps* the likeness of the original Cretan Bull.

Minos could not bear to destroy such a beautiful creature, and therefore reneged upon his promise to Poseidon. It was for this reason that Poseidon punished Minos with the unnatural deceit of Pasiphae.

Pasiphae is the sister of Aeetes of Colchis, a very ancient place of proto-mythology. In a skip-back or mythological reversion to a similar tale, but from very ancient times, Pasiphae is said to have engendered Asterius, later called the Minotaurus, or the Bull of Minos. Asterius is in some instances the Ancient of Days, who is the Master of cycles and the Stars.

Minos eventually gained dominion over the seas, because his mother was Europa, born of the purest of late Phoenician stock. As an important interjection here, I do apologize because it has just struck me that we have become over absorbed with Greek and Egyptian mythology. This story seems to be a true Phoenician myth! A myth to explain the union of the people of Zeus with the Phoenicians, and also why Crete was always different from other Greek lands

Minos defeated Athens and demanded seven boys and seven maidens to be sacrificed to the Minotaurus. This number, seven, has been related by numerous times to the Pleiades which reside in the constellation of Taurus. It was said that these Pleiades were represented to be the daughters of Atlas. The seven most ancient saints of Ireland and Brittany have been spoken of above. This number seven is the number of circuits of the classical labyrinth. Seven is naturally also the seven heavenly bodies, the days of the week, the mean time of each of the four phases of the moon, during its average 28 day cycle.

Many of the European labyrinths were called after the classical city of Troy. As an artificial shell of a cow plays a part of the story of Crete, so likewise, an artificial shell of a horse is the trickery that turns the fortune of the war over the city of Troy. Indeed, the Trojans claimed that the rape and abduction of Helen from the Greeks was only retribution for their rape of Europa from their lands and nations. Even later, the Turks, who overran the continent up to Vienna, retorted that they were only exacting their revenge for the sack of Troy and the war over Helen.

Jerusalem and Jericho are also cities related to the magic of the Labyrinth. The trumpeters made seven circuits of the latter city, before a great out-cry and piercing trumpet-tone raised the walls of that famous city.

Singing and dancing to the light of the moon, in traditional and formalized fashion in special dancing places is common among ancient peoples. Near to our home place in Ireland is a locale by the River Anner called Mullinarinka, *the dancing ring* or *the dancing mill.* The translation in Irish for the stream would be Moon River since Aine *(pron. Awnne)* is the name of the moon.

The Sacred Geometry

The classical labyrinth symbol, which is found world wide, perfectly demonstrates *Golden Mean* proportions. We should draw a tangent base line near the entrance, and another parallel at the opposite side of the spiral. If we connect these parallel lines with a perpendicular, which is then divided in half —we observe that the tip of an imagined erect penis touches this mid line. The point where this erection crosses into the womb of the spiral is precisely .618, or **Phi,** of half the entire body of the spiral.

We have already discussed, at great length, that the Golden Mean is the symbol of all creation from raw matter. It is the governing proportion of imposing form upon lifeless material. It is therefore the universal symbol of fecundity and life. As in the myth about the Cretean Labyrinth, the labyrinth meant that it was a holy site of fecundity.

Ancient people inscribed this symbol upon rocks at places where animals mated or gave birth, easily and successfully. Animals seek out special underground water spirals that assist with delivery, or better guarantee the journey of sperm to the seed. These places were later regarded as holy, because they also facilitated other human and natural functions such as speeches of tribal leaders, common councils or the deliberation of judges.

Appendix 6

Mezo America Culture

Upon first inspection the Aztec, Mayan and Olmec cultures present a very flamboyant artistry of color and form. But when we consider the rain forest environment, tropical flowers the spectacular parrots, birds and jungle fauna, we learn to appreciate their special style. Students of the classics have been brought up to admire the pristine formality of Egyptian style. Conjure up a picture of the gracious Nile, bringer of life and sustenance, flowing through the expansive desert, and you might see a connection between art and environment in the land of Egypt.

I was extremely disgusted when I heard of the tale of the Mayan Priests who were delighted at the formidable *lagrimations* of the children which they were conducting to sacrifice to the rain god —because their tears forebode a plentiful downpour of the life giving rain! Yet, with all due respect, I do not fully credit the callous way this story was told. And furthermore, there is no dependable Nile in Yucatan —rain is actually a matter of survival, life and death for a very large population.

The more I studied these Native Americans, the more I began to understand them and to like them and their art forms. Curiously located at exact opposite sides of the world, the Meso Americans and the people of

India were the only ones to use the concept of zero. As well, each of their cosmologies recognizes human history extending over periods of millions of years. The comparison of India and Middle America is an interesting topic which some people are working on at the present time. What we would like to do is to compare the Meso-Americans with ancient Atlantic Culture; and even our own modern thinking.

Because, if you strip away the colors and the environment of Middle America, you will get a person who thinks naturally and cosmologically — just like all those ancient people that we have discussed in our text above. We do not need to invent a new study or a new worldview to deal with these people. They fit in too well and even serve to illuminate a portion of our story about all our human ancestors.

Mary Miller and Karl Taube write in *The Gods and Symbols of Ancient Mexico and the Maya,* "According to Aztec accounts, the gods gathered at *Tamoanchan* following previous destructions of the earth. They drew blood from their own bodies to generate a new race of humans; *Quetzalcoatl,* in particular, sprinkled blood from his penis on ancient bones he stole from the underworld. Then, in an act of auto-sacrifice...the god, *Nanahuatzin* immolated himself on a bonfire to create the sun, and *Tecuciztecatl,* followed suit becoming the moon...probably all ancient Mezoamerican peoples **were held in the thrall of this "blood debt," in which humans endlessly owed gods human blood and flesh.** In the Mayan...*Popol Vuh,* the gods destroy successive generations of living beings until a race of humans learns to praise their makers and nourish them through prayer and blood sacrifice."

Every Christian can appreciate the idea of a "blood debt" which is our own personal sacrifice *in return* for the ultimate sacrifice that the god made for us and all of humanity. This is one of the reasons that Christianity thrived in this very kindred culture. The Catholic priest, Landa, was surprised to find native forms of ritual baptism complete with serpent-tailed *aspergillum* for specific rites of cleansing and purification of newborns up to three year old children.

But, in terms of Atlantic culture, some of the resemblances are remarkable. Of course, there are Pleiades cycles, pyramids and symbols of actual *Earth-holders,* and many other similarities. Also, most Mezoamerican burials are accompanied by real dogs or ceramic dogs *(we have discussed the dog's graves in Ireland and the relation of dogs with the exaltation of the moon in Taurus)* .The dead also received a piece of jade or a coin in their mouth to pay for their canoe ride over the waters *(the river Styx)* to heaven. Also, as in Atlantic and Egyptian cosmology, the Mayan gods travel in canoes, especially the heavenly rain gods, the Chac's. We have spoken of the ancient concept of warring elements of contentious natures battling with one another. In *The Gods and Symbols (p.41)* it says that the Aztec term, *atl-tlachinolli,* is composed of the terms for **water** *(atl)* and **fire** *(tlachinolli).* This combination is their actual phrase for the word and concept of war.

But, above all these things, we are most amazed to be able to interpret their creation myth along pure Atlantic cosmological lines. In their mythology, the Mexica *(the true name of the Aztecs)* came from an island in a lake. This place was called Aztlan, *"place of whiteness, or of herons".* They replicated this place in their design of Tenochtitlan, the island city of the Aztecs upon which Mexico City was founded.

We will remember from above that the god, Quetzalcoatl, *sprinkled blood from his penis on ancient bones* in order to create a new race of beings after a destruction of the world. The place where the gods gathered is in the region of the geographic co-ordinant of Scorpio, which is related to the private parts, like the penis. *We have already related this geography and time period to the nakedness of Noah and the castration of Uranus.* The idea of reviving humans from ancient bones is that the Galactic Cosmic time period has long ago moved on to Morocco and further onward into the Mediterranean. This story is perfectly in tune with the cosmological philosophy that we have attempted to uncover within this book. The myth perfectly conveys the cosmic meaning.

Appendix 7

The Western Coastal Regions of the Americas

The Western United States exhibits a geographical and a geological panorama which comprises some of the most ancient vestiges on our planet. There is a place in the depths of the Colorado River Grand Canyon which exhibits the oldest exposed stratification upon the entire planet.

When we look at some of the earliest antique maps of the coastlines of the Americas, we notice some stunning abnormalities.

There is a large island off the coast of California. The romance of *Amadis de Gaula,* which every respectable Conquistador carried with him to the New World, featured this island as *Californax,* home of the war-like Amazon women. We could possibly think that this map could be a representation of this coast prior to the time of this large island falling into the ocean. This kind of geological activity is not unusual and reflects the nature of the North American coastline which gradually, and at other times, dramatically and monstrously falls into the sea.

I have always though it too much of a coincidence that the *Californax* of the Amazons, should mimic the Hespera of the Moroccan Amazons.

Other maps show a significant bulge on the western coast of South America. There are many indications of the dramatic elevation of the Andes

Mountains as a consequence of a mighty coastal submergence. Could this old map also be an ancient representation?

Maps exist which portray a believable *North-West Passage,* which connects the Atlantic with the Pacific. These maps motivated many a northern exploration, including one of the possible quests of Lewis and Clark. Even without ice, northern geographical drift has closed this wonder passage of the ancient world.

There is another very peculiar map of the northern regions which exhibits a massive connection of land between Asia and Alaska. This is not shown as an ice covered land-bridge but as an actual piece of terra firma. It may be assumed that like the other abnormalities this map became the inspiration for the theory of Asians crossing to the Americas. This is because in the context of the biblical thinking of the Church, aboriginal Native Americans pose an unpleasant theoretical difficulty; as well as a dogmatic conundrum.

We would therefore like to examine the history of these coastlands in order to establish a useable picture of their antiquity.

Prehistoric Man of the Santa Barbara Coast (1929) by David Banks Rogers commands our interest and our attention. His unbiased examination is so intriguing because he so believably describes the monstrous geological forces at play upon the California coast. His examination of the geology on the islands of Santa Cruz and Santa Rosa led him to report that the, **"original structure of the land having been completely inverted."** Upon this stage Banks Rogers describes the immense antiquity of three diverse prehistoric people whose footprints and impressions still remained undisturbed upon these virgin coastlands.

Prehistoric populations and geological upheaval on the California coast are important to our interpretation of the cosmic theme of cosmic cycles. For us, Jerusalem is the global geography related to the Galactic Cycle's position in **Aries.** California is directly 180 degrees on the other side of the world, which is the region of **Scorpio** and **Libra.** As we said, if you put a pole through Jerusalem, the other hemi-sphere of that pole is mostly ocean. This creates the impression that land is just being ground away along the subduction plate of the California coast. While this fact is obvious to any novice student of geology, my question is, "Why isn't land being replaced on this side of the globe, and why is the majority of this territory covered by ocean?"

Rogers says *(p.34)* that he was able to piece together a picture of a succession of distinct cultures, possibly of races, that had each run its course and completely vanished from the region, and that the first of these people had arrived at a period so remote that even the climatic conditions differed greatly from those to which we are accustomed.

In describing Santa Cruz Island, Rogers writes *(p.277)*, "The island has apparently undergone repeated transformations through the agency of coastal upheavals. A section of the sea floor of the Miocene age was lifted above the surface, broken and torn, and its crevices filled with igneous intrusions. This new born land, of whose extent we know nothing, endured for a time and was swallowed by the sea. This cycle was repeated at least three times, probably many more than that, previous to the Pleistocene Period. Upon at least four occasions, torrents of melted stone were poured forth, each of these outpourings of a different nature from that which preceded or followed it…A map of this part of the western coast of the American continent in early Pleistocene time would probably present an entirely different appearance from that with which we are now acquainted…instead of an island dotted sea…we should see a wide extent of fertile forest land. We know that these dense forests were the haunts of mammals that are now extinct. Among these were herds of elephants, of at least two species, droves of horses, giant ground-sloths, saber-toothed cats and huge wolves…At some time preceding the close of the Pleistocene Period, there occurred a tremendous remodeling of the coastal region…in some places one hundred miles in width were suddenly swallowed by the sea…" Bones of these prehistoric animals are found within the uplifted strata of rocks and within the La Brea Tar Pits of Los Angeles.

I do not know why, but I had always been under the impression that California was an empty virgin territory at the time of the coming of the Europeans. Nothing could be further from the truth. Rogers writes *(p.8)*, "The reports that reached the King of Spain of the teaming population of Alta California, all immersed in the darkest paganism, aroused in him a zeal to gather into the church these throngs of potential neophytes." On the same page he writes, "Apparently no effort was made in these early contacts with the yet unspoiled race to obtain a knowledge of its past history or religious beliefs, or to compile a vocabulary of the various dialects encountered. These were said to have varied greatly, even in adjoining villages, and to have been unintelligible to those a few leagues away."

Rodgers concludes *(p.266)* that, "We have here the remains of the most extensive unbroken Indian settlement, of which we have knowledge, on the American continent north of the Mexican boundary." He is lead to this conclusion by the extraordinary depth of the camp debris throughout the Channel Islands, which in many places reached to the depth of 14 to 20 feet!

My Irish wife, Nuala, was taught in school that Columbus discovered a virgin territory, not as yet populated with human kind. Indeed, I remember getting much the same impression –because the history books always called it **the New World.** How would it be, if this New World turns out to be *the really Old World?* And that we are consciously destroying the most important anthropological records existing on our planet?

The European conquest of North and South America involved the most hateful genocide and culture destruction witnessed upon our planet. No apology can explain, nor make right, what happened. Yet, this is what happens in the world on the level of politics and nations. I would just ask intelligent students not to ameliorate, nor defend these actions. Quite simply put, it was a subversive and brutal conquest of an innocent and friendly native people.

David Banks Rogers is amazed at some of his findings. We will offer a conglomeration of some of his statements: "There are everywhere evidences of the former existence of a teeming prehistoric race *(p.274)*. The formation appears to be of considerable thickness and is composed of alternating beds of sand and clay…It is from this deposit that remains of elephants have recently been taken…for it definitely places the connection of these islands with the mainland as late as the Pleistocene time *(p.273)*…the close of the Pleistocene Period, there occurred a tremendous remodeling of the coastal region. Areas, approximating in some places one hundred miles in width were suddenly swallowed by the sea *(p.278)*. Probably the most interesting of all the products of Canalino craftsmanship were the seaworthy boats *(p.333-339)* large and staunch boats…exactness…live coals were thrown in with the lump asphaltum…the resultant fire would convert the asphaltum to the consistency of molasses, at which stage it would enter every crevice and orifice…very light…elicited praise from the early Spanish explorers…night voyages…round trips of 150 miles…a maritime people for some time *(p.341)."*

Rogers then mentions the Oak Grove People *(p.342)* whom the native

Canalino called, "the Ancient, Ancient Ones...a people that lived in the land long before we came." Rogers deduces from their camp sites and building projects that during the long history of these ancient people that they experienced, "a period of tempestuous storms and of a volume of rainfall unknown in our now temperate climate *(p.343)*"

Rogers compares these ancient ones to the many instances of lost people, such as the Ohio Mound Builders, the Cliff Dwellers of Mesa Verde, the Easter Islanders, the Khmers of Angkor, "and others whose passing has to the present remained shrouded in mystery...Every village of the Oak Grove People appears to have been deserted at approximately the same time *(p.355)."*

Prehistoric Man of the Santa Barbara Coast by David Banks Rogers gives us such an insightful look at the former geography, geological forces, animal life, historic and pre-historic natives that one really feels that he has created a vibrant picture of a very ancient time in California. He therefore provides us with an exemplary context that we may refer to and use.

The very idea that about 100 miles of coastline could disappear at one instance is most intriguing and frightening for California residents. If our cosmological picture of the advance of culture and the continuation of cosmic cycles is correct –we cannot imagine that the massive deterioration of the coastline of the Western Americans will miraculously stop and cease. Of course, we are speaking of cycles and events which may not happen for thousands or even millions of years.

Professor Banks Rogers is also surrounded by some mystery and controversy. Namely, it is reported that he established a small museum on the grounds or nearby to the University of Santa Barbara, which, most unfortunately, was burned down. Some people who had seen his collection have reported that it contained unusual artifacts not reported in his annals. But then again, the same sort of mystery was reported of Schliemann, the discoverer of Troy, who was said to have held artifacts of Atlantis in his private collection. Maybe these were just things which did not readily compare to the usual findings?

APPENDIX 8

Someone Lived Here Before Us –
Covering up the Antiquity of Humankind

Dennis Cassinelli, the author of *Gathering Traces of the Great Basin Indians*, originated this wonderful title for his first chapter, *Someone Lived Here Before Us*.

Cassinelli tells us of the Lovelock Cave, 22 miles south of Lovelock, Nevada, on the shore of ancient Lake Lahontan, "The habitation of the cave can be traced back to about 4700 years ago...Some of the bodies were nearly perfectly mummified by the dry conditions in the cave. Some of the mummies were found to have red hair. One skeleton was of a man who measured 6'6" in height." Also among the 10,000 artifacts discovered in 1912-1924, there appeared eleven tulle reed duck decoys –perfectly preserved, but now hidden away in a storage room at the Museum of the American Indian in New York City.

The greater majority of people are shocked at the idea that ancient cultures and civilizations occupied their place in the world thousands and millions of years before the present day. These same people are very frightened by the idea that generations and generations have come and gone through destruction, famine and disease, because this realization speaks to their own mortality and the inevitable calamities of the natural world.

The propaganda against a far reaching antiquity over millions of years is a world wide concerted effort. Academics do not like this notion of great antiquity either because it is not so easy to teach as the simplistic notion of absolute *straight-line progress*. Scientists, also, are adverse to the idea because they have adopted straight-line thinking and progressive Evolution. In their mind, degeneration or devolution is not a possible thesis. Politicians actively hate the idea because they are the ultimate champions of forward movement, because they continually and openly swear to make things better than they are.

Politicians and governments have always favored the idea of the emptiness of the Americas. Some of my European friends were taught that Columbus had discovered a land almost without people. Or, if there were people there, their population was small in relation to the size of the geography. Also, the native culture was primitive, their people migratory, and their religion archaic and/or savage and their sciences non-existent. The Americas have been continually publicized as the *New World,* a virgin palette upon which the conquerors could impose their designs. But, from the knowledge that we have hoped to have gained from this book, the Americas are not the New World, but the Americas are the very **Old and Ancient World.**

Even the Native Americans have problems with the idea that America is a very old territory that was inhabited for millions of years in the past. I have heard rumors that they secretly hold some mementos of ancient people who preceded them here on these shores. The discovery of Kennewick Man led to the conclusion that there may have been distinct other races living here prior to our Native Americans. Poor Kennewick Man was spirited away and locked up some where that he would not be any more trouble to anyone, and even subject to judicial proceedings! Never has a dead skeleton come back to life and create such controversy and fuss.

The most accepted theory of the origin of the peoples of the Americas is that they were of Asian origin, having crossed over by way of the Bering Straight and Alaska. George Erikson in *Atlantis in America (p.56)* tells us that this theory was put forward by a priest of the Roman Catholic Church, Fray Jose de Acosta in 1590. The Beringia migration from Siberia was contrived to disassociate the Lost Tribes of Israel with any connection with the Americas —an idea which the Church was the first to advanced. Erickson writes, "Later, science seized on the idea, and, as it often has, followed the Church's lead, incorporating religious dogma into scientific dogma. A rather flimsy theory, based on no actual research, received universal acceptance from the scientific community and found its way into our body of scientific knowledge. It has remained there long enough that it is now considered conventional wisdom." All Native Americans discount this theory. They all claim that they were placed here by the Creator Spirit. Most probably, Fray Jose de Acosta, got his idea from the Benedict Arias Montanus world map of 1572 published in Antwerp —which clearly shows a massive land connection between Alaska and Asia

The Pedra Furada site at the Capivara National Park in Brazil has provided hard scientific evidence of paintings and human habitation of a high spiritually developed culture from a time 58,000 years BC. In 1986 Drs. Guidon and Delibrias reported C-14 dates of 48-32,000 BP. In the *Athena Review (vol.3, no.2:Peopling of the Americas)*, newer and more refined dating techniques have pushed back the dates to 60K. Human remains were a type of modern Homo Sapiens of the Late Pleistocene in Europe. The Garrincho sample however exhibits an endo-exo cranial fossa (hole in the bone through which arteries pass) and other archaic traits.

The researchers also noted an extraordinary climate change at 7000 BC, from an extremely wet climate of rich vegetation to a much dryer and more temperate climate. David Banks Rogers in his *Prehistoric Man of the Santa Barbara Coast* also reported the **identical** climate change at the same time period (7000 BC) of the Oak Grove Dwellers. On *p.344* he reports of artifacts and a great highway he found 40 feet below the surface of Tecolote Canyon, deposited there by horrendous floods.

Some fanatics have actually threatened to kill the investigators of Pedra Furada. Dr. Niede Guidon says, "I cannot understand why. Perhaps because when you are the first to discover something, people want to kill you because you disturbed the placid waters of the lake. The theories on the peopling of America are only theories…a theory is not a law, but may and must be changed each time new facts are discovered."

Regarding the antiquity of the Americas, it has always impressed me that at the time of the European Conquest of these regions that there were 500 and more distinct language groups identified in the northeastern part of South America —language groups which were as different from each other as the present day Chinese language is to the English language. This type of radical differentiation of language groups is never the result of recent population movements, such as the supposed Siberian invasion. These language groups typify a paradigmatic creation-like context of extreme antiquity in a tranquil and undisturbed setting reminiscent of the Garden of Eden.

Recently I met Winifred Jones, the great-great-granddaughter of Dr. William Jones M.D., to whom the famous Calaveras Skull was first shown. In 1866 workers at the Bald Mt. Mine in Calaveras, California uncovered a skull encrusted within the wall of a mine shaft 130 feet below the surface and also beneath a layer of lava. Once again, because such a find was evidence for the many million year old habitation of the earth, let alone the Americas –this find was laughingly discredited and spirited away to the recesses of the Peabody Museum.

This *Calaveras* is the Spanish name for **skull,** because of the extraordinary findings of hundreds of skulls in the area and river bed. This seems to testify to some extraordinary natural disaster which took so many lives at one time. Also, it was the practice of the gold-seekers to use hydraulic mining by directing powerful water hoses at the hillsides adjacent to the gold carrying rivers. This process uncovered other skulls, skeletons, and plentiful evidence of ancient tools and artifacts buried deep beneath the ground (c. Whitney, *The Auriferous Gravels of the Sierra Nevada of California.* 1880; Wright, *Man and the Glacial Period.* 1897; Becker, *Antiquities from under Toulumne Table Mountain in California.* 1891).

Unfortunately, these finds, while often reported, were never properly categorized or recorded and have disappeared from an extraordinary body of unique evidence. Only the Great Gold Rush could have produced such a wholesale *earth-exposure-mining* technique as water blasting the hillsides. But, like the Spanish conquest of Peru and Mexico, the greed for gold obliterated a special opportunity to gather ancient traditions and unique information.

I have tried diligently to reconstruct and gain information on these extraordinary finds. But, shortly after these discoveries appear it seems that someone has instituted a cover-up which was cleverly documented by reasonable academic analysis. In *U.C. Archaeological Survey #12; California Archaeology: 13-16,* it is reported that peculiar, petrified and gigantic skulls and bones from a race distinct from the Indians had been discovered in the

Mammoth Cavern in Calaveras. On further examination, it became evident that the skulls were neither petrified nor gigantic —having acquired several layers of sulphate of lime dripping from the cavern. Their cranial development was similar to those of present Indians, though one of the skulls appears to have, "a very intellectual character." The study concludes with the mention of a very long list of other caves where similar remains were obviously thrown into the deep almost vertical cavities of these deep repositories.

Curiously, the Sierra Miwok, the historic inhabitants of this region, cremate or bury their dead under stone mounds. In their tradition the caverns are inhabited by stone giants who come forth at night searching for human victims, "to be carried to the depths to be devoured. The thought of tossing corpses of fellow tribal members into caves to be eaten by this monster was abhorrent to the recent Indians."

W.J. Wallace who wrote the article suggests that carbon-14 dating might at some time be carried out on some of the gathered materials. In his footnotes he references other caves and findings, among them near Cool, "yielded human bones and those of extinct animals."

In conclusion, it seems evident that much of the gathered material which is now in storerooms needs to be reexamined by bi-partisan experts who will furnish impartial evidence for both sides of this debate over extreme antiquity.

Lastly, there is the instance of the controversial *Neale Mortar and Pestle* discovered in gravel close to bed rock at Tuolumne Table Mountain. These artifacts are estimated to be between 33-55 million years old according to *Forbidden Archeology by Cremo & Thompson*. The geologist, George F. Becker attested to J.H. Neale's statements that the find had been deposited 1400 feet from the mouth of the tunnel, and 200 feet beyond the edge of solid lava in the prevolcanic auriferous gravels. Stone tools and fragments of human bones were also discovered by the miners at this site, within the gravel layers.

There are universal instances of the traditions and memories of ancient people being willfully effaced by those who came behind them. The story of both North and South Native Americans is a testimony of this cruel fact. We have rehearsed the case of the Fomorians of Ireland whose genealogies were banned by edict in order to destroy their memory. It is evident that this practice was also used in Greece, where the roots of more ancient people were submerged into the ancestry of the later conquerors. Finally, we would like to note a new movement in Egyptology, called *Khemitology*. One book that I read by Stephen S. Mehler, *The Land of Osiris*, dealt with Egyptian proto-culture of many tens of thousands of years ago, when the Nile flowed on the western side of the Pyramids. This book has some interesting photos and arguments, especially concerning the healing power of water and sound. In general human terms we should realize that the conscious obliteration of the memory of the *people who lived here before us* is a very natural human reaction. That is just the way life is, and the way we are. However, it just makes life hell for the researcher into antiquity and the truth.

Peruvian archaeologist, Ruth Solis, is the director of the site at Caral in Peru. She has uncovered a vast 150 acre complex of buildings, pyramids and plazas of, what some believe may be the oldest urban center in the Americas. Evidence of trade and exchange between coastal fishing regions and produce from the Andes suggests that Caral may be a significant model of early mercantile civilization. The main pyramid covers an area of four football fields and reaches a height of 60 feet. Attached to this pyramid area is a large sunken amphitheater with a capacity for several hundreds during civic and religious ceremonies. The abundance of condor bone flutes and llama bone cornets places Caral at a high level of culture. From this mother city, 17 other pyramid city complexes emerged scattered over a 35 square mile area. Because this site is under-funded, significant analysis of dating and astronomical alignment is as yet unavailable.

Finally, when we look at *Science Frontiers: Some Anomalies and Curiosities of Nature*, compiled by William R. Corliss *(1994)*, we should soberly consider the genuine wealth of evidence of ancient occupation of the Americas. The following are accounts taken from this work: Decades ago, Gutorn Gjessing pointed out that the identical Red Paint Culture was found in Norway as that existed in Atlantic North America. No one paid much attention to that, but more recent carbon-14 dating has shown that the identical cultures had identical carbon-14 dates of about 7,000 years ago. It is now admitted that this was a high latitude culture that obviously sailed the stormy north Atlantic and stretched from northwest Europe over to America from Labrador into New York State (p.21).

Corliss also mentions sites where human occupation may be earlier than at Pedra Furada in Brazil. There is the Calico site in California which has rendered some dates of 20,000 years ago. While in some of the deeper layers, estimates have come in at about 200,000 years old.

Other sites bearing evidence of human habitation in extreme antiquity are mentioned: Old Crow River in the Yukon, Alaska (100K-BP); Meadowcroft Rockshelter, Pennsylvania (16K-BP); Monte Verde, Chile (33K-BP); Toca de Esperanza, Brazil (3Million-BP); Orogrande, New Mexico (35K-BP); Yuha Pinto Wash, Imperial Valley, California (50K-BP); Fort Morgan, Colorado (30K-BP); Valsequillo, Mexico (250K-BP).

I imagine that in the near future, no one will ever doubt man's continual existence here on earth. We say *continual*, in the sense that we cannot put a simple start date for God's creation. We are now only at the forefront of gaining a general acceptance for this philosophically obvious viewpoint, that mankind has been around forever. However, it is now definitely time to stop the apologizing, and require the rest of the academic community to recognize the facts as they come forward *–someone lived here before us!*

As a final note, the cave called the Grotto of the Cosmos, near Xique-Xique in central Brazil is believed to be the oldest astronomical observatory in the Americas. Notches marking the winter solstice and red sun and comet figures probably belong to a 10,000 year old culture, which adopted the site from people who were in evidence some 300,000 years ago.

We really need not get too excited about the reluctance of academics to catch up with all these exciting new discoveries. For their position is much like that of the Catholic Church investigating miracles and apparitions of Our Lady. As befits their position of leadership, both these bodies need to sit back for a while to take time to review information as it develops.

BIBLIOGRAPHY

(Note: "LCL" signifies The Loeb Classical Library, Harvard University Press, Cambridge, MA, and William Heinemann Ltd., London. Also "LCL" always indicates a translator's work from Greek and Latin into English.)

Abbott, Patrick. *Natural Disasters*. Boston: McGraw Hill, 2004.

Albiruni. *Vestiges of the Past*. Trans. C. E. Suchau under the title *The Chronology of Ancient Nations*. London: Allen, 1879.

Allcroft, A. H. *The Circle and the Cross*. London: Macmillan, 1927.

Amadis de Gaula. by Vasco Lobeira. Trans. R. Southey. London: Smith, 1872.

an Lega, Mac. *Stair Ercuil*. Trans. G. Quinn. Irish Texts Society, Dublin, 1939.

Andre, Patrick. *La Cite Gallo-Romaine des Venetes*. Vannes, France: Societe Polymathique, 1971.

Annals of the Kingdom of Ireland. see J. Keating.

Apollodorus. *The Library*. Trans. Sir J. G. Frazer. LCL, 1921.

Apocryphal New Testament. Printed for W. Hone. London, (n/d).

Apuleius, L. *The Golden Ass*. Trans. R. Graves. London: Penguin, 1950.

Armstrong, J. *The History of the Island of Minorca*. Dublin, 1756.

Aristotle. *On the Cosmos*. Trans. D. J. Furley. LCL, 1965.

Aristotle. *Athenian Constitution*. Trans. H. Rackham. LCL, 1935.

Arrian. *History of Alexander* and *Indica*. Trans. I. Robson. LCL, 1966.

Asimov. *Biographical Encylopedia of Science and Technology*. London: Pan, 1964.

Athenaeus. *Deipnosophis*. Trans. C. B. Gulick. LCL, 1969.

Aveni, Anthony. *Skywatchers*. Austin, TX: University of Texas Press, 2001.

Babrius and Phedrus. Trans. B. E. Perry. LCL, 1965.

Bachofen, J. J. *Mutterecht und Urrsligion*. Leipzig: Kroner, 1898.

Bagster's Critical New Testament. London: Bagster, 1925.

Baker, M. *Garden Folklore*. London: Sphere, 1979.

Bengtsson, F. G. *The Long Ships*. New York: Ballantine, 1966.

Bede. *Historical Works*. Trans. J. E. King. LCL, 1965.

Boll, Franz. *Sphaera*. Teubner. Leipzig, 1903.

Boll, Franz. *Aus derOffenbarung Johannis*. Amsterdam: Hakkert, 1967.

Bouche-Leclercq, A. *L'Astrologie Grecque*. Paris: Leroux, 1899.

Brown, L. A. *The Story of Maps*. Boston: Little Brown, 1949.

Butler, Rev. A. *The Lives of the Fathers, Martyrs & Saints*. Dublin: Virtue, 1898.

Buxton, Simon. *The Shamanic Way of the Bee*. Vermont: Destiny Books, 2004.

Caesar. *Alexandrian, African, Spanish Wars: Gallic War.* Trans. A. G. Way. LCL, 1978.

Callimachus, Lycophron, Aratus. Trans. A. W. & G. R. Mair. LCL, 1977.

Carrigan, Rev. W. *The History and Antiquities of the Diocese of Ossory.* Dublin: Sealy, 1905.

Cassinelli, Dennis. *Gathering Traces of the Great Basin Indians.* Reno, NV: Western Books, 1996.

Celsus. *De Medicinia.* Trans. W. G. Spencer. LCL, 1961.

Childe, V. G. *New Light on a Most Ancient East.* No information.

Childress, David H. *Lost Cities of Africa & Arabia.* Kempton, IL: Adventures Unlimited Press, 1997.
Also, his works in The Lost City Series: *China, Lemuria, South America, North & Central America, and Atlantis.*

Clement of Alexandria. Trans. G. W. Butterworth. LCL, 1919.

Codex Iuris Canonici. Herder: Friburgi Brisgoviae, 1918.

Corliss, William R. *Science Frontiers: The Sourcebook Project.* Maryland, 1994.

Cramer, F. H. *Astrology in Roman Law and Politics: Vol. 37.* Philadelphia: American Philosophical Society, 1954.

Croll, Dr. J. *Climate and Time.* No information.

Crone, G. R. *Maps and Their Makers.* London: Hutchinson University Library, 1955.

Culin, S. *Chess and Playing Cards.* Washington, DC: U.S. National Museum, 1898.

De Barandiaran, J. M. *Mitologia Vasca.* San Sebastian: Txtertoa, 1979.

De Landa, Friar Diego. *Yucatan, Before and After the Conquest.* New York: Dover, 1978–2004.

De Prorok, Count Byron. *In Quest of Lost Worlds.* New York: E. P. Dutton, 1935. (*Stockton Public Library*)

de Vries, J. *Kelten aund Germanen.* Bern: Franke, 1960.

Dionysius of Halicarnassus. *Roman Antiquities.* Trans. E. Cary. LCL, 1937.

Dirge of Ireland. O'Connell. 1704. (see O'Brennan)

Dome of the Rock. Edited by Landay. *Newsweek.* New York, 1970.

Eisler, R. *The Royal Art of Astronomy.* London: Joseph, 1946.

Egypt: Architecture, Sculpture, Painting. Edited by K. Lange & M. Hirmer. New York: Phaidon, 1968.

Eusebius. *The Eclesiastical History.* Trans. K. Lake. LCL, 1926.

Fell, B. *America B.C.* New York: Pocket Books, 1978.

Fenagh, The Book of St. Caillin. Trans. D. H. Kelly. Dublin, 1875.

Gavrinis. Archeologique Kergal. Fontenay-Le Fleury, (n/d).

Gadalla, M. *Egyptian Divinites.* North Carolina: Tehuti, 2001.

Getty, E. *The Island of Tory. Ulster Journal.* vol. i & iii, (n/d).

Gellius, Aulus. *The Attic Nights.* Trans. J. C. Rolfe. LCL, 1970.

Greek Anthology. Trans. W. R. Patton. LCL, 1970.

Greek Choliambic Poets. Trans. A. D. Knox. LCL, 1953.

Greek Mathematical Works. Trans. I. Thomas. LCL, 1939.

Gregory, Lady. *Gods and Fighting Men.* Dublin: Murray, 1904.

Grimm, Bruder. *Kinder und Hausmarchen.* Zurich: Manesse, (n/d).

Grosjean, R. *Filiitosa.* Promenades Archeologiques. (no place, n/d).

Guide de la Bretagne Mysterieuse. Edited by Gwenc'hlan Le Scouezec. Paris: Princesse, 1979.

Hancock, G. *Fingerprints of the Gods.* England: Heinemann, 1995.

Hancock, G. *The Message of the Sphinx.* New York: Crown, 1996.

Hansen, L. Taylor. *The Ancient Atlantic.* Wisconsin: Amherst Press, 1969. (*California Institute Of Arts Library*)

Hapgood, Charles. *Maps of the Ancient Sea Kings.* Boston: Chilton, 1966.

Healy, Rev. Dr. J. *Ireland's Ancient Schools and Scholars.* Dublin: Gill, 1902.

Heath, Sir T. *Aristarchus of Samos.* Oxford: Claredon, 1913.

Henry, F. *Croix Sculptees Irelandaises.* Dublin: Three Candles, 1964.

Hesiod. *Theogony; The Homeric Hymns; Homerica.* Trans. H. G. Evelyn-White. LCL, 1977.

Herodotus. *Histories.* Trans. A. D. Godley. LCL, 1920.

Hitching, F. *The World Atlas of Mysteries.* London: Pan, 1978.

Hofner, T. *Uber Isis und Osiris.* Darmstadt, Germany: Wisenschaftliche Buchgesellschaft, 1967.

Homer. *The Illiad, The Odyssey*. Trans. A. T. Murray. LCL, 1924.

Horace. *The Odes and Epodes*. Trans. C. E. Bennett. LCL, 1914.

Hubert, H. *The Rise of the Celts*. New York: Knopf, 1934.

Jarno, J. V. *Nos Ancetres, Les Venetes*. La Baule: Paludiers, 1979.

Jeans, Sir J. *The Stars in their Courses*. Cambridge University, 1931.

Jenkins, A. C. *Wild Animals*. New York: Albany Books, 1979.

Josephus. *Jewish Antiquities; Against Apion*. Trans. H. St. J. Thackeray. LCL, 1976.

Joyce, P. W. *A Social History of Ancient Ireland*. London: Longmans, 1903.

Keane, M. *Towers and Temples of Ancient Ireland*. Dublin: Hodges, 1867.

Keating, Rev. J. *General History of Ireland, 1625*. Edited by D. O'Connor. Dublin: Duffy, 1861.

Laertius, Diogenes. *Lives of the Eminent Philosophers*. Trans. R. D. Hicks. LCL, 1966.

Lobeira, Vasco. *Amadis de Gaula*. Trans. R. Southey. London: Smith, 1872.

Logan, P. *The Holy Wells of Ireland*. London, Smythe, 1980.

Mackenzie, W. G. *The Races of Scotland & Ireland*. Paisley, Scotland: Gardner, 1923.

Madden, A. C. *The Beaker Wedge Tomb at Moyturra*. R. S. A. I. *Journal*, vol. 99, 1969.

Maher, J. *Romantic Slievenamon.* Callan, Ireland, 1923.

Manetho. *Aegyptiaca.* Trans. W. G. Waddell. LCL, 1940.

Manilius. *Astronomica.* Trans. G. P. Gould. LCL, 1977.

Mapp, W. *The Quest of the Holy Grail.* Edited by P. M. Matarasso. England: Penguin, 1969.

Mehler, Stephen S. *The Land of Osiris.* Chicago: Adventures Unlimited Press, 2001.

Michelin Guide Brittany. London, 1979.

Miller, Mary, & Karl Taube. *The Gods and Symbols of Ancient Mexico and the Maya.* London: Thames and Hudson, 1993.

Miller, Mary, & Simon Martin. *Courtly Art of the Ancient Maya.* San Francisco: Thames and Hudson, 2004.

Minor Latin Poets. Trans. J. W. & A. Duff. LCL, 1934

Monmouth, J. *The History of the Kings of Britain.* Edited by L. Thorpe. England: Penguin, 1966.

Morris, H. *The First Battle of Magh Turedh. R. S. A. I. Journal.* North Ireland, May, 1928.

Murphy, S. *Stone Mad.* London: Routledge and Paul, 1966.

Neugenbauer & Parker. *Egyptian Astronomical Texts: The Early Decans.* Brown University Press, 1960.

Newgrange. Midlands East Tourism. Mullingar, Ireland, 2003.

Nonnos. *Dionysiaca.* Trans. H. J. Rose & L. R. Lind. LCL, 1960.

Nordenskiold, A. E. *Fascimile Atlas; The Early History of Cartography.* Stockholm, 1889. New York: Dover, 1973.

O'Brennan. *Ancient Ireland.* Dublin: Mullany, 1855.

O'Curry, E. *The Manuscript Materials of Ancient Irish History.* Dublin: Hinch & Traynor, 1878.

O'Donovan, J. *The Fomorians and Lochlanns. Ulster Journal of Archaeology,* vol. 9. North Ireland, 1861.

O'Dugan. *The Legend of Balor on Tory Island.* As told by E. O'Donovan. Library of R. I. A. Dublin, 1896.

Ogygia, Rerum Hibernicarum: Chronologica. London: Roderico O'Flaherty, 1685.

O'Hanlon, Rev. J. *Lives of the Irish Saints.* Dublin: Duffy, 1934.

O'Kearney, N. *Folk Lore.* Kilkenny Arch. Society, 1960.

O'Rahilly, T. H. *Early Irish History and Mythology.* Dublin Institite of Advanced Studies, Dublin, 1946.

O'Siochain, P. A. *Ireland: A Journey into Lost Time.* Dublin: Foilsiuchain Eireann, 1982.

Ovid. *Metamorphosis.* Trans. M. M. Innis. Baltimore: Penguin, 1955.

Pauly-Wissowa Real-Enzyklopadie des Klassischen Altertumwissenschaft. Stuttgart, 1912.

Pausanius. *Description of Greece.* Trans. W. H. S. Jones. LCL, 1918.

Perrault. *Fairy Tales.* Edited by G. Brerton. London: Penguin, 1957.

Philo. *On the Giants.* Trans. F. H. Colson. LCL, 1968.

Pittau, M. *La Sardegna Nuragica.* Sassari, Sardinia: Dessi, 1980.

Plato. *Timaeus & Critias.* Trans. R. G. Bury. LCL, 1929.

Pliny. *Natural History.* Trans. J. Rackham & D. E. Eicholz. LCL, 1945.

Plotinus. *The Enneads.* Trans. A. H. Armstrong. LCL, 1966.

Plutarch. *Concerning the Face that appears in the Face of the Moon.* Trans. H. Cherniss & W. C. Helmbold. LCL, 1968.

Plutarch. *Isis and Osiris; The E at Delphi; The Obsolesence of Oracles.* Trans. F. C. Rabbit. LCL, 1969.

Plutarch. *Lives.* Trans. B. Perrin. LCL, 1914.

Power, P. *Sex and Marriage in Ancient Ireland.* Cork: Mercier, 1976.

Preuschen, E. *Die apokryphen gnostischen Adamschriften aus dem Armenishen.* Giessen: J. Ricker, 1900.

Procopius. *Buildings.* Trans. H. B. Dewing. LCL, 1940.

Ptolemy. *Tetrabiblos.* Trans. F. E. Robbins. LCL, 1940.

Roe, H. M. *The High Crosses of Western Ossory.* Kilkenny Archaeological Society, 1976.

Rogers, Prof. David B. *Prehistoric Man of the Santa Barbara Coast.* Santa Barbara Museum, CA, 1929.

Rooth, A. B. *The Raven and the Carcass. Folklore Fellows Communication,* vol. 186. Helsinki, 1962.

Rowse, A. L. *The Tower of London.* London: Weidenfeld & Nicolson, 1972.

Royal Irish Academy Dictionary. R. I. A. Dublin, 1940.

Santillana & Dechend. *Hamlet's Mill*. Boston: Godine, 1977.

Schwaller De Lubicz, R. A. *Sacred Science (1982); The Egyptian Miracle. (1985); The Temples of Karnak. (1999)*. Rochester, VT: Inner Traditions.

Schwaller De Lubicz, Isha. *Her-Bak. Egyptian Initiate*. New York: Inner Traditions, 1978.

Seneca. *Naturales Questiones*. Trans. T. H. Corcoran. LCL, 1971.

Sextus Empiricus. *Works*. Trans. R. G. Bury. LCL, 1971.

Sherlock, T. *Discourses*. Dublin: Dyton & Ewing, 1767.

Sicilus, Diodorus. *Histories*. Trans. C. H. Oldfather. LCL, 1933.

Silius Italicus. *Punica*. Trans. C. Duff. LCL, 1968.

Smith, C. *History of Waterford*. Waterford, Ireland, 1746.

Spanuth, J. *Atlantis of the North*. London: Sidgwick & Jackson, 1979.

Saint Jerome. *Select Letters*. Trans. F. A. Wright. LCL, 1950.

Saward, Jeff. *Labyrinths & Mazes*. New York: Sterling, 2003.

Spence, L. *The Myths of Mexico and Peru.*London: Harrap, 1917.

Spence, L. *The History of Atlantis*. London: Rider, 1926.

Stair Ercuil. by Mac an Lega. Trans. G. Quinn. Irish Texts Society, Dublin, 1939.

Stegeman, V. *Astrologie und Universalgeschichte.* Leipzig: Teubner, 1930.

Strabo. *The Geography.* Trans. H. L. Jones. LCL, 1917.

Sudhoff, Heinke. *Ancient Seafarers.* 1991. *Internet 2004.*

Sudhoff, K. *Iatromathematiker.* Breslau: Kern's, 1902.

Teresi, Dick. *Lost Discoveries.* New York: Simon & Schuster, 2002.

Tertulian. *Apology de Spectaculis.* Trans. T. R. Glover. LCL, 1966.

Theophrastus. *The Characters.* Trans. J. M. Edmonds. LCL, 1953.

Thompson, Richard L. *Mysteries of the Sacred Universe.* Florida: Govardhan Hill, 2000.

Tompkins, P. *Secrets of the Great Pyramid.* England: Penguin, 1978.

Underwood, G. *The Pattern of the Past.* London: Abacus, 1974.

Varro. *De Linga Latina.* Trans. R. G. Kent. LCL, 1938.

Vasari, G. *The Lives of the Painters, Sculptors and Architects.* London: Dent, 1970.

Verdera, Nito. *South America on Ancient Maps. Internet.2004.*

Vitriuvius. *On Architecture.* Trans. F. Granger. LCL, 1962.

Webster, Rev. W. *Basque Legends.* London: Griffith & Farran, 1879.

Wheeler, J. T. *Tales from Indian History.* Calcutta: Thacker, 1892.

Whishaw, E. M. *Atlantis in Spain.* Kempton, IL: Adventures Unlimited, 1997.

Wilson, C. *The Atlas of Holy Places & Sacred Sites*. New York: D. K. Publishing, 1996.

Wolfel, D. J. *Die Kanarischen Inseln*. Bamberg: Paideuma, 1950.

Yeats, W. B. *Fairy and Folk Tales of Ireland*. London, Pan, 1973.

Zapp, I. *Atlantis in America*. Kempton, IL: Adventures Unlimited, 1998.

Zarate. *The Discovery and Conquest of Peru*. Trans J. M. Cohen. London: Penguin, 1968.

Credits & Thanks for the Images:

Salisbury Cathederal from Underwood's *Pattern of the Past*
Ancient Irish Crosses by courtesy of Irish Commissioners of Public
    Works, Dublin.
Maps from Nordenskiold, *Fascimile Atlas*. Stockholm 1889
Dendera Zodiac from *Monuments of Egypt*. Napoleonic Edition.
Image of Atlas & Hercules by courtesy of Biblioteque Nationale de
    Paris.
Nuraghe from *La Sardenga Nuragica* by Masimo Pittau

Printed in the United States
38575LVS00003B/31

9 780976 498162